The BIG BOOK *of* —

HEALTHY
SMOOTHIES
AND JUICES

The BIG BOOK of
HEALTHY SMOOTHIES AND JUICES

More Than 500 Fresh and Flavorful Drinks for the Whole Family

Avon, Massachusetts

Published by
Adams Media, a division of F+W Media, Inc.
57 Littlefield Street, Avon, MA 02322. U.S.A.
www.adamsmedia.com

Contains material adapted and abridged from *The Everything® Green Smoothies Book* by Britt Brandon with Lorena Novak Bull, copyright © 2011 by F+W Media, Inc., ISBN 10: 1-4405-2564-1, ISBN 13: 978-1-4405-2564-3; *What Color Is Your Smoothie?* by Britt Brandon, copyright © 2012 by F+W Media, Inc., ISBN 10: 1-4405-3616-3, ISBN 13: 978-1-4405-3616-8; and *The Everything® Giant Book of Juicing* by Teresa Kennedy, copyright © 2013 by F+W Media, Inc., ISBN 10: 1-4405-5785-3, ISBN 13: 978-1-4405-5785-9.

ISBN 10: 1-4405-8037-5
ISBN 13: 978-1-4405-8037-6
eISBN 10: 1-4405-8038-3
eISBN 13: 978-1-4405-8038-3

Printed in the United States of America.

10   9   8   7   6   5   4   3   2   1

Always follow safety and commonsense cooking protocol while using kitchen utensils, operating ovens and stoves, and handling uncooked food. If children are assisting in the preparation of any recipe, they should always be supervised by an adult.

This book is intended as general information only, and should not be used to diagnose or treat any health condition. In light of the complex, individual, and specific nature of health problems, this book is not intended to replace professional medical advice. The ideas, procedures, and suggestions in this book are intended to supplement, not replace, the advice of a trained medical professional. Consult your physician before adopting any of the suggestions in this book, as well as about any condition that may require diagnosis or medical attention. The author and publisher disclaim any liability arising directly or indirectly from the use of this book.

Many of the designations used by manufacturers and sellers to distinguish their product are claimed as trademarks. Where those designations appear in this book and F+W Media, Inc. was aware of a trademark claim, the designations have been printed with initial capital letters.

Cover design by Erin Alexander.
Cover images © Tetiana Vitsenko/natika/123RF.

This book is available at quantity discounts for bulk purchases.
For information, please call 1-800-289-0963.

CONTENTS

P **Pregnant-Friendly:** While all the smoothies and juices in this book are healthy and therefore good for women who are expecting, those marked with this logo are specially recommended for a pregnancy diet.

V **Vegan**

PART I SMOOTHIES 17

6 Green Smoothies 127

11 Vegetable Juices 287

12 Kid-Friendly Juices 323

13 Juices for Healthy Living ...337

Standard U.S./Metric Measurement Conversions 387

Index 388

INTRODUCTION

The smoothies and juices in this book are lifesavers—literally. If you want more energy, better digestion, smoother skin, and a healthier attitude, you need to join the growing ranks of people who've made smoothies and juices an essential part of their lives.

The Big Book of Healthy Smoothies and Juices offers you more than 500 savory or sweet choices for delicious drinks. Whether you want to nurture your digestion, boost your calcium for better bones, or improve your memory, you'll find the right juice or smoothie within these pages—everything from a Sinful Strawberry Cream smoothie for a warm summer day to Heirloom Tomato Juice or a Night on the Town Tonic. There are recipes for pregnant women, nursing mothers, on-the-go parents, and a special selection of kid-friendly drinks.

These foods take minutes to prepare, but you and your family will feel their benefits all day. They're easy on your budget and can be easily transported to work or school. They'll give you more energy and stamina to make the most of your day, and your kids will love them.

Whether you're constantly on the go, stuck behind a desk all day, working around the house, or in a combination of those situations, a healthy diet is key to your well-being. You'll find that as you integrate these smoothies and juices into your diet, you'll increase your consumption of essential vitamins, antioxidants, and phytochemicals. Cooked foods often lose their natural nutrients; smoothies and juices retain them.

It's possible that you're already a devotee of the smoothie/juice lifestyle. If so, you'll find plenty of innovative recipes here to supplement those you already make. On the other hand, if you're a smoothie/juicer beginner, there's lots of great advice here on how to get started. You don't need fancy kitchen equipment—just a blender and/or a food processor or juicer. Nor do you need a lot of special foods. You can make healthy smoothies and juices out of practically anything, and, as you'll find in these pages, you can use these foods in combinations that may astonish you.

So get ready to blend, juice, and process your way to a new, healthy, happy lifestyle.

PART I
SMOOTHIES

CHAPTER 1

THE SMOOTHIE REVOLUTION

Although the value of a diet rich in greens, fruits, and vegetables has been well known for quite some time, the health-conscious smoothie has not been commonplace until recent years. It has also been only in recent years that much of the information has been provided identifying the Standard American Diet—high in bad fats, low in quality protein and carbohydrates—as the main culprit in multiple health issues that strike people of all ages and backgrounds. With the breakthrough of raw food diets, the proven health benefits of diets low in refined carbohydrates, and illnesses that have shown marked improvement with the implementation of a more green-focused diet, fresh fruit and vegetable smoothies now appeal to more people.

The powers of healing and the benefits from consuming rich greens in smoothies are particularly astounding. Abundant vitamins, minerals, antioxidants, amino acids, omega-3s, healthy fats, phytochemicals, and proteins that can change the natural processes of your body for the better are unleashed in every "green" smoothie you consume!

What Are Healthy Smoothies?

A healthy smoothie is a mixture of greens and/or fruit blended together until a desirable, smooth texture is achieved. While there are many smoothie combinations that target specific needs or areas of the body, the main reasons to consume healthy smoothies are to eat more vegetables and fruits on a daily basis, enjoy the smoothie combinations you choose from this book and create on your own, and live a healthier and happier lifestyle as a result of this major nutritional shift in your daily life. Integrating these smoothies into your average day without extra time, money, or hassle is also easily done. It takes only minutes to prepare, blend, and enjoy these treats, and requires only a blender and the vegetables and fruits of your choosing. The entire process is easy to understand and apply to any schedule—no matter how hectic.

From children to adults, and pregnant women to raw-food enthusiasts, everyone is including healthy smoothies in their diets. Those who desire a faster metabolism and those who suffer from serious ailments can all get extra benefits from green smoothies and the powerful ingredients packed in each sip. Combinations can be mixed, matched, and manipulated to create any type of smoothie desired. Bright morning smoothies and sweet dessert smoothies are filled with important nutrition and tasty additions while savory smoothies can be made from a number of ingredients to satisfy any salty or spicy craving.

Greens and Nutrition

Green smoothies are smoothies with greens blended into them. They differ from juices (which you'll find in Part II of this book) in that they're a complete food—they still have fiber. Most people know that greens are very nutritious but struggle to eat enough of them—they're not the easiest vegetables to prepare tastefully while maintaining all of the important vitamins and minerals your body requires. Steaming, sautéing, baking, and roasting vegetables causes them to lose the vitamins and minerals you're trying to obtain by eating them in the first place. Absorbing the nutrients from greens presents another challenge—you may not get the full benefits from your average meal or salad containing greens because greens can be difficult to digest and tedious to chew to the point where digestion would be easy. Blended greens in smoothies have already been ripped apart and are effectively "predigested," allowing for almost immediate absorption.

Although many people suffer from irregularity, few know of the power of fiber held in a serving of greens. A type of carbohydrate that resists the body's digestive enzymes and acids, soluble fiber forms a gel-like substance in the digestive tract that binds with cholesterol so it can't be reabsorbed by the body. Insoluble fiber (often referred to as "nature's broom") moves food through the digestive system more quickly, reducing instances of constipation. Increasing your daily intake of deep green vegetables and certain fruits can make irregularity a thing of the past.

Healthy Smoothies Versus the Standard American Diet

When you take into consideration that the Standard American Diet is packed with high levels of sugars, sodium, saturated fats, and preservatives from the types of foods consumed and how those foods are prepared, the healthy smoothie can be a very important addition to any diet. Regular consumption of empty calories and dangerous additives can easily be changed, and consuming these nutrient-dense smoothies just once a day can reverse the adverse affects of such nutrient-deficient lifestyles. Between a skipped breakfast, a lunch on the run from a fast food place, and a dinner made from ingredients packed with sodium, trans fats, and dangerous preservatives, the average consumer rarely fulfills the suggested serving sizes of fruits and vegetables in a normal day, and ends up suffering from the symptoms and illnesses that result from important deficiencies. All of these ailments can be reversed and improved with green smoothies and their powerful ingredients.

Supplement Your Diet Naturally

Symptoms and illnesses that arise from a vitamin deficiency can only be cured by that particular vitamin. Deep-green vegetables are a one-stop shop for ensuring you fulfill your body's needs for vitamins and negate any possible illnesses and symptoms that could arise from being deficient. Also, of the eight essential amino acids that we need for bodily functions such as muscle repair, manufacturing hormones, mental functions, sleep, memory, and physical and mental energy, your body produces none of them naturally, so you need to get them from the foods you consume.

The Benefits of Healthy Smoothies
The vegetables, fruits, and herbs used in green smoothies are rich in powerful antioxidants known for enhancing brain function, combating negative effects of stress, improving cardiovascular health, and reversing the aging process.

How many essential amino acids do you think are in a processed and unidentifiable fast food hamburger? Whatever the answer may be, it can't compare to what's in the 2 cups of raw vegetables and 2 cups of raw fruits you'll be blending into your green smoothie. If you know you are lacking in vitamins, minerals, or amino acids, green healthy smoothies are a great way to meet and exceed your dietary needs. Green smoothie ingredients pack a powerful amount of the vitamins and minerals required to keep body and mind working at their fullest potential.

VITAMINS

- **Biotin.** Found in the deep-green leafy vegetables, biotin is responsible for cell growth, maintaining a steady blood sugar level, and the metabolism of fats and amino acids. It also strengthens hair and nails.
- **Carotenes.** Vibrant orange and yellow vegetables and leafy greens get their color from these amazing provitamins (substances converted by the body into vitamins). They are powerful antioxidants that provide protection from free radicals and aid in cancer prevention. Important phytochemicals lutein, lycopene, and beta-carotene are released with the tearing of these vegetables and provide the body with enormous protection from illness and disease.
- **Vitamin A.** Carrots and dark-green and yellow vegetables hold this important vitamin, known for its role in providing vision health and proper cell growth.
- **Vitamin B_1.** Also known as thiamine, B_1 aids in every process, including nervous system processes, muscle function, metabolism of carbohydrates, and the production of healthy digestive enzymes as well as electrolyte flow. This vitamin can be found in apples, beans, and nuts.
- **Vitamin B_2.** Also known as riboflavin, this vitamin, found mainly in broccoli and asparagus, aids cells in their growth, maintains proper functioning, and produces energy.
- **Vitamin B_3.** Also known as niacin, this hormone-regulating vitamin assists the adrenal glands in production of sex- and stress-related hormones, lowers LDL ("bad" cholesterol) while raising HDL ("good" cholesterol), and recently has been thought to improve symptoms of arthritis. It is found in green vegetables, beans, and nuts.
- **Vitamin B_5.** Also known as pantothenic acid, this vitamin is responsible for synthesizing and metabolizing the fats, carbohydrates, and proteins for all necessary bodily functions. Good sources of B_5 are avocados, kale and other cabbage family vegetables, and sweet potatoes.
- **Vitamin B_6.** Also known as pyridoxine, B_6 is found in peas, carrots, and spinach and is responsible for the synthesis of important neurotransmitters serotonin and norepinephrine.
- **Vitamin B_{12}.** Also known as cobalamin, this vitamin aids in blood formation and energy production, and is necessary for the metabolism in every cell throughout the body.
- **Vitamin C.** Found in most citrus fruits and in vibrant-colored and deep-green vegetables, vitamin C is well known for its immune-system-boosting properties, but is also necessary

for iron absorption and supports the growth and repair of cartilage, collagen, muscle, and blood vessels.

- **Vitamin D.** This vitamin is produced in our bodies as a result of exposure to the sun. You can get helpful supplies of vitamin D from fortified dairy products to protect your body from autoimmune diseases, cancers, osteoporosis, and hypertension.
- **Vitamin E.** This fat-soluble antioxidant has been known for stimulating skin repair and strengthening cells, but it is absolutely necessary in removing free radicals from the body's systems. It is found in abundance in spinach, collards, and dandelion greens, as well as turnips and beets.
- **Vitamin K.** This fat-soluble compound is extremely helpful in blood clotting, and is found in the deep-green leafy vegetables.

MINERALS

- **Boron.** Found in spinach, cabbage, and carrots, as well as apples, pears, and grapes, this mineral maintains the health of bones and teeth by metabolizing calcium, magnesium, and phosphorus. It has also been cited for building muscle and promoting mental clarity and brain functioning.
- **Calcium.** Although well known for maintaining the strength of bones and teeth, calcium also plays a vital role in maintaining regularity of the heart and helping to metabolize iron efficiently. Found in kale, broccoli, and collard greens, calcium is especially important for women who are pregnant, nursing, or menstruating.
- **Chromium.** This weight-loss helper is powerful in effective fatty-acid metabolism and works together with insulin to maintain the proper use of sugar in the body.
- **Copper.** Found in most green vegetables, copper is another mineral that aids in the absorption of iron; it also helps to maintain cardiovascular health and can promote fertility in both men and women.
- **Selenium.** Found in deep-green vegetables and in asparagus and mushrooms, selenium is helpful in weight loss by stimulating the metabolism, and effective in disease prevention by acting as an antioxidant against free radicals that cause health issues like arthritis, cancer, and heart disease.
- **Magnesium.** This mineral is helpful in maintaining proper functioning of the muscles and the nervous system. Health problems resulting from low levels of magnesium include hypertension, diabetes, osteoporosis, and certain digestive disorders.
- **Potassium.** Working with sodium to maintain a proper balance of the body's water, potassium is mainly required for the metabolism of carbohydrates and the synthesis of proteins.

- **Sodium.** This mineral is important in maintaining proper muscle control and optimal nerve functioning, as well as correcting the body's distribution of fluid and maintaining proper pH balance.
- **Iron.** Although all people require adequate amounts of iron (found in dark-green vegetables), vegans and pregnant or menstruating women are in a different bracket, requiring much more. Iron is a commodity for lifestyles requiring additional protein because it is essential for strengthening the immune system, and is found in great amounts in the proteins of red blood cells.

Greens and Healing

With many diagnoses, doctors' orders normally include a change of diet, and that changed diet usually includes increasing fruits and vegetables while decreasing refined carbohydrate and sugar intake. The studies, statistics, and testimonies of those who have introduced greens into their diet speak loudly in terms of the resulting physical and mental health improvements. Researchers at Harvard Medical School tracked the health of more than 22,000 physicians and found that those who ate at least 2½ servings of vegetables daily reduced their risk of heart disease by almost 25 percent. At the University of California, Berkeley, researchers found that a high intake of fruits and vegetables also reduced the risk of cancer by an average of 50 percent. And a vegan diet rich in fruits and vegetables has reportedly reduced diabetes indicators and shown an increase in immune protection against arthritis.

Immediate Benefits

Many people who add green smoothies to their diet experience the benefits within a matter of days or a few short weeks. These benefits include more energy, mental clarity, better digestion, and clearer skin.

Women and men have found that their hair feels stronger, thicker, and more lustrous as a result of taking important vitamins like calcium, magnesium, and biotin that are found in greens. Men and women have reported a sense of mental clarity that can be compared to "the clearing of a fog" when they started consuming green smoothies; almost every mineral, vitamin, and phytonutrient found in deep greens can aid in mental and physical processes.

Reduce Your Health Risks

From improving the condition of hair, skin, and nails to renewing mental clarity and increased stamina, green smoothies combine the perfect ingredients to provide the essential vitamins, minerals, and nutrients to achieve almost any change desired. Vitamins necessary to sustain life and maintain healthy lifestyles can be found in deep greens and fruits. Folate (vitamin B_9), found in many of the greens, is an important B vitamin needed especially by pregnant women in order to ensure that the fetus is protected from spinal defects like spina bifida. The protein provided by vegetable sources far surpasses that of meats of any variety; a deep-green vegetable like broccoli can deliver a healthy dose of protein without the unhealthy saturated fats of an animal protein source.

The powerful ingredients found in green smoothies have alleviated conditions even as severe as osteoarthritis, osteoporosis, Alzheimer's disease, and various cancers. The phytochemicals found in these greens have been proven to have antioxidant activity that protects cells from oxidative damage and reduces the risks for certain cancers. If you like cabbage, you'll be pleased to learn that it contains indoles that stimulate enzymes that make estrogen less effective, and can reduce the risk of breast cancer!

Preparation and Storage Tips

In order to prepare a healthy smoothie, all that's needed are the fruits and vegetables of your choosing (according to recipes that sound appetizing to you) and a high-speed blender capable of emulsifying the greens and additions. The blender can be completely based on your needs and choosing. In most reviews of blenders on the market today, healthy smoothie consumers compare them based upon a few major factors: power, noise, capacity, and ease of cleanup.

- **Power.** The power of your blender will determine how quickly and efficiently your smoothie and its ingredients can be liquefied and blended. If time or texture are of no importance, this factor may not require much attention.
- **Noise.** Noise can be of no importance or of the utmost importance when it comes to selecting the perfect blender. If you plan on blending your smoothie prior to the rest of your house waking, it might be smart to invest in a quieter version that will still get the job done nicely.
- **Capacity.** Capacity is extremely important, considering you will be putting cups of fruits and vegetables, along with other ingredients, into the same canister. You will need enough room for the blending to be efficient. Also, be sure to take into consideration that you

will need enough room in your blender for the adequate amount of ingredients for your desired number of servings.

- **Ease of cleanup.** Although cleanup may also seem like a nonissue at first thought, consider your schedule or routine when making this purchase. Do you need it to be dishwasher safe? Will the blender require special tools for cleaning? Is there a recommended strategy to keep the blender clean while also ensuring a long lifespan?

The two most commonly used brands are Blendtec and Vitamix. Although these high-speed emulsifying machines come at a higher cost than your average blender, their quality, efficiency, and capabilities can make even those reluctant to purchase a new one consider making a swap. If you plan to use blenders for this precise purpose, more familiar brand names like KitchenAid, Black & Decker, and Krups also provide smoothie makers or blenders that will leave you delighted.

Pure Smoothies

Creating a green smoothie with organic fruits and vegetables ensures that your tasty treat is free of dyes, pesticides, and preservatives.

Shelf Life

The prep time required for the ingredients starts as soon as you get your greens, fruits, and vegetables home. Although greens will remain green for days or weeks, their powerful antioxidants, vitamins, and minerals dissipate from the time of picking, so eating them as soon as possible will give you the most nutrition out of every ounce. Lettuces and greens should be washed and stored in an airtight bag or container with paper towels or something that can absorb excess water from the leaves. Vegetables such as carrots, turnips, and beets should be rid of their stems and green tops in order to prevent drying the vegetables out. Both fruits and vegetables with hard outer skins or rinds should be peeled prior to blending, and pits should always be removed. After blending your green smoothie, you can even take it to go in any insulated container that will help maintain its temperature and freshness, or you can store it in an airtight glass container in your refrigerator for up to three days (although it probably won't last that long!).

Pantry Essentials

The simplicity of green smoothies is found in what is required to create one: a blender, a knife for food prep, and the greens, fruits, and vegetables of your choosing. That's it! Whether you'd like to use your tried-and-true kitchen blender or you'd rather opt for a high-horsepower emulsifying machine, the choice is yours. A cutting board, peeler, and knife will help in preparing your fruits and vegetables with ease and assist in quick cleanup. In most cases, you may want to soak and rinse your greens in cold water, but rinsing by hand can be done just as easily. Salad spinners offer the option of spinning off any excess water from your greens.

Save Time and Money!
In a fraction of the time required to make an entire meal, you can prep, blend, and enjoy a more nutritious healthy smoothie. Smoothies can also cut down on the cost of preparing an entire meal.

Depending on the type, taste, or texture you desire, your ingredients will be the main priority throughout the smoothie-making process. The choice of greens, vegetables, and fruits that you'd like to combine in your smoothie are essential, and you can always stock up on any of the suggested additions you find appealing. Although certain fruits and vegetables may not be available locally or seasonally depending on the time of year, freezing is always an option that will allow you to enjoy your favorite ingredients year round.

Additional Ingredients

Soy and protein powders, spirulina, coconut milk, almond milk, rice milk, kefir, Greek yogurt, and cacao are tasty ingredients you can blend into your own green smoothies. These ingredients are widely available and can change the taste experience completely. The bottom line is that what you need in your pantry is what *you* would like in your green smoothie. Try one ingredient, or try them all—it's up to you!

CHAPTER 2

WHAT GOES INTO A HEALTHY SMOOTHIE?

Deep-green, organic produce is the best choice for your smoothies. Organic produce doesn't expose you to the dangerous chemicals used in commercial agriculture, ensuring that you'll get maximum nutrients from the fruits and vegetables you use. If you're concerned about the "pricey" cost of organic from your local market, consider that growing fruits and vegetables in your backyard garden is the easiest way to save money and prevent your ingredients from being contaminated by herbicides or pesticides. If you don't have the time or space to grow your own, purchase locally or regionally grown organic produce in your local health food store, farmers' market, or supermarket.

Leafy Greens

Your green smoothie isn't complete without a dose of vibrant leafy greens. Research shows that leafy greens are one of the most concentrated sources of nutrition. They supply iron; calcium; potassium; magnesium; vitamins K, C, E, B_6, and B_{12}; and folate in abundance.

Leafy greens provide a variety of phytonutrients, including beta-carotene and lutein, which protect cells from damage and eyes from age-related problems. A few cups of dark green leaves also contains small amounts of omega-3 fatty acids and nine times the RDA for vitamin K, which regulates blood clotting, protects bones from osteoporosis, and may reduce the risk of atherosclerosis by reducing calcium in arterial plaques.

A Dieter's Delight

Because greens have very few carbohydrates and a lot of fiber, they take the body a long time to digest. If you're on a diet, leafy greens can be your best friend; they fill you up, but they have very few calories and no fat. In fact, most greens have such little impact on blood glucose that many low-carb diets consider them free foods.

Types of Greens

Leafy greens run the gamut in taste, from arugula—which ancient Romans considered an aphrodisiac because of its peppery taste—to iceberg lettuce, which is crunchy and sweet with a very mild flavor. Here are some of the most popular leafy greens used for smoothies:

- **Lettuce.** Deep green lettuce is a good source of calcium, chlorophyll, iron, magnesium, potassium, silicon, and vitamins A and E. All types help rebuild hemoglobin, add shine and thickness to hair, and promote hair growth. Iceberg contains natural opiates that relax the muscles and nerves. Lettuce is strong and works best in combination with other vegetables. Wash carefully, refrigerate, and use within a few days.
- **Frisée and escarole.** Both from the endive family, frisée is the curly leafed, light-green variety with a mild flavor while escarole is a more broad-leafed deep green that can be bitter if not selected carefully. Choose leaves from the inner part of the head. Both varieties are high in vitamins A and K, folate, and beta-carotene and are known for fighting depression and calming food cravings.
- **Parsley.** Packed with chlorophyll, vitamins A and C, calcium, magnesium, phosphorus, potassium, sodium, and sulfur, parsley helps stimulate oxygen metabolism, cell respiration, and regeneration. Wash, refrigerate, and use within five days.
- **Spinach, kale, and Swiss chard.** Popeye was right all along: You'll be strong to the finish if you eat your spinach, kale, and chard, which are similar in nutritional value and provide ample supplies of iron, phosphorus, fiber, and vitamins A, B, C, E, and K. Wash thoroughly and bag loosely in the refrigerator. Use within four days.
- **Watercress.** This delicate, leafy green veggie has a slightly pungent taste and is packed with vitamin C, calcium, and potassium. It also contains acid-forming minerals, which make it ideal for intestinal cleansing and normalizing, and chlorophyll, which stimulates metabolism and circulatory functions. Refrigerate and use within five days.
- **Wheatgrass.** This juice from wheat berries contains many anti-aging properties, including vitamins A, B complex, and E; chlorophyll; a full spectrum of minerals; and various enzymes. Refrigerate and use within four days.

Cruciferous Veggies

From broccoli and cauliflower to Brussels sprouts, kale, cabbage, and bok choy, the members of the cruciferous or cabbage family pack a nutritional wallop. They contain phytochemicals, vitamins, minerals, and fiber that are important to your health. Studies show that sulforaphane—one of the phytochemicals found in cruciferous vegetables—stimulates enzymes in the body that detoxify carcinogens before they damage cells.

Here's a rundown of the most delicious and nutritious root crops:

- **Broccoli.** Packed with fiber to help regularity, broccoli is also surprisingly high in protein, and it's packed with calcium, antioxidants, and vitamins B_6, C, and E. Because of its strong flavor, broccoli works best combined with other vegetables in juices, rather than juiced alone. Wash well and use within four days to get maximum nutrients.
- **Cabbage.** Another member of the fiber-filled cruciferous family, cabbage comes in many different varieties, from round green, white, and red cabbages to Savoy cabbage, with delicate, crinkly leaves. Other members of the cabbage family you can use in your smoothies include kale, collard greens, Brussels sprouts, and Chinese cabbage. All have large stores of vitamins B_6 and C. Kale and collard greens also have a lot of vitamin A and calcium. Members of the cabbage family are also packed with minerals.
- **Cauliflower.** Like other cruciferous vegetables, because of its strong flavor, cauliflower works best as a contributing player rather than a solo act. High in vitamin C and fiber, it has a more delicate taste than other cruciferous veggies. Use within four days or refrigerate for up to a week.

Root Vegetables

Classified by their fleshy underground storage unit or root, which is a holding tank of nutrients, root vegetables are low in fat and high in natural sugars and fiber. Root veggies are also the perfect foods to eat when you need sustained energy and focus.

Powerhouse Veggies

Some of the most nutritious root veggies include those with orangey skins, including carrots, squash, and sweet potatoes. The orange skin signifies that they contain beta-carotene, a powerful antioxidant that fights damaging free radicals.

Here are some delicious and nutritious root vegetables to include in your smoothies:

- **Beets.** Both the beet greens and beet roots are blendable and highly nutritious. The roots are packed with calcium, potassium, and vitamins A and C. Choose small to medium beets with fresh green leaves and roots. Use greens within two days and beet root within two weeks.
- **Carrots.** Carrots lend a mild, sweet taste to smoothies and taste equally delicious on their own. Carrots are packed with vitamins A, B, C, D, E, and K, as well as calcium,

phosphorus, potassium, sodium, and trace minerals. Carrots stimulate digestion; improve hair, skin, and nails; have a mild diuretic effect; and cleanse the liver, helping to release bile and excess fats. Remove foliage when you get home, because it drains moisture and nutrients from the carrots. Refrigerate and use within a week.

- **Celery.** High in vitamin C and potassium with natural sodium, celery has a mild flavor that blends well with other veggies. Its natural sodium balances the PH of the blood and helps the body use calcium better. Choose firm, bright-green stalks with fresh green leaves. Refrigerate for up to a week.

- **Fennel.** Similar to celery in nutrients and high in sodium, calcium, and magnesium, fennel has a licorice-like taste that enhances the taste of juices made from vegetables with a strong flavor. Choose fennel bulbs the size of tennis balls with no bruising or discoloration. Refrigerate and use within five days.

- **Garlic.** A member of the lily family, this aromatic bulb, high in antioxidants for reducing cholesterol and heart disease, adds flavor and tang. Use one or two cloves per quart. Choose firm, smooth heads and store in a cool, dry place. Use within two weeks.

- **Ginger.** Technically a rhizome and native to Asia, ginger has a sweet, peppery flavor that enhances juice. Buy large, firm nodules with shiny skin. Refrigerate and use within a week.

- **Parsnips.** Cousins to the carrot, parsnips are packed with vitamin C, potassium, silicon, and phosphorus. Choose large, firm parsnips with feathery foliage. Refrigerate and use within a week.

- **Potatoes.** High in vitamins C and B and potassium, potatoes add a light flavor to smoothies. Store in a cool, dry place and use within two weeks.

- **Radishes.** Small but mighty in taste and loaded with vitamin C, iron, magnesium, and potassium, radish juice cleanses the nasal sinuses and gastrointestinal tract and helps clear up skin disorders. Use a handful to add zing. Refrigerate and use within a week.

- **Turnips and turnip greens.** Ounce for ounce, turnip greens have more calcium than milk. The root supplies calcium, potassium, and magnesium. Together, they neutralize overly acidic blood and strengthen bones, hair, nails, and teeth. Store turnips at room temperature, scrub well, and use within two weeks. Refrigerate greens and use within a week.

- **Sweet potatoes and yams.** High in beta-carotene, vitamin C, calcium, and potassium, these two vegetables have a similar taste and can be substituted for one another in recipes. Store in a cool, dry place.

- **Green onions.** Green onions are high in disease-fighting antioxidants and have the mildest flavor of the onion family, making them ideal for blending. They also have antibacterial properties that fight infections and skin diseases. Green onions should be firm and deep green in color. Refrigerate, and use within a week.

Veggies from the Vine

From acorn squash to zucchini, vegetables straight from the vine deliver a cornucopia of nutrients and fiber. Vine vegetables are also especially easy to grow in small, compact gardens or in containers on patios.

- **Cucumbers.** With their mild flavor, cukes complement other vegetables and go well with herbs. Cucumbers are high in vitamin A and silica, which help repair connective tissue and skin. Buy firm, dark-green cucumbers with a slightly bumpy skin. Use within four days.
- **String beans.** High in B vitamins, calcium, magnesium, potassium, protein, and sulfur, string beans are good for your overall metabolism as well as your hair, skin, and nails. They have a strong flavor and taste best when combined with other vegetables.
- **Summer squash and zucchini.** Rich in B vitamins and niacin, calcium, and potassium, summer squash has a bland flavor that works best with other vegetables. It helps cleanse and soothe the bladder and kidneys. Store in a cool, dry place. Use within a few weeks.
- **Tomatoes.** Tomatoes are a good source of lycopene, which has been proven to have anti-cancer properties, and vitamin C and potassium, which cleanse the liver and add to the body's store of minerals, especially calcium. Fresh tomato juice also stimulates circulation. Store at room temperature.
- **Bell peppers.** High in vitamin C, red peppers are also high in vitamin A and are much sweeter than the green variety. Peppers contribute to beautiful skin and hair, while red peppers stimulate circulation and tone and cleanse the arteries and heart muscle. Store at room temperature. Before blending, wash gently with a mild castile soap, pull out the large clump of seeds, and remove the cap.

Berries

Red, blue, purple, or black—no matter what the color or size, berries are wonder foods that are loaded with phytochemicals, antioxidants, and other vitamins and minerals that help prevent cancer and many other diseases. Cranberries and blueberries also contain a substance that can prevent bladder infections.

- **Cranberries.** High in vitamins C, A, and B complex including folate, cranberries help prevent bladder infections by keeping bacteria from clinging to the wall of the bladder. Cranberries help reduce asthma symptoms, diarrhea, fever, fluid retention, and skin disorders, as well as disorders of the kidney, urinary tract, and lungs. Cranberries also facilitate weight loss.
- **Blueberries and blackberries.** Both berries are packed with saponins, which improve heart health, as well as disease-fighting antioxidants, vitamin C, minerals, and phytochemicals.
- **Raspberries.** Raspberries contain plenty of vitamin C and potassium, and are 64 calories per cup.
- **Strawberries.** Strawberries are loaded with vitamin C, iron, calcium, magnesium, folate, and potassium—essential for immune-system function and for strong connective tissue. Strawberries also provide just 53 calories per cup.

Tree and Vine Fruits

From apples to watermelon, fruits of the tree and vine provide an abundance of life-enhancing and disease-fighting vitamins, minerals, antioxidants, and phytochemicals.

Fruits of the Tree

Tree fruits are as American as apple pie, and are highly versatile players in making green smoothies, contributing a wide range of flavors, colors, and textures. Here are some of the most popular fruits:

- **Apples.** Rich in vitamins A, B_1, B_2, B_6, B_9 (folate) and C; biotin; and a host of minerals that promote healthy skin, hair, and nails, apples also contain pectin, a fiber that absorbs toxins, stimulates digestion, and helps reduce cholesterol. Apples are extremely versatile and blend well with other juices.
- **Apricots.** Apricots are high in beta-carotene and vitamin A and are a good source of fiber and potassium.
- **Cherries.** With abundant vitamins A, B, and C; niacin; and minerals, cherries are potent alkalizers that reduce the acidity of the blood, making them effective in reducing gout, arthritis, and prostate disorders.
- **Grapefruit.** Rich in vitamin C, calcium, phosphorus, and potassium, the pink and red varieties of grapefruit are sweeter and less acidic than white grapefruit. Grapefruit helps strengthen capillary walls, heal bruising, and reduce ear disorders, fever, indigestion, scurvy, varicose veins, obesity, and morning sickness.
- **Lemons.** Lemons are high in citric acid and vitamin C, so a little goes a long way in juicing. Their high antioxidant content and antibacterial properties relieve colds, sore throats, and skin infections and also help reduce anemia, blood disorders, constipation, ear disorders, gout, indigestion, scurvy, skin infections, and obesity.
- **Oranges.** An excellent source of vitamins C, B, and K; biotin; amino acids; and minerals, oranges cleanse the gastrointestinal tract, strengthen capillary walls, and benefit the heart and lungs. Oranges help reduce anemia, blood disorders, colds, fever, heart disease, high blood pressure, liver disorders, lung disorders, skin disorders, pneumonia, rheumatism, scurvy, and obesity.
- **Limes.** Similar to lemons in nutrients but not as acidic or cleansing, limes can be substituted for lemons in juice recipes.
- **Peaches and nectarines.** High in beta-carotene and vitamins B and C, niacin, and minerals, peaches and nectarines cleanse the intestines and help relieve morning sickness.
- **Pears.** Packed with fiber and vitamins C and B, niacin, and the minerals phosphorus and calcium, pears help reduce disorders of the bladder, liver, and prostate as well as constipation.
- **Plums.** Plums are high in vitamins C and A, copper, and iron, and their benzoic and quinic acids are effective laxatives. Plums help with anemia, constipation, and weight loss.
- **Grapes.** High in caffeic acid, which helps fight cancer, grapes are also packed with bioflavonoids, which help the body absorb vitamin C. Grapes also contain resveratrol, a nutrient that helps prevent liver, lung, breast, and prostate cancer, and saponins, a nutrient that binds with cholesterol and prevents the body from absorbing it.

Melons

Melons are the juiciest fruit by far, and naturals for fresh smoothies. They come in many varieties, including canary, cantaloupe, casaba, Crenshaw, and honeydew. They are sweet and fun summertime thirst quenchers.

All varieties are full of vitamins A, B complex, and C and promote skin and nerve health. Melons provide enzymes and natural unconcentrated sugars that help aid digestion.

Best Melons for Smoothies

Cantaloupe, honeydew, and watermelon are among the most popular melons in the United States.

- **Cantaloupe** is high in beta-carotene, vitamin C, and potassium. It alleviates disorders of the bladder, kidney, and skin and reduces constipation.
- **Honeydew** is high in potassium and vitamin C. When blended into smoothies, it promotes energy. It alleviates disorders of the bladder, kidney, and skin and reduces constipation.
- **Watermelon** is high in electrolytes and rich in vitamin A and potassium. It quenches thirst and also helps cleanse the kidney and bladder. Watermelon helps reduce discomfort associated with aging, arthritis, bladder disorders, constipation, fluid retention, kidney disorders, pregnancy, prostate problems, and skin disorders, and it promotes weight loss.

Tropical Fruit

You can find a bounty of tropical fruit in your local supermarket, even if you live in a cold climate, including:

- **Avocados.** Although frequently mistaken for a vegetable, the avocado is actually a member of the pear family. Avocados are rich in vitamins A, C, and E. Ripe avocados can be refrigerated for up to five days.

- **Bananas.** Bananas are a great source of potassium, an essential electrolyte, as well as magnesium and vitamin B_6.
- **Kiwifruit.** Kiwi are rich in vitamins A and C and contain nearly as much potassium as bananas. Their fuzzy skins contain valuable antioxidants and can also be used in marinades for tenderizing meats.
- **Mangos.** Like other orange-colored produce, mangos are packed with beta-carotene.
- **Papayas.** Papayas are loaded with papain, an enzyme that promotes digestion and has been shown to protect the stomach from ulcers. Papayas are also rich in vitamins A and C, and have an abundance of natural sugars. Papayas can also help reduce acidosis, acne, heart disease, tumors, ulcers, and blood disorders.
- **Pineapple.** A great source of potassium, calcium, iron, and iodine, fresh pineapple is worth the hassle required to prepare it for smoothies. Using a strong knife, slice off the top and bottom of the pineapple so it sits flat on your cutting board, and then slice off the peel.

Other Additions

You can boost the taste and nutritional value of your green smoothies with supplements that include soy and nutritional powders and herbal additions.

Best Soy and Powder Additives

Soy and powders can give your smoothies a rich, flavorful taste and texture and boost the nutrient value.

- **Silken tofu**, a soy product, adds flavor and texture and is rich in isoflavones, which may prevent cancer and osteoporosis and help reduce heart disease.
- **Flaxseed** is high in omega-3 acids as well as lecithin, which facilitates digestion.
- **Wheat germ**, high in vitamin E, thiamine, and copper, adds protein and fiber to juice.
- **Bee pollen** is high in protein; vitamins A, B, C, and E; calcium; and magnesium.

Best Herbal Helpers

Herbs lend phytochemicals and fresh taste and aroma to smoothies.

- **Basil** provides vitamins C and A plus beta-carotene.
- **Chives** provide calcium, phosphorus, and several vitamins.
- **Cilantro** is renowned for its anticholesterol, antidiabetic, and anti-inflammatory effects.
- **Dill** is rich in antioxidants and dietary fibers that help control blood cholesterol levels.

- **Mint**, including peppermint and spearmint, has the ability to cut off the blood supply to cancer tumors.
- **Oregano** is among the best sources of vitamin K, and it has antioxidants that prevent cellular damage caused by oxidation of free radicals.
- **Rosemary** provides carnosic acid, which shields the brain from free radicals and lowers the risk of stroke and neurodegenerative diseases.
- **Tarragon** is packed with minerals and vitamins C, B$_6$, A, and E, and may help transfer nutrients to your muscles.

Milk and Yogurt Additions

There are a variety of dairy and nondairy products you can add to your green smoothies to create a delicious, creamy consistency. Some of the most popular additions include:

- **Coconut milk.** Although most people assume coconut milk is the water drained from the coconut, coconut milk is actually derived from the flesh of the coconut. Not only is coconut milk known for its antiviral, antibacterial, and anticarcinogenic properties, it contains a healthy type of easily metabolized saturated fat that is also found in breast milk and is known to promote healthy brain and bone development.

Coconuts Save Lives!

During World War II, blood shortages were resolved by doctors using the coconut water from young, green coconuts. Because coconut water has the same electrolyte balance as blood, it was found to be the perfect substitute for blood plasma.

- **Soymilk.** The FDA, American Heart Association, and American Cancer Society all promote soymilk as a healthy part of a balanced diet. Containing various anticarcinogens, soymilk has been shown to promote health by preventing breast and prostate cancers, reducing bad cholesterol (LDL), reversing bone loss associated with osteoporosis, preventing diabetes and kidney disease, and helping with symptoms related to menopause. When selecting a soymilk, try to find one with a low sugar content or with more naturally occurring sugars.
- **Almond milk.** Rich in copper, manganese, magnesium, potassium, vitamin E, selenium, and calcium, almond milk offers a strong, healthy, protein-packed alternative to cow's milk. Using almond milk in a green smoothie will lend a nutty background taste.

Make Your Own Almond Milk

If the price or ingredients of store-bought almond milk has you considering homemade options, follow these simple directions to create your very own almond milk: grind ¼–½ cup of almonds in coffee grinder until fine, then combine in a blender with a cup of pure water for up to 3 minutes. Strain remaining almond bits using a coffee filter.

- **Rice milk.** Processed from brown rice, rice milk has less protein and more carbohydrates than the other milk alternatives, but boosts the body's natural processes with loads of B_1 for vitality; B_5 for hair, skin, and nails; B_6 and folic acid for promoting the healthy metabolism of protein and carbohydrates; and E for normalizing reproductive health.
- **Kefir.** Although this fermented milk is a dairy product, it is an easily digested addition to any smoothie that can even be safely consumed by most people with milk allergies. Toting the vitamins B_1, B_{12}, and K and biotin, kefir (which means "feel good" in Turkish) is well known for promoting digestive health with its beneficial yeast and probiotic bacteria.
- **Greek yogurt.** Greek yogurt contains an average of 20 grams of protein (compared to the 10 grams in the average yogurt) and has about half the carbohydrates (9 grams versus 15–17 grams) of other yogurts—and can also have half the sodium! Because of the triple-strained process it undergoes to remove the whey and water for its creamy texture, Greek yogurt is also much thicker and creamier than other yogurts, without the addition of unhealthy thickening agents.

CHAPTER 3

FRUIT SMOOTHIES

APPLES, BANANAS, AND CHERRIES

APPLE-NANA

Simple and sweet, this smoothie takes the flavors of apples and bananas that you know and love, and blends them together in a cool, icy treat. The addition of pure apple juice gives this already sweet concoction a kick of apple deliciousness that helps blend everything together for a taste that's just right!

INGREDIENTS

1 banana, peeled

1 yellow apple, cored

1 cup all-natural, organic apple juice (not from concentrate)

1 cup ice

Yields: 2 cups

Per 1 cup serving • Calories: 91 • Fat: 0g • Protein: 1g • Sodium: 1mg • Fiber: 3g • Carbohydrates: 24g

1. In a blender, combine the banana, apple, and apple juice with ½ cup ice, and blend until thoroughly combined.

2. While blending, add remaining ice until desired consistency is achieved.

AN APPLE PIE DAY

The cloves in this smoothie add a flavor reminiscent of apple pie and add to the immunity-strengthening health benefits already present in the spinach, apples, and coconut milk. Although most consider cloves an essential when it comes time to make pies for the holidays, Ayurvedic healers utilize this spice for its healing powers.

INGREDIENTS

2 cups spinach

1 teaspoon ground cloves

1 teaspoon cinnamon

3 apples, peeled and cored

1½ cups coconut milk

Yields: 1 quart

Per 1 cup serving • Calories: 232 • Fat: 18g • Protein: 3g • Sodium: 24mg • Fiber: 2g • Carbohydrates: 19g

1. Place the spinach in the blender.

2. Add the spices, followed by the apples.

3. Add coconut milk slowly while blending until desired texture is achieved.

APPLE-GINGER DELIGHT

The smooth, creamy Greek yogurt, apples, and ginger combine in this recipe for a truly delicious treat. Enjoy!

INGREDIENTS

1 cup romaine lettuce

2 apples, cored and peeled

½" ginger, peeled

½ cup Greek yogurt

Yields: 3–4 cups

Per 1 cup serving • Calories: 88 • Fat: 0g • Protein: 4g • Sodium: 18mg • Fiber: 3g • Carbohydrates: 19g

1. Combine romaine, apples, ginger, and half of the yogurt in a blender and blend until thoroughly combined.

2. Add remaining yogurt while blending until desired texture is achieved.

Cravings for Sweets

Everybody is familiar with the common craving. Cravings may vary from person to person—you may crave salty or sweet, for example. Either way, apples have been known to curb most cravings, and they also create a feeling of fullness. When a craving hits, eat an apple with a full glass of water and wait 30 minutes. Chances are your craving will have subsided and you will have replaced a higher calorie option with a nutritious snack!

GREAT GRANNY SMITH

With a sweet-tart taste that so many people love, Granny Smith apples have even spun off into candy flavors. Try serving this smoothie the next time your kids want sour apple candy.

INGREDIENTS

1 cup spinach

3 Granny Smith apples, peeled and cored

2 bananas, peeled

2 cups purified water

Yields: 3–4 cups

Per 1 cup serving • Calories: 112 • Fat: 0g • Protein: 1g • Sodium: 9mg • Fiber: 3g • Carbohydrates: 29g

1. Combine spinach, apples, bananas, and 1 cup of water in a blender and blend until thoroughly combined.

2. Add remaining water while blending until desired texture is achieved.

ICED APPLES AND SPICE

This frosty smoothie will likely make you think of a delicious apple pie. Even though you get a nutritional boost from the vitamin C and quercetin in the apples and the minerals in the spices, the smoothie tastes so great that you may forget to focus on its powerful health benefits.

INGREDIENTS

2 yellow apples, cored

1 teaspoon ground cinnamon

1 teaspoon ground cloves

1 teaspoon ground ginger

1 cup all-natural, organic apple juice (not from concentrate)

1 cup ice

Yields: 2 cups

Per 1 cup serving • Calories: 140 • Fat: 1g • Protein: 1g • Sodium: 8mg • Fiber: 3g • Carbohydrates: 36g

1. In a blender, combine the apples, cinnamon, cloves, ginger, and apple juice with ½ cup ice, and blend until thoroughly combined.

2. While blending, add remaining ice until desired consistency is achieved.

RED APPLE DAPPLE

Simple and sweet, this smoothie needs only the tartness of cherries and the unique deliciousness of apples to make it zing! Tons of rich antioxidants, like the quercetin in apples, fill every sip of this delicious smoothie treat that can do double-duty as breakfast or dessert. You'll promote overall health while fending off colds and allergies.

INGREDIENTS

2 red apples, cored

1 cup cherries, pitted

1½ cups all-natural, organic apple juice (not from concentrate)

1 cup ice

Yields: 3 cups

Per 1 cup serving • Calories: 141 • Fat: 0g • Protein: 1g • Sodium: 5mg • Fiber: 3g • Carbohydrates: 36g

1. In a blender, combine the apples, cherries, and 1 cup apple juice with ½ cup ice, and blend until thoroughly combined.

2. While blending, add remaining apple juice and ice until desired consistency is achieved.

BANANA BANGER

If you're a peanut butter lover, this recipe is for you. Replacing common peanut butter, which may be full of sodium, sugar, and trans fats, with all-natural almond butter, which packs protein, healthy fat, and great taste, this smoothie ensures that you'll provide your metabolism with the clean fuel it needs to function at its best.

INGREDIENTS

2 bananas, peeled

2 tablespoons natural almond butter

1 cup plain kefir

1 cup water

1 cup ice

Yields: 2 cups

Per 1 cup serving • Calories: 140 • Fat: 3g • Protein: 6g • Sodium: 64mg • Fiber: 2g • Carbohydrates: 25g

1. In a blender, combine the bananas, almond butter, kefir, and ½ cup water with ½ cup ice, and blend until thoroughly combined.

2. While blending, add remaining water and ice until desired consistency is achieved.

BANANA NUT BLEND

Waking up to the sweet aroma of fresh-baked banana bread can't be topped . . . until you taste this smoothie!

INGREDIENTS

¼ cup walnuts

1 cup vanilla almond milk

1 cup romaine lettuce

2 bananas, peeled

Yields: 3–4 cups

Per 1 cup serving • Calories: 99 • Fat: 6g • Protein: 2g • Sodium: 39mg • Fiber: 2g • Carbohydrates: 12g

1. Combine walnuts and ½ cup almond milk in a blender and blend until walnuts are completely emulsified.

2. Add romaine, bananas, and remaining ½ cup almond milk while blending until desired texture is achieved.

Walnuts and Antioxidants

When you think of antioxidant-rich foods, walnuts probably aren't your first thought, but just ¼ cup of walnuts carries almost 100 percent of your daily value of omega-3 fatty acids, and is loaded with monounsaturated fats. Of the tree nuts, walnuts, chestnuts, and pecans carry the highest amount of antioxidants, which can prevent illness and reverse oxidative damage done by free radicals.

BANANAS WITH Bs

Bananas are packed with vitamins B$_6$ and C, making them a delicious way to get more of these ultra-important vitamins, which promote energy and a healthy metabolism. Combined with creamy kefir, bananas ensure that the health benefits and the taste of this smoothie provide a scrumptious way to live healthfully.

INGREDIENTS

2 bananas, peeled

1 cup plain kefir

1 cup water

1 cup ice

Yields: 3 cups

Per 1 cup serving • Calories: 115 • Fat: 0.5g • Protein: 5.5g • Sodium: 64mg • Fiber: 2g • Carbohydrates: 24g

1. In a blender, combine the bananas, kefir, and ½ cup water with ½ cup ice, and blend until thoroughly combined.

2. While blending, add remaining water and ice until desired consistency is achieved.

BANANA SPLIT

If you're like most people, banana splits brings back memories of carefree childhood bliss. Here, instead of using processed ice cream and additives, this smoothie uses all-natural ingredients that work together to improve immunity and cell health. This puts a healthy spin on a not-so-healthy timeless classic.

INGREDIENTS

2 bananas, peeled

½ cup coconut meat

¼ cup cherries, pitted

1 cup plain kefir

1 cup water

1 cup ice

Yields: 3 cups

Per 1 cup serving • Calories: 127 • Fat: 1g • Protein: 6g • Sodium: 64mg • Fiber: 2g • Carbohydrates: 26g

1. In a blender, combine the bananas, coconut meat, cherries, kefir, and ½ cup water with ½ cup ice, and blend until thoroughly combined.

2. While blending, add remaining water and ice until desired consistency is achieved.

BASIC BANANA BLEND

There's nothing easier than a simple recipe of just a few ingredients. This basic concoction of smooth, beautiful bananas needs nothing else but water and ice to be an enticing smoothie that packs tons of flavor and nutrition, with just a quick whirl of the blender.

INGREDIENTS

2 bananas, peeled

1 cup water

1 cup ice

Yields: 2 cups

Per 1 cup serving • Calories: 105 • Fat: 0.4g • Protein: 1g • Sodium: 1mg • Fiber: 3g • Carbohydrates: 27g

1. In a blender, combine the bananas and water with ½ cup ice, and blend until thoroughly combined.

2. Add remaining ice as needed and blend until desired consistency is achieved.

BLISSFUL BANANAS

Even though this delicious smoothie is full of vitamins and minerals, its benefits don't stop there. The carbohydrate- and fiber-rich combination of bananas and oats in this delightful blend makes for a satisfying snack or meal that will fuel your body, keep you focused, and satisfy your hunger.

INGREDIENTS

2 bananas, peeled

¼ cup rolled oats

2 cups water

1 cup ice

Yields: 2 cups

Per 1 cup serving • Calories: 143 • Fat: 1g • Protein: 3g • Sodium: 2mg • Fiber: 4g • Carbohydrates: 34g

1. In a blender, combine the bananas, oats, and 1 cup water with ½ cup ice, and blend until thoroughly combined.

2. While blending, add remaining water and ice until desired consistency is achieved.

CHERRIES AND SPICE

Creamy, spicy, and sweet, this smoothie is a delicious way to add some nutritious fruit servings to your diet. The vitamin C in the deep red berries helps protect against cardiovascular disease and prenatal problems. This tasty recipe takes healthy living to a whole new level!

INGREDIENTS

2 cups cherries, pitted

1 tablespoon grated ginger

1 teaspoon ground cloves

1 teaspoon ground nutmeg

1 cup vanilla almond milk

1 cup ice

½ cup water

Yields: 3 cups

Per 1 cup serving • Calories: 106 • Fat: 1g • Protein: 2g • Sodium: 32mg • Fiber: 3g • Carbohydrates: 27g

1. In a blender, combine the cherries, ginger, cloves, nutmeg, and almond milk with ½ cup ice, and blend until thoroughly combined.

2. While blending, add the water and remaining ice until desired consistency is achieved.

VERY CHERRY VANILLA

Needing nothing more than three simple ingredients, this smoothie combines sweet cherries, flavorful vanilla bean, and creamy vanilla almond milk for a very vanilla spin on an already delicious treat. Packed with loads of valuable nutrition, this is one smoothie you'd never guess was designed to promote health.

INGREDIENTS

2 cups cherries, pitted

1 vanilla bean's pulp

1 cup vanilla almond milk

1 cup ice

Yields: 3 cups

Per 1 cup serving • Calories: 102 • Fat: 1g • Protein: 1g • Sodium: 30mg • Fiber: 2g • Carbohydrates: 26g

1. In a blender, combine the cherries, vanilla bean pulp, and almond milk with ½ cup ice, and blend until thoroughly combined.

2. While blending, add remaining ice until desired consistency is achieved.

BERRIES

BERRY, BERRY DELICIOUS

The sweet tang of oranges, strawberries, and blueberries combine beautifully with the romaine in this smoothie to develop a deliciously refreshing treat.

INGREDIENTS

1 cup romaine lettuce

2 oranges, peeled

1 cup strawberries

1 cup blueberries

1 cup vanilla almond milk

Yields: 3–4 cups

Per 1 cup serving • Calories: 121 • Fat: 1g • Protein: 2g • Sodium: 40mg • Fiber: 5g • Carbohydrates: 29g

1. Combine the romaine, oranges, berries, and ½ cup of almond milk in a blender and blend until thoroughly combined.

2. Add remaining almond milk while blending until desired texture is achieved.

Citric Acid and Flavor

Lemon, lime, and orange juices are commonly used in foods and drinks with the main purpose of enhancing the flavors of the main ingredient. A small amount of acidic citrus juice can add a depth to the flavors of fruits or vegetables, and the result in smoothies containing berries is an amplified sweetness of the berries' natural flavors.

BERRIES FOR BABY 🅿

When Mama's happy, everyone's happy. Satisfying and refreshing ingredients combine here for a flavorful smoothie you can enjoy guilt free.

INGREDIENTS

1 cup watercress

2 bananas, peeled

1 cup blueberries

1 cup strawberries

2 cups kefir

Yields: 3–4 cups

Per 1 cup serving • Calories: 167 • Fat: 4g • Protein: 5g • Sodium: 67mg • Fiber: 5g • Carbohydrates: 29g

1. Combine watercress, bananas, berries, and 1 cup kefir in a blender and blend until thoroughly combined.

2. Add remaining kefir as needed while blending until desired consistency is achieved.

A BERRY DELICIOUS END TO THE DAY

When you want something sweet and fruity and a berry smoothie sounds just perfect, treat yourself to this homemade version that offers more health benefits than a store-bought treat and the peace of mind from knowing exactly what's in it.

INGREDIENTS

1 cup iceberg lettuce

1 pint strawberries

1 pint blueberries

1 banana, peeled

½ cup vanilla almond milk

½ cup ice cubes (optional)

Yields: 3–4 cups

Per 1 cup serving • Calories: 111 • Fat: 1g • Protein: 2g • Sodium: 22mg • Fiber: 5g • Carbohydrates: 27g

1. Combine iceberg, strawberries, blueberries, banana, and almond milk in a blender until thoroughly combined.

2. Add optional ice cubes, if desired, while blending until desired texture is achieved.

Berries and the Bladder

Although many people consider them just tasty fruits, berries are well known superfoods that can improve health and prevent illness. In addition to contributing to strong heart health, blueberries and cranberries promote bladder health by fighting off *E. coli* bacteria, the culprit in urinary tract infections.

A BERRY GREAT MORNING

This smoothie is packed with rich antioxidants, powerful phytochemicals, and loads of protein that will get you moving and keep you moving!

INGREDIENTS

2 cups mixed baby greens

1 pint raspberries

1 pint blueberries

1 banana, peeled

1 cup vanilla soymilk

Yields: 1 quart

Per 1 cup serving • Calories: 94 • Fat: 2g • Protein: 3g • Sodium: 28mg • Fiber: 6g • Carbohydrates: 19g

1. Combine greens, berries, and banana and blend thoroughly.

2. While blending, add soymilk slowly until desired texture is achieved.

Blueberries and Raspberries for a Healthy Life

Combining raspberries and blueberries in the same smoothie gives your immune system a boost you'd never expect. The vitamins and phytochemicals that burst from these berries and make their skin vibrant red and purple are what also fight off the cancers, carcinogens, and mental health risks that you'd rather steer clear of!

BERRY BANANAS

The deliciously sweet flavors of berries, bananas, and almond milk blend perfectly with the light, crisp romaine to develop a green smoothie that beats any takeout smoothie around.

INGREDIENTS

1 cup romaine lettuce

1 pint blueberries

1 pint raspberries

2 pints strawberries

2 bananas, peeled

1 cup vanilla almond milk

1 cup Greek yogurt

Yields: 4–6 cups

Per 1 cup serving • Calories: 230 • Fat: 2g • Protein: 9g • Sodium: 66mg • Fiber: 11g • Carbohydrates: 49g

1. Combine romaine, berries, bananas, and almond milk in a blender and blend until thoroughly combined.

2. Add Greek yogurt while blending until desired texture is achieved.

RED BERRY ROUNDUP

Made with four different varieties of vibrant red berries, this is a delicious, creamy smoothie full of rich phyto-chemicals and vitamins A and C for top-notch immunity-building defenses. Along with great nutrition from the berries, you'll benefit from good bacteria in the probiotic-rich kefir.

INGREDIENTS

½ cup strawberries

½ cup raspberries

½ cup cranberries

½ cup cherries, pitted

1 cup strawberry kefir

½ cup water

1 cup ice

Yields: 3 cups

Per 1 cup serving • Calories: 88 • Fat: 0g • Protein: 5g • Sodium: 64mg • Fiber: 3g • Carbohydrates: 17g

1. In a blender, combine the strawberries, raspberries, cran-berries, cherries, kefir, and water with ½ cup ice, and blend until thoroughly combined.

2. While blending, add remaining ice until desired consistency is achieved.

BLUEBERRY SUPREME

Blueberries take center stage in this antioxidant-packed, day-brightening recipe!

INGREDIENTS

1 cup iceberg lettuce

2 pints blueberries

1 banana, peeled

½ cup rice milk

Yields: 3–4 cups

Per 1 cup serving • Calories: 128 • Fat: 1g • Protein: 2g • Sodium: 16mg • Fiber: 5g • Carbohydrates: 32g

1. Combine iceberg, blueberries, banana, and half of the rice milk in a blender and blend until thoroughly combined.

2. Add remaining rice milk while blending until desired texture is achieved.

CRAZY FOR CRANBERRIES

Cranberries lend a tart sweetness to any smoothie, and when paired with delicious ginger, there's no end to the amazing depth of flavors. Helping to maintain urinary tract health, the cranberry's powerful benefits make this smoothie a great option for everyone of every age and gender.

INGREDIENTS

2 cups cranberries

1 tablespoon grated ginger

1 cup vanilla rice milk

1 cup ice

Yields: 3 cups

Per 1 cup serving • Calories: 65 • Fat: 1g • Protein: 1g • Sodium: 32mg • Fiber: 3g • Carbohydrates: 18g

1. In a blender, combine the cranberries, ginger, and rice milk with ½ cup ice, and blend until thoroughly combined.

2. While blending, add remaining ice until desired consistency is achieved.

RASPBERRY DELIGHT

This smooth blend of raspberries and banana packs vitamins and minerals into a deliciously sweet dessert. With the added nutrition from the lettuce, rice milk, and yogurt, this smoothie offers protein, iron, folate, and other B vitamins galore!

INGREDIENTS

1 cup iceberg lettuce

2 pints raspberries

1 banana, peeled

½ cup rice milk

½ cup Greek yogurt

Yields: 3–4 cups

Per 1 cup serving • Calories: 141 • Fat: 1g • Protein: 5g • Sodium: 28mg • Fiber: 11g • Carbohydrates: 30g

1. Combine iceberg, raspberries, banana, and rice milk in a blender and blend until thoroughly combined.

2. Add Greek yogurt while blending until desired texture is achieved.

RASPBERRY TART MORNING START

Raspberries and lime join to make a sweet and tart smoothie that will open your sinuses and sweeten your morning. This blend will please all of your taste buds!

INGREDIENTS

1 cup Greek yogurt

1 cup romaine lettuce

2 pints raspberries

½ lime, peeled

Yields: 3 cups

Per 1 cup serving • Calories: 118 • Fat: 1g • Protein: 8g • Sodium: 26mg • Fiber: 11g • Carbohydrates: 22g

1. Pour ½ cup yogurt in a blender, followed by the romaine, raspberries, and lime. Blend.

2. Continue adding remaining yogurt while blending until desired texture is achieved.

Fight Cancer with Sweetness

With each providing a sweet and tart flavor, limes and raspberries are extremely powerful additions to any day. Rich in antioxidants and packing powerful anticancer properties, these two fruits pair up to keep your immune system running at its best.

RIDICULOUS RASPBERRIES 'N' CREAM

The delightful tastes of strawberry kefir and coconut milk get all jazzed up with the splendid addition of raspberries in this delicious, nutritious smoothie. The rich red ingredients deliver an antioxidant blast that will keep your body healthy and moving in the right direction!

INGREDIENTS

2 cups raspberries

1 cup strawberry kefir

1 cup coconut milk

1 cup ice

Yields: 2 cups

Per 1 cup serving • Calories: 355 • Fat: 25g • Protein: 11g • Sodium: 110mg • Fiber: 8g • Carbohydrates: 27g

1. In a blender, combine the raspberries, kefir, and ½ cup coconut milk with ½ cup ice, and blend until thoroughly combined.

2. While blending, add remaining coconut milk and ice until desired consistency is achieved.

SINFUL STRAWBERRY CREAM

When a craving for something sweet and delicious hits, this is a simple go-to you're sure to enjoy. Rich, sweet, and creamy, this recipe will simultaneously satisfy your sweet tooth and your daily values of important vitamins and minerals.

INGREDIENTS

1 cup spinach

2 pints strawberries

1 banana, peeled

1 cup kefir

Yields: 3–4 cups

Per 1 cup serving • Calories: 126 • Fat: 3g • Protein: 4g • Sodium: 39mg • Fiber: 5g • Carbohydrates: 24g

1. Combine spinach, strawberries, banana, and ½ cup kefir in a blender container and blend until thoroughly combined.

2. Add remaining kefir while blending until desired texture is achieved.

Kefir Versus Milk

If you've never indulged in this awesome milk alternative, now may be the perfect time. Kefir contains a plethora of vitamins, beneficial probiotic bacteria, and rich enzymes that promote healthy growth, optimize digestion, and fight illness. The best part is that almost every grocery store that carries milk products will carry kefir, so the switch is as easy as walking farther down the aisle.

SPARKLING STRAWBERRY

The "sparkle" of this smoothie comes from the delectable addition of ginger that makes every sip a striking one! Antioxidants for immunity, protein for strength and endurance, and probiotics for good bacteria protection—the combination of ingredients in this recipe helps make living better that much tastier.

INGREDIENTS

2 cups strawberries

1 tablespoon grated ginger

1 cup strawberry kefir

1 cup ice

Yields: 3 cups

Per 1 cup serving • Calories: 78 • Fat: 0g • Protein: 5g • Sodium: 64mg • Fiber: 2g • Carbohydrates: 14g

1. In a blender, combine the strawberries, ginger, and kefir with ½ cup ice, and blend until thoroughly combined.

2. While blending, add remaining ice until desired consistency is achieved.

Antioxidants: When They're Good

In theory, antioxidants provide some measure of immunity from cancer. However, a new study from Sweden suggests that people who already have cancer would be unwise to take extra antioxidants, since they seem to allow small tumors to proliferate. But if you're cancer-free, make antioxidants a part of your daily diet.

STRAWBERRIES 'N' GREENS

If you love strawberries, you'll be happy to enjoy one of your favorite fruits while also getting one full serving of your daily requirement of greens. Agave nectar comes into this smoothie to sweeten the flavor, but only if needed.

INGREDIENTS

½ cup dandelion greens

2 pints strawberries

1 cup vanilla soymilk

1 tablespoon agave nectar, to taste
(optional)

Yields: 3–4 cups

Per 1 cup serving • Calories: 85 • Fat: 1g • Protein: 3g • Sodium: 31mg • Fiber: 4g • Carbohydrates: 17g

1. Add dandelion greens, strawberries, and ½ cup soymilk in a blender and blend until combined.

2. Slowly add remaining soymilk while blending until desired consistency is achieved.

3. Stop blending periodically to check for desired sweetness, and drizzle in agave nectar until desired sweetness is achieved.

Strawberries for Sight

Rich in the antioxidants that give them their vibrant red color, this sweet berry is also rich in vitamins A, C, D, and E; B vitamins including folate; and phytochemicals that join forces to help you maintain healthy eyes and strong vision. Strawberries may help delay the onset of macular degeneration.

SWEET STRAWBERRY START

Sweet strawberries are a delicious food to kick off your morning routine. Blended with bananas and creamy kefir, this recipe makes for a nutritious, complex carbohydrate–rich jump-start that will give you long-lasting energy.

INGREDIENTS

2 cups strawberries

1 banana, peeled

1 cup strawberry kefir

½ cup coconut milk

1 cup ice

Yields: 4 cups

Per 1 cup serving • Calories: 140 • Fat: 6g • Protein: 5g • Sodium: 52mg • Fiber: 2g • Carbohydrates: 18g

1. In a blender, combine the strawberries, banana, kefir, and coconut milk with ½ cup ice, and blend until thoroughly combined.

2. While blending, add remaining ice until desired consistency is achieved.

CITRUS

SPLENDID CITRUS

Booming with the strong flavors of pineapple, orange, grapefruit, lemon, and lime, this sweet and tart smoothie will liven your senses while providing you with a boost in physical and mental health.

INGREDIENTS

2 large kale leaves

1 cup pineapple, peeled and cubed

1 large orange or 2 small oranges, peeled

1 grapefruit, peeled

½ lemon, peeled

½ lime, peeled

Yields: 1 quart

Per 1 cup serving • Calories: 73 • Fat: 0g • Protein: 2g • Sodium: 8mg • Fiber: 3g • Carbohydrates: 18g

1. Combine kale and all fruits in a blender in the order listed.

2. Blend until desired consistency is reached.

Feed Your Brain!

With four servings of fruit and two servings of vegetables, the vitamin and mineral benefits are obvious, but this citrusy green mix is also especially high in iron and folate. Necessary for optimal brain function, folate is especially important for pregnant and nursing women.

GREAT GRAPEFRUIT

The grapefruit and cucumber combine in this smoothie to offer a refreshing zing to your morning with vitamins and nutrients that will wake you up and keep you feeling fresh throughout the day!

INGREDIENTS

1 cup baby greens

2 grapefruits, peeled

1 cucumber, peeled and sliced

¼ cup purified water

Yields: 1 quart

Per 1 cup serving • Calories: 59 • Fat: 0g • Protein: 1g • Sodium: 3mg • Fiber: 2g • Carbohydrates: 14g

1. Combine greens, grapefruit, and cucumber with half of the water and blend.

2. Add remaining water slowly while blending until desired consistency is reached.

Why Grapefruit Is Great

Although the grapefruit is known for being rich in vitamin C, this citrus fruit has been used not only for building immunity but also for treating symptoms of illness. The next time you start feeling feverish, the best thing to take may just be a healthy helping of grapefruit, which would make this smoothie the perfect option!

LUSCIOUS LEMON-LIME

The tartness of lemons and limes is mellowed with crisp romaine and sweet agave nectar. The kefir gives a creamy texture with protein and essential vitamins. These ingredients combine in a delicious smoothie that will make you feel awake and refreshed.

INGREDIENTS

1 cup romaine lettuce

2 lemons, peeled

2 limes, peeled

½ cup kefir

1 tablespoon agave nectar

Yields: 2–3 cups

Per 1 cup serving • Calories: 111 • Fat: 2g • Protein: 3g • Sodium: 36mg • Fiber: 5g • Carbohydrates: 17g

1. Combine romaine, lemons, limes, and kefir and blend until thoroughly combined.

2. Add agave nectar slowly while blending, stopping periodically to taste, until desired sweetness and texture is achieved.

Balance Your Body

Lemons and limes don't just have the acidity and tang to make you pucker up—they are incredibly healthy, too. Those same small, sour fruits that can bring a tear to your eye actually promote a balanced alkaline level in your body.

SUBLIME LIME

The tart taste of lime in this smoothie is balanced nicely with the sweet and thickening banana, making a sweet treat that may give your face a reason to pucker up momentarily!

INGREDIENTS

1 cup spinach

2 limes, peeled and deseeded

1 banana, peeled

½ cup purified water

Yields: 3–4 cups

Per 1 cup serving • Calories: 51 • Fat: 0g • Protein: 1g • Sodium: 10mg • Fiber: 2g • Carbohydrates: 14g

1. Combine spinach, limes, and banana in a blender with half of the water and blend until thoroughly combined.

2. If needed, add remaining water while blending until desired consistency is achieved.

Limes and Joints

Although many patients suffering from arthritis decide to exercise and eat differently, few know the powerful effects limes can have on joints! These vitamin C–filled fruits can pack a punch in getting arthritis symptoms to a minimum and making everyday life seem less achy where the limbs bend.

LICKITY LIME AND BERRIES

The tart sensation of limes gets chilled out with the sweet tastes of strawberries, raspberries, and creamy kefir. When there's a delicious blend like this one that packs a one-two punch of vitamins A and C for immunity-strengthening benefits, it's pretty easy to live healthy!

INGREDIENTS

1 cup strawberries

1 cup raspberries

1 lime, peeled and deseeded

1 cup strawberry kefir

1 cup ice

½ cup water

Yields: 2 cups

Per 1 cup serving • Calories: 110 • Fat: 1g • Protein: 8g • Sodium: 96mg • Fiber: 5g • Carbohydrates: 20g

1. In a blender, combine the strawberries, raspberries, lime, and kefir with ½ cup ice, and blend until thoroughly combined.

2. While blending, add water and remaining ice until desired consistency is achieved.

ORANGE YOU GLAD YOU WOKE UP FOR THIS!

While waking yourself with orange juice may be delicious and nutritious, this spin on the traditional morning juice drink takes the cake! Made with real, whole oranges that provide quality nutrition from their abundant beta-carotene, vitamin C, and fiber, this delicious creamy spin on your favorite glass of OJ may make tomorrow morning's wakeup call a little easier to bear.

INGREDIENTS

4 oranges, peeled and deseeded

1 scoop vanilla protein powder

1½ cups vanilla almond milk

1 cup ice

Yields: 2 cups

Per 1 cup serving • Calories: 253 • Fat: 3g •
Protein: 15g • Sodium: 68mg • Fiber: 6g •
Carbohydrates: 52g

1. In a blender, combine the oranges, protein powder, and 1 cup almond milk with ½ cup ice, and blend until thoroughly combined.

2. While blending, add remaining almond milk and ice until desired consistency is achieved.

COCONUTS, MANGOS, AND MELONS

CALMING COCONUT COOLER

If you're out of ideas for bedtime treats that contribute more than sugar, fat, and calories, you're looking at the right recipe! Here smooth chamomile tea meets with the natural, unique sweetness of coconut and ginger for a nutritious, sensational-tasting smoothie that will set your mind at ease and gently rock you off to sleep.

INGREDIENTS

1½ cups coconut meat

1½ cups cooled chamomile tea

1 tablespoon grated ginger

1 cup ice

Yields: 2 cups

Per 1 cup serving • Calories: 215 • Fat: 20g • Protein: 2g • Sodium: 12mg • Fiber: 5g • Carbohydrates: 10g

1. In a blender, combine the coconut meat, chamomile tea, and grated ginger with ½ cup ice, and blend until thoroughly combined.

2. While blending, add remaining ice until desired consistency is achieved.

COCONUT CREAM DREAM

Coconut cream pies are a delicious dessert, but have too many empty calories and too few vitamins and minerals. This recipe blends the star ingredients of coconut cream pie in a healthy green smoothie.

INGREDIENTS

1 cup romaine lettuce

Flesh of 2 mature coconuts

1 tablespoon lemon juice

1 banana, peeled

¼" ginger, peeled

½ cup almond milk

½ cup Greek yogurt

Yields: 3–4 cups

Per 1 cup serving • Calories: 177 • Fat: 67g • Protein: 10g • Sodium: 72mg • Fiber: 19g • Carbohydrates: 41g

1. Combine romaine, coconut flesh, lemon juice, banana, ginger, and almond milk in a blender until thoroughly combined.

2. Add the yogurt while blending until desired texture is achieved.

CRAZY FOR COCONUTS

Combining uniquely flavored, vitamin B–packed coconut meat and coconut milk with the light flavors of pure vanilla bean makes for one delicious smoothie that also provides health benefits galore, including better blood quality and improved mood.

INGREDIENTS

1 cup coconut meat

1 vanilla bean's pulp

2 cups coconut milk

1 cup ice

Yields: 3 cups

Per 1 cup serving • Calories: 173 • Fat: 16g • Protein: 1g • Sodium: 25mg • Fiber: 2g • Carbohydrates: 6g

1. In a blender, combine the coconut meat, vanilla bean pulp, and coconut milk with ½ cup ice, and blend until thoroughly combined.

2. While blending, add remaining ice until desired consistency is achieved.

EASY ISLAND TIME

Coconut meat, banana, and pineapple each lends its own unique flavor and texture to this delicious smoothie. But this combo provides more than just beauty and taste; the vitamin C and phytochemicals like bromelain improve immunity, tune up system functioning, and make this smoothie an all-around winner!

INGREDIENTS

1 cup coconut meat

1 banana, peeled

½ cup pineapple

2 cups coconut milk

1 cup ice

Yields: 4 cups

Per 1 cup serving • Calories: 163 • Fat: 12g • Protein: 1g • Sodium: 19mg • Fiber: 3g • Carbohydrates: 14g

1. In a blender, combine coconut meat, banana, pineapple, and coconut milk with ½ cup ice, and blend until thoroughly combined.

2. While blending, add remaining ice until desired consistency is achieved.

MANGO MADNESS

The color of this smoothie is vibrant, and the beta-carotene, vitamins A and E, and strong variety of minerals found in it help strengthen your bones and protect your vision.

INGREDIENTS

½ cup dandelion greens

½ cup romaine lettuce

2 mangos, peeled and pit removed

1 banana, peeled

½ cup purified water

Yields: 3–4 cups

Per 1 cup serving • Calories: 130 • Fat: 1g • Protein: 1g • Sodium: 12mg • Fiber: 4g • Carbohydrates: 34g

1. Combine dandelion greens, romaine, mangos, banana, and half of the water in a blender and blend thoroughly.

2. While blending, add remaining water until desired texture is achieved.

Mangos and Complexion

If you suffer from any type of skin abnormalities such as rashes, eczema, or even clogged pores, you'll be happy to know that mangos contain minerals, phytochemicals, and phenols that can improve the condition of your skin. The sweet taste of a mango smoothie with the added benefit of clearer skin is a definite win-win!

MANGO SUPREME

Mangos and bananas make one sweet combination, and with the amazing amounts of vitamins, minerals, and phytochemicals you get from blending them with rich greens, this smoothie is the perfect combination of delightful taste and sound nutrition.

INGREDIENTS

1 cup iceberg lettuce

2 mangos, peeled and pit removed

1 banana, peeled

2 cups purified water

Yields: 3–4 cups

Per 1 cup serving • Calories: 96 • Fat: 0g • Protein: 1g • Sodium: 7mg • Fiber: 3g • Carbohydrates: 25g

1. Combine iceberg, mangos, banana, and 1 cup of water in a blender and blend until thoroughly combined.

2. Add remaining water while blending until desired texture is achieved.

COOL CUCUMBER MELON

The mix of romaine, cucumbers, honeydew, and mint in this recipe combines beautifully to develop one of the most crisp, refreshing smoothies you'll taste.

INGREDIENTS

1 cup romaine lettuce

1 sprig mint leaves

3 cucumbers, peeled

½ honeydew melon, peeled, seeds removed

½ cup kefir

Yields: 3–4 cups

Per 1 cup serving • Calories: 86 • Fat: 1g • Protein: 3g • Sodium: 43mg • Fiber: 3g • Carbohydrates: 17g

1. In a blender, combine romaine and mint leaves followed by the cucumbers, melon, and half of the kefir and blend until thoroughly combined.

2. Add remaining kefir while blending until desired texture is achieved.

Cucumbers and Skin

If you're exfoliating, hydrating, and moisturizing your skin but still feel like you're not reaching that desired clarity and glow, try working on your complexion from the *inside*. Packed with the powerful combination of vitamin A and silica, cucumbers can help repair connective tissue and skin. So, instead of buying that new and improved face cream, add a couple of servings of cucumbers to your diet for the healthy skin you desire!

GINGER MELON STRESS MELTAWAY ♥

Although pregnancy is an amazing experience of excitement and anticipation, stress and moodiness can make it unbearable at times. Calm your nerves while quieting cravings with this delicious combination of watercress, melons, citrus, and ginger.

INGREDIENTS

1 cup watercress

½ cantaloupe, rind and seeds removed

½ honeydew, rind and seeds removed

1 tangerine, peeled

½" ginger, peeled

1 cup red raspberry tea

Yields: 3–4 cups

Per 1 cup serving • Calories: 94 • Fat: 0g • Protein: 2g • Sodium: 45mg • Fiber: 2g • Carbohydrates: 24g

1. Combine watercress, cantaloupe, honeydew, tangerine, and ginger in a blender and blend until thoroughly combined.

2. While blending, add tea as needed until desired consistency is achieved.

SPLENDID MELON

While endive is more commonly found in salads or as a garnish, this green is a wonderful base to this smoothie. The cantaloupe and honeydew melon add sweet nectar that will quench any need your body may have.

INGREDIENTS

1 cup endive

1 cantaloupe, peeled and seeds removed

1 honeydew, peeled and seeds removed

½ cup ice cubes (optional)

Yields: 3–4 cups

Per 1 cup serving • Calories: 185 • Fat: 1g • Protein: 4g • Sodium: 93mg • Fiber: 5g • Carbohydrates: 47g

1. Combine endive, cantaloupe, and honeydew in a blender and blend thoroughly until desired texture is achieved.

2. If a thicker consistency is desired, ice can be added while blending until desired consistency is reached.

Cantaloupe Promotes Energy

In a single serving of cantaloupe, there are a variety of vitamins and minerals that promote great health, including over 100 percent of the Recommended Daily Allowance (RDA) of vitamins C and A. One of the most astounding benefits of this fruit is its major role in speeding up metabolism, specifically the metabolism of carbohydrates.

WACKY WATERMELON

Watermelon's amazing taste isn't the only great thing about this fruit. Packed with vitamins, minerals, nutrients, and a ton of water, it satisfies your sweet tooth while quenching your thirst at the same time.

INGREDIENTS

1 cup iceberg lettuce

½ sprig mint leaves

2 cups watermelon

1 cucumber, peeled

Purified water, to taste (optional)

Yields: 3–4 cups

Per 1 cup serving • Calories: 32 • Fat: 0g • Protein: 1g • Sodium: 4mg • Fiber: 1g • Carbohydrates: 7g

1. Combine the iceberg, mint, watermelon, and cucumber in a blender and blend until thoroughly combined.

2. Add additional water, if necessary, while blending until desired texture is achieved.

Water-Melon

The average person has a hard time getting the recommended daily 8 to 10 glasses of water. Whether the flavorless drink is unappealing, sweet and sugary drink alternatives are more desirable, or the actual consumption of 64 ounces seems tedious, hydrating can be difficult. The alternative to drinking your daily water requirement is to consume some of it through fruits and vegetables that contain a lot of water. With the high water content of the ingredients in this smoothie, you may not even need to add any additional fluid!

WONDERFUL WATERMELON

This delicious smoothie is full of hydrating watermelon, smooth bananas, and creamy coconut milk that will brighten your day. With flu-fighting quercetin and cancer-fighting lycopene in every sip of this simple splendor, your vitality can improve without any effort at all!

INGREDIENTS

2 cups watermelon

1 banana, peeled

1 cup coconut milk

1 cup ice

Yields: 3 cups

Per 1 cup serving • Calories: 214 • Fat: 16g • Protein: 3g • Sodium: 11mg • Fiber: 1g • Carbohydrates: 19g

1. In a blender, combine the watermelon, banana, and coconut milk with ½ cup ice, and blend until thoroughly combined.

2. While blending, add remaining ice until desired consistency is achieved.

PEACHES AND PEARS

PEACHY BERRY

If you love peaches and berries, combining them with the baby greens in this smoothie delivers sweet tastes with vitamins and nutrients.

INGREDIENTS

1 cup baby greens

2 peaches, pitted and peeled

1 cup strawberries

1 banana, peeled

½ tablespoon ginger, sliced or grated

Purified water, to taste (optional)

Yields: 3–4 cups

Per 1 cup serving • Calories: 92 • Fat: 1g • Protein: 2g • Sodium: 3mg • Fiber: 4g • Carbohydrates: 23g

1. Add all ingredients to a blender and blend until thoroughly combined.

2. Add water, if necessary, while blending until desired texture is achieved.

Organic Alert!

Although peaches can be found in almost every grocery store and fruit stand during their season as well as year-round in the grocer's freezer, it is an important fruit to purchase organic. Because of its thin flesh, it is more susceptible to the pesticides and preservatives used in the nonorganic growing process. Although they are pricier than nonorganic varieties, buying organic peaches is important for your health and your family's.

JUST PEACHY

Peaches can add a sweet nectar taste to almost anything. In this recipe, they brighten the fresh taste of romaine.

INGREDIENTS

1 cup romaine lettuce

3 peaches, pitted (peel removed optional)

1 banana, peeled

½ cup water

Yields: 3–4 cups

Per 1 cup serving • Calories: 72 • Fat: 0g • Protein: 1g • Sodium: 2mg • Fiber: 3g • Carbohydrates: 18g

1. Combine romaine, peaches, banana, and ¼ cup of water in a blender and blend until thoroughly combined.

2. Add remaining water while blending until desired texture is achieved.

CREAMY PEAR PERFECTION

Pears and protein powder that provide your muscles with all of the necessary nutrition for repair make for a creamy spin on "healthy" drink options. Delicious and unique, this smoothie gets even better with the addition of probiotic-rich kefir for immunity-protecting power.

INGREDIENTS

2 pears, cored

1 scoop vanilla protein powder

1 cup plain kefir

1 cup ice

Yields: 2 cups

Per 1 cup serving • Calories: 158 • Fat: 1g • Protein: 19g • Sodium: 94mg • Fiber: 3g • Carbohydrates: 19g

1. In a blender, combine the pears, protein powder, and kefir with ½ cup ice, and blend until thoroughly combined.

2. While blending, add remaining ice until desired consistency is achieved.

A DARING PEARING

Because pears aren't in season year round, the frozen option is available at almost any grocery store, and will make equally delicious green smoothies.

INGREDIENTS

1 cup spinach

3 pears, peeled and cored

1 banana, peeled

1 cup purified water

Yields: 3–4 cups

Per 1 cup serving • Calories: 105 • Fat: 0g • Protein: 1g • Sodium: 9mg • Fiber: 5g • Carbohydrates: 28g

1. Combine spinach, pears, banana, and ½ cup water in a blender and blend until thoroughly combined.

2. Add remaining water while blending until desired texture is achieved.

PEAR PASSION SMOOTHIE

Adding protein for muscle repair, probiotics for immune system support, and antioxidants for cell protection, the protein powder, kefir, and cinnamon make this pear smoothie a nutrition bonanza.

INGREDIENTS

2 pears, cored

1 cup plain kefir

1 scoop vanilla protein powder

1 teaspoon cinnamon

1 cup water

1 cup ice

Yields: 3 cups

Per 1 cup serving • Calories: 107 • Fat: 1g • Protein: 13g • Sodium: 63mg • Fiber: 2g • Carbohydrates: 13g

1. In a blender, combine the pears, kefir, protein powder, cinnamon, and water with ½ cup ice, and blend until thoroughly combined.

2. While blending, add remaining ice until desired consistency is achieved.

PEAR SPLENDOR

Pears give this smoothie its unique sweetness and taste while the banana adds a smooth texture. Packed with vitamins and nutrients, this smoothie is a tasty, fiber-filled delight!

INGREDIENTS

1 cup spinach

2 pears, cored and peeled

1 banana, peeled

1 cup almond milk

Yields: 3 cups

Per 1 cup serving • Calories: 136 • Fat: 1g • Protein: 1g • Sodium: 59mg • Fiber: 5g • Carbohydrates: 33g

1. Combine spinach, pears, banana, and ½ cup almond milk in a blender and blend until smooth.

2. While blending, continue adding remaining almond milk until desired texture is achieved.

The Power of Copper

A little-known fact about the pear is that just 1 serving contains a powerful amount of copper. A strong and very important mineral, copper works wonders in fighting the process of free radical damage to cells. Not only does this mean that a pear can help you fight off cancer and disease, but the aesthetic effects of anti-aging are pretty attractive, too!

PERFECT PEARS

Pears are practically perfect on their own, but when paired with pure apple juice, which adds an extra boost of flavor and a perfected texture, this pear smoothie becomes a sweet, simple, and delicious jolt of energy-promoting nutrition from its rich concentration of vitamin C and plentiful B vitamins.

INGREDIENTS

2 pears, cored

1 cup all-natural, organic apple juice (not from concentrate)

1 cup ice

Yields: 2 cups

Per 1 cup serving • Calories: 92 • Fat: 0g • Protein: 1g • Sodium: 5mg • Fiber: 3g • Carbohydrates: 23g

1. In a blender, combine the pears and apple juice with ½ cup ice, and blend until thoroughly combined.

2. While blending, add remaining ice until desired consistency is achieved.

PLEASANTLY PEAR

With its variety of fruits coupled with romaine, this smoothie has vitamins, minerals, and antioxidants galore, providing your body with unsurpassed nutrition.

INGREDIENTS

1 cup romaine lettuce

2 pears, peeled and cored

1 apple, peeled and cored

1 banana, peeled

½ cup purified water

Yields: 3–4 cups

Per 1 cup serving • Calories: 132 • Fat: 0g • Protein: 1g • Sodium: 4mg • Fiber: 6g • Carbohydrates: 35g

1. Combine romaine, pears, apple, banana, and ¼ cup water in a blender and blend thoroughly.

2. While blending, add remaining water until desired texture is achieved.

Fiber Effects of Pears

Fiber helps keep your digestive tract functioning optimally. Why not enjoy a green smoothie that packs a whopping amount of fiber from greens, pears, and apples? This delicious smoothie can get your digestive system working at its full potential and make irregularity a thing of the past.

VANILLA-PEAR PERFECTION

Although pears taste delicious on their own, adding the naturally aromatic vanilla bean's pulp raises its deliciousness level just a bit. Great taste isn't the only perk of this smoothie; you also get disease-fighting antioxidant benefits from the vanillin in each and every sip. Rich, creamy, and flavorful, this smoothie blends together an amazing fruit, a delicious spice, and smooth vanilla almond milk for a cool creation that's sure to amaze.

INGREDIENTS

2 pears, cored

1 vanilla bean's pulp

1 cup vanilla almond milk

1 cup ice

Yields: 2 cups

Per 1 cup serving • Calories: 77 • Fat: 1g •
Protein: 3g • Sodium: 60mg • Fiber: 4g •
Carbohydrates: 13g

1. In a blender, combine the pears, vanilla bean pulp, and almond milk with ½ cup ice, and blend until thoroughly combined.

2. While blending, add remaining ice until desired consistency is achieved.

CHAPTER 4

SWEET SMOOTHIES

CACAO CRAZINESS

Chocolate cravings can end in guilty consumption of sugar- and fat-laden candy that leads to the need for more exercise. Satisfy those cravings with pure cacao in a smoothie like this, and candy cravings will be a thing of the past.

INGREDIENTS

¼ cup almonds

2 cups purified water

1 cup watercress

2 tablespoons powdered natural cacao

2 bananas, peeled

2 apples, peeled and cored

Yields: 3–4 cups

Per 1 cup serving • Calories: 153 • Fat: 5g • Protein: 3g • Sodium: 7mg • Fiber: 4g • Carbohydrates: 27g

1. Combine almonds and 1 cup of water in a blender and emulsify until no almond bits remain.

2. Add watercress, cacao, bananas, apples, and remaining water while blending until desired consistency is achieved.

Sweet Antioxidant Protection

When in need of powerful antioxidants that protect, reach no further than a heaping helping of raw cacao. The plant that actually delivers the cocoa we're oh-so-familiar with, cacao is known as a superfood for providing an abundance of antioxidants. Protect your body and the hard work you've put into making it an efficient machine by adding raw cacao in sweet or savory smoothies for an extra hit of health!

CHOCOLATEY DREAM

Ahhhh, chocolate! It's pretty difficult to find someone who doesn't like chocolate, and this smoothie has the perfect blend of ingredients to satisfy any chocolate craving.

INGREDIENTS

1 cup watercress

2 tablespoons raw powdered cocoa

2 bananas, peeled

2 cups almond milk

Yields: 3–4 cups

Per 1 cup serving • Calories: 104 • Fat: 2g • Protein: 2g • Sodium: 80mg • Fiber: 3g • Carbohydrates: 23g

1. In a blender, combine the watercress and cocoa powder, followed by the bananas and 1 cup of the almond milk and blend until thoroughly combined.

2. Add remaining almond milk while blending until desired texture is achieved.

Chocolate Is Healthy?

Chocolate has been determined to be beneficial in the daily diet! Now, don't take this as a go-ahead to dive into that huge bag of M&M's. Powdered, unprocessed cocoa is the chocolate shown to provide the most benefits. Although the candy bar alternative may seem more gratifying, the sugar content, trans fats, and milk products may be the reason they haven't yet been labeled superfoods.

GO, COCOA!

Bursting with flavor, this smoothie provides more nutrition than you would think. Vitamins, minerals, and antioxidants beam from each ingredient!

INGREDIENTS

1 cup romaine lettuce

2 bananas, peeled

1 tablespoon raw cocoa powder

½ vanilla bean's pulp

2 cups almond milk

Yields: 3–4 cups

Per 1 cup serving • Calories: 102 • Fat: 2g • Protein: 2g • Sodium: 77mg • Fiber: 3g • Carbohydrates: 23g

1. Combine romaine, bananas, cocoa powder, vanilla bean pulp, and 1 cup almond milk in a blender and blend until thoroughly combined.

2. Add remaining almond milk while blending until desired texture is achieved.

Fight Cancer with Cocoa

With almost every candy bar available consisting of milk products, devout vegans are left to purchase hard-to-find vegan candy, or create their own desserts at home. With the purchase of raw carob or cocoa powder, your kitchen can be turned into a chocolate shop of homemade delectable delights! Providing strong cancer-fighting antioxidants, these raw forms of chocolate bliss can extend your life while satisfying your sweet tooth.

GO NUTS FOR CHOCOLATE!

Even some of the most dedicated vegans have a soft spot for chocolate. This recipe allows you to create your own thrifty, quick, and easy chocolate smoothies at home while still adhering to the vegan lifestyle.

INGREDIENTS

¼ cup almonds

1 cup vanilla almond milk

2 tablespoons raw powdered cocoa

1 cup watercress

1 banana, peeled

1 tablespoon agave nectar (optional)

Yields: 3–4 cups

Per 1 cup serving • Calories: 143 • Fat: 7g
• Protein: 4g • Sodium: 56mg • Fiber: 4g •
Carbohydrates: 19g

1. Combine almonds and ½ cup almond milk in a blender and blend until almonds are completely emulsified.

2. Add cocoa, followed by the watercress, banana, nectar, and remaining ½ cup almond milk while blending until desired texture is achieved.

HYDRATING HONEY

Full of potassium from the bananas, this smoothie helps to maintain a healthy fluid balance of the body. And the amazingly rich honey brings some extra antioxidants—which help to keep cells healthy and protected from catastrophic cancerous mutations—with a unique sweetness that will really get your taste buds buzzing.

INGREDIENTS

2 bananas, peeled

1 cup water

1 tablespoon all-natural, organic honey

1 cup ice

Yields: 2 cups

Per 1 cup serving • Calories: 138 • Fat: 0.4g
• Protein: 1g • Sodium: 2mg • Fiber: 3g •
Carbohydrates: 36g

1. In a blender, combine the bananas, water, and honey with ½ cup ice, and blend until thoroughly combined.

2. While blending, add remaining ice until desired consistency is achieved.

THE JOY OF ALMONDS

If that Almond Joy candy is what satisfies your sweet tooth, this smoothie is for you. Packed with the flavors of almonds and coconut, this creamy smoothie will surely become one of your favorites!

INGREDIENTS

½ cup almonds

2 cups coconut milk

1 cup romaine lettuce

Flesh of 2 mature coconuts

1 banana, peeled

Yields: 3–4 cups

Per 1 cup serving • Calories: 210 • Fat: 100g • Protein: 13g • Sodium: 56mg • Fiber: 21g • Carbohydrates: 44g

1. Combine the almonds and ½ cup of coconut milk in a blender and emulsify until most remnants of the almonds have been liquefied, adding more liquid as needed.

2. Add the romaine, coconut flesh, banana, and 1 cup of coconut milk and blend until thoroughly combined.

3. Add remaining coconut milk, if needed, while blending until desired texture is achieved.

MAPLE-CINNAMON OATMEAL

When a steaming hot bowl of oatmeal doesn't do the trick, maybe the opposite is exactly what you need! Cool, creamy, and sweet, this smoothie takes the delicious flavors of rolled oats, aromatic cinnamon, and sweet maple syrup and combines them in a concoction that will take the place of hot oatmeal in anyone's heart.

INGREDIENTS

1 banana, peeled

½ cup rolled oats

1 teaspoon organic, pure maple syrup

1 teaspoon ground cinnamon

1 cup vanilla almond milk

1 cup ice

Yields: 2 cups

Per 1 cup serving • Calories: 175 • Fat: 3g • Protein: 6g • Sodium: 64mg • Fiber: 4g • Carbohydrates: 34g

1. In a blender, combine the banana, oats, maple syrup, cinnamon, and almond milk with ½ cup ice, and blend until thoroughly combined.

2. While blending, add remaining ice until desired consistency is achieved.

MINTY BLISS

The ingredients here blend together to create a sweet treat with a creamy texture; this smoothie may be satisfying enough to bump your favorite ice cream out of its number one spot!

INGREDIENTS

1 cup iceberg lettuce

¼ cup whole mint leaves

1 pint raspberries

1 cup almond milk

½ cup Greek yogurt

Yields: 3–4 cups

Per 1 cup serving • Calories: 86 • Fat: 1g • Protein: 5g • Sodium: 54mg • Fiber: 6g • Carbohydrates: 16g

1. Combine the iceberg, mint, raspberries, and almond milk in a blender and blend until thoroughly combined.

2. Add yogurt while blending until desired texture is achieved.

A SWEET BEET TREAT

When you're looking for a sweet treat, beets are vitamin- and nutrient-packed vegetables that offer up a sweet taste comparable to many fruits. This recipe is just one of the many greens-and-beet combinations that you'll enjoy!

INGREDIENTS

1 cup beet greens

3 beets

1 banana, peeled

1 cup almond milk

½ cup ice cubes (optional)

Yields: 3–4 cups

Per 1 cup serving • Calories: 77 • Fat: 1g • Protein: 2g • Sodium: 107mg • Fiber: 3g • Carbohydrates: 17g

1. Combine beet greens, beets, banana, and ½ cup almond milk in a blender container and blend until thoroughly combined.

2. Add remaining almond milk and ice, if desired, while blending until desired texture is achieved.

Beet Greens

While the actual beets are what have the reputation for being sweet, nutritious, delicious little veggies, the roots and greens of the beet are also edible and highly nutritious. Full of calcium, potassium, and vitamins A and C, the roots and leaves of these powerful deep-purple veggies are a healthy addition to any diet.

PUMPKIN SPICE

Who doesn't love the sweet aroma of freshly baked pumpkin pie? This recipe will be as sweet and tempting as a heaping helping of the not-so-nutritious baked alternative, but with all of the delicious and nutritious goodness that pumpkin provides.

INGREDIENTS

½ cup pumpkin, cubed or diced

1 cup vanilla soymilk

1 cup romaine lettuce

1 teaspoon cloves

1 tablespoon ginger, grated

½ cup Greek yogurt

Yields: 3–4 cups

Per 1 cup serving • Calories: 66 • Fat: 1g • Protein: 6g • Sodium: 51mg • Fiber: 1g • Carbohydrates: 7g

1. Combine pumpkin and ½ cup soymilk in a blender until completely emulsified.

2. Add romaine, cloves, ginger, and yogurt and blend until thoroughly combined.

3. If needed, add remaining soymilk while blending until desired consistency is achieved.

The Power of Pumpkin

Rich in vitamins and nutrients, this beta-carotene–rich squash contains a surprising amount of nutrition. Pumpkin contains more than 140 percent of your daily value of vitamin A in just ½ cup. By consuming pumpkin with ginger, yogurt, and soymilk in this smoothie, you'll be getting a high-protein, vitamin-rich treat that will satisfy your need for pumpkin pie any time of year.

SWEET POTATO PIE

This delicious smoothie—with flavors reminiscent of sweet potato pie—makes a healthy alternative to the real thing; it's got vitamins, minerals, and antioxidants galore.

INGREDIENTS

2 sweet potatoes, peeled and cut for blender's ability

2 cups vanilla soymilk

1 teaspoon cloves

½"–1" knob of ginger

1 cup spinach

Yields: 3–4 cups

Per 1 cup serving • Calories: 111 • Fat: 2g • Protein: 4g • Sodium: 91mg • Fiber: 3g • Carbohydrates: 19g

1. Combine the sweet potatoes with 1 cup vanilla soymilk in a blender and blend until sweet potato is completely emulsified.

2. Add cloves, ginger, and spinach and blend until thoroughly combined.

3. Add remaining soymilk while blending until desired texture is achieved.

VANILLA CHILLER

The simple flavor of vanilla is satisfying all on its own, but this smoothie pairs it up with aromatic cloves, sweet maple syrup, and the creaminess of kefir for a light, bright, and flavorful treat. And if that's not exciting enough, vanilla is full of vanillin, an antioxidant that protects all of the body's systems against free radical damage.

INGREDIENTS

2 vanilla beans' pulp

1 teaspoon ground cloves

1 teaspoon all-natural, organic maple syrup

2 cups plain kefir

1 cup ice

Yields: 2 cups

Per 1 cup serving • Calories: 163 • Fat: 4g • Protein: 14g • Sodium: 194mg • Fiber: 0.4g • Carbohydrates: 23g

1. In a blender, combine the vanilla bean pulp, cloves, maple syrup, and kefir with ½ cup ice, and blend until thoroughly combined.

2. While blending, add remaining ice until desired consistency is achieved.

CHAPTER 5

VEGETABLE SMOOTHIES

AWESOME ASPARAGUS

Rich in vitamins K, A, C, folate, and other Bs, and a variety of minerals like iron and zinc, this veggie's benefits surpass many others. Introducing 1 cup of asparagus to your daily diet promotes heart health, digestive health and regularity, and satisfies a daily serving requirement of vegetables.

INGREDIENTS

1 cup romaine lettuce

1 cup asparagus

1 green onion

1 celery stalk

1 garlic clove

2 cups purified water

Juice of ½ lemon

Yields: 3–4 cups

Per 1 cup serving • Calories: 12 • Fat: 0g • Protein: 1g • Sodium: 3mg • Fiber: 1g • Carbohydrates: 3g

1. Combine romaine, asparagus, onion, celery, garlic, and 1 cup of purified water in a blender and blend until thoroughly combined.

2. Add remaining water and lemon juice while blending until desired texture and taste are achieved.

SWEET ASPARAGUS Ⓥ

The sweet tang of oranges and lemons blends with the unique taste of asparagus and watercress to give this smoothie a wide variety of taste sensations.

INGREDIENTS

1 cup watercress

1 cup asparagus

1 lemon, peeled

1 orange, peeled

1 cup purified water

Yields: 3–4 cups

Per 1 cup serving • Calories: 33 • Fat: 0g • Protein: 2g • Sodium: 6mg • Fiber: 2g • Carbohydrates: 8g

1. Combine watercress, asparagus, lemon, orange, and ½ cup water in a blender and blend until thoroughly combined.

2. Add remaining water while blending until desired texture is achieved.

AMAZING AVOCADOS Ⓥ

If you're looking to add the good fats that can be found in nuts, seeds, and certain fruits to your diet, avocados should definitely be in your kitchen. The creamy texture of avocados makes a perfect addition to salads, soups, and smoothies.

INGREDIENTS

1 cup spinach

2 avocados, peeled and seeds removed

1 lime, peeled

1 cup purified water

1 cup vegan Greek yogurt

Yields: 3–4 cups

Per 1 cup serving • Calories: 200 • Fat: 15g • Protein: 8g • Sodium: 38mg • Fiber: 7g • Carbohydrates: 13g

1. Combine spinach, avocados, lime, ½ cup water, and ½ cup yogurt in a blender and blend until thoroughly combined.

2. Add remaining water and yogurt while blending until desired texture is achieved.

Avocados and Oral Cancer

Although avocados have been found to fight the cancer-causing free radicals of colon, breast, and prostate cancers, the most notable protective benefit avocados create in the human body is the protection against oral cancer. With a 50 percent mortality rate most commonly due to late detection, oral cancer is a preventable cancer that can be guarded against with the addition of just 2 ounces of avocado to your diet.

GUACAMOLE, ANYONE? Ⓥ

This vibrant smoothie includes all of the wonderful ingredients of the much-loved, extremely healthy snack.

INGREDIENTS

1 cup watercress

1 avocado, peeled and seed removed

1 lime, peeled

1 tomato

1 green onion

1 celery stalk

¼ cup cilantro

1 cup purified water

Yields: 3–4 cups

Per 1 cup serving • Calories: 95 • Fat: 7g • Protein: 2g • Sodium: 19mg • Fiber: 5g • Carbohydrates: 8g

1. Combine watercress, avocado, lime, tomato, onion, celery, cilantro, and ½ cup water in a blender and blend until thoroughly combined.

2. Add remaining water while blending until desired texture is achieved.

Flaxseed in Your Smoothie

Although most of the protein powders available are sweet flavors, you can find plain ones that will add protein without altering the taste. A different type of health-benefiting addition good in savory smoothies is ground flaxseed. Rich in omega-3s, powerful in fighting cancers, and well known for regulating blood pressure, these slightly nutty-tasting seeds boost your green smoothie to a super green smoothie!

BABY, BE HAPPY Ⓟ

This simple recipe makes a deliciously sweet veggie smoothie you're sure to enjoy. Iron-rich spinach and peas combine with vitamin-rich carrots for a splendid creation that will satisfy your increasing iron needs.

INGREDIENTS

1 cup spinach

1 cup sweet peas

3 carrots, peeled

2 cups red raspberry tea

Yields: 3–4 cups

Per 1 cup serving • Calories: 46 • Fat: 0g • Protein: 2g • Sodium: 76mg • Fiber: 3g • Carbohydrates: 9g

1. Combine spinach, peas, carrots, and 1 cup of tea in a blender and blend until thoroughly combined.

2. Add remaining tea as needed while blending until desired consistency is achieved.

BROCCOLI BLASTOFF

Broccoli and kale add a great dose of protein to this smoothie. If you're looking for even more protein, there is the delightful option of protein powders in a variety of flavors that would blend nicely with savory smoothies such as this.

INGREDIENTS

2 kale leaves

1 cup broccoli

½ red bell pepper

2 celery stalks

1 green onion

1–2 garlic cloves, depending on size

2 cups purified water

Yields: 3–4 cups

Per 1 cup serving • Calories: 23 • Fat: 0g • Protein: 1g • Sodium: 18mg • Fiber: 1g • Carbohydrates: 1g

1. Combine kale, broccoli, pepper, celery, onion, garlic, and 1 cup of water in a blender and blend until thoroughly combined.

2. Add remaining water as needed while blending until desired consistency is achieved.

BLAZING BROCCOLI

Everybody grew up hearing "You need to finish your broccoli." It's one veggie that has a bad reputation. The truth is that broccoli is one of the most powerfully packed superfoods you can find!

INGREDIENTS

1 cup spinach

1 cup broccoli

1 carrot, peeled

1 green pepper, cored

½ lime, peeled

2 cups purified water

Yields: 3–4 cups

Per 1 cup serving • Calories: 24 • Fat: 0g •
Protein: 1g • Sodium: 27mg • Fiber: 2g •
Carbohydrates: 6g

1. Combine spinach, broccoli, carrot, pepper, lime, and 1 cup of purified water in a blender and blend until thoroughly combined.

2. Add remaining water while blending until desired texture is achieved.

BROCCOLI CARROT ⓥ

Broccoli is not only a vitamin- and mineral-packed green veggie, it also contains more protein than most other veggie options. Vegans and vegetarians can find a good source of extra protein in this vibrant green vegetable.

INGREDIENTS

1 cup romaine lettuce

1 cup broccoli

2 carrots

2 cups purified water

Yields: 3–4 cups

Per 1 cup serving • Calories: 22 • Fat: 0g •
Protein: 1g • Sodium: 32mg • Fiber: 2g •
Carbohydrates: 5g

1. Combine romaine, broccoli, carrots, and 1 cup of water in a blender and blend until thoroughly combined.

2. Add remaining water while blending until desired texture is achieved.

MEMORY MAINTAINER

Protecting your brain was never this delicious! The vitamins, minerals, and antioxidants that promote optimal functioning of your mental processes also prevent the brain's deterioration from illness and disease. This is one smoothie you won't forget!

INGREDIENTS

1 cup romaine lettuce

½ cup broccoli

½ cup cauliflower

1 tomato

1 garlic clove

2 cups purified water

Yields: 3–4 cups

Per 1 cup serving • Calories: 16 • Fat: 0g • Protein: 1g • Sodium: 12mg • Fiber: 1g • Carbohydrates: 3g

1. Combine romaine, broccoli, cauliflower, tomato, garlic, and 1 cup of water in a blender and blend until thoroughly combined.

2. Add remaining water as needed while blending until desired consistency is achieved.

AN ORANGE BROCCOLI BLEND Ⓥ

Thanks to the fiber, vitamins, and minerals in each of these ingredients, this smoothie is tasty and hearty enough to replace any meal.

INGREDIENTS

1 cup romaine lettuce

1 cup broccoli

1 zucchini

2 carrots, peeled

2 cups purified water

Yields: 3–4 cups

Per 1 cup serving • Calories: 30 • Fat: 0g • Protein: 2g • Sodium: 37mg • Fiber: 2g • Carbohydrates: 6g

1. Combine romaine, broccoli, zucchini, carrots, and 1 cup of water in a blender and blend until thoroughly combined.

2. Add remaining water while blending until desired texture is achieved.

RAPID RECOVERY

Tasty and powerful, this recipe's ingredients provide protein from intensely vitamin- and mineral-rich veggies. The addition of the lemon and garlic benefit your body by promoting a healthy metabolic level for more efficient fat burning.

INGREDIENTS

1 cup watercress

1 cup broccoli

1 celery stalk

½ lemon, peeled

1 garlic clove

2 cups Greek yogurt

Yields: 3–4 cups

Per 1 cup serving • Calories: 78 • Fat: 0g • Protein: 13g • Sodium: 67mg • Fiber: 1g • Carbohydrates: 7g

1. Combine watercress, broccoli, celery, lemon, garlic, and 1 cup of yogurt in a blender and blend until thoroughly combined.

2. Add remaining yogurt as needed while blending until desired consistency is achieved.

Yogurt for Rapid Recovery

We know protein delivers recovery aid to our muscles, but what is the best type to deliver maximum benefits and reap the most rewards? Chicken, beef, pork, and fish all come with saturated fats and aren't suitable for vegetarian athletes. If you're not interested in a protein shake of the powdered variety, turn to Greek yogurt! It has lower carbs (9 grams or less) than regular yogurt, not to mention twice the protein (20 grams) and half the sodium.

CABBAGE CARROT

Cabbage is one of those important yet neglected veggies, most commonly eaten on St. Paddy's Day or as cole slaw at picnics—not the most nutritious ways to prepare it. This recipe blends tasty green cabbage with carrots and ginger to deliver a sweet smoothie with a bite!

INGREDIENTS

1 cup green cabbage

3 carrots, peeled

2 celery stalks

1" ginger, peeled and sliced

2 cups purified water

Yields: 3–4 cups

Per 1 cup serving • Calories: 30 • Fat: 0g • Protein: 1g • Sodium: 54mg • Fiber: 2g • Carbohydrates: 7g

1. Combine cabbage, carrots, celery, ginger, and 1 cup water in a blender and blend until thoroughly combined.

2. Add remaining water while blending until desired texture is achieved.

CAROTENE AGAINST CANCER

The potent healing powers of beta-carotene are unleashed in this delicious blend of carrots and sweet potatoes. It's a satisfying treat for any sweet tooth, and you'll be protecting your health with each delicious sip!

INGREDIENTS

1 cup romaine lettuce

3 carrots, peeled

1 cup sweet potato

¼" ginger, peeled

2 cups chamomile tea

Yields: 3–4 cups

Per 1 cup serving • Calories: 50 • Fat: 0g • Protein: 1g • Sodium: 53mg • Fiber: 3g • Carbohydrates: 12g

1. Combine romaine, carrots, sweet potato, ginger, and 1 cup of tea in a blender and blend until thoroughly combined.

2. Add remaining tea as needed while blending until desired consistency is achieved.

CARROT ASPARAGUS Ⓥ

This blend is yet another recipe that can easily have its vitamin and mineral content improved with the addition of ground flaxseed. The addition of flaxseed to this smoothie would lend a delicious hint of nutty flavor.

INGREDIENTS

1 cup watercress

1 cup asparagus

2 carrots, peeled

2 cups water

Yields: 3–4 cups

Per 1 cup serving • Calories: 20 • Fat: 0g • Protein: 1g • Sodium: 28mg • Fiber: 2g • Carbohydrates: 4g

1. Combine watercress, asparagus, carrots, and 1 cup water in a blender and blend until thoroughly combined.

2. Add remaining water while blending until desired texture is achieved.

Flaxseed

Flaxseed is a common product found in almost every grocery store. Available organic, nonorganic, ground, and whole, flaxseed can be found in aisles with nuts or near produce. You can purchase the whole seed product and use them in sandwiches, salads, and main dishes by using a coffee grinder and grinding them until thoroughly powdered. If the thought of grinding your own flaxseed sounds intimidating or time consuming, the ground product may be a wiser option.

CARROT COMMANDO

Carrots, spinach, and apples combine for a delightfully sweet and filling smoothie. They provide loads of the important vitamins and minerals needed for optimal functioning of all your body systems.

INGREDIENTS

1 cup spinach

4 carrots, peeled

2 apples, peeled and cored

2 cups purified water

Yields: 3–4 cups

Per 1 cup serving • Calories: 65 • Fat: 0g • Protein: 1g • Sodium: 50mg • Fiber: 3g • Carbohydrates: 16g

1. Combine spinach, carrots, apples, and 1 cup of water in a blender and blend until thoroughly combined.

2. Add remaining water as needed while blending until desired consistency is achieved.

Carrots for Flushing an Athlete's Fat Stores

Among the many capabilities of the carrot, one little-known responsibility is its contribution to the liver's cleansing power. Carrots aid the liver's cleansing process by keeping it squeaky clean and helping to more efficiently move excess bile and fat stores out of the body. With this important vegetable's assistance, you could have fewer digestive disorders, better regularity, and an overall "lighter" feeling from its toxin-, fat-, and fluid-flushing abilities.

CAULIFLOWER TO THE RESCUE

This sweet veggie can give a great boost to anyone in need of improved brain and heart health. Including this powerful ingredient in a delicious veggie smoothie makes a great recipe even greater!

INGREDIENTS

1 cup romaine lettuce

1 cup cauliflower

2 carrots, peeled

1 apple, peeled and cored

2 cups chamomile

Yields: 3–4 cups

Per 1 cup serving • Calories: 40 • Fat: 0g • Protein: 1g • Sodium: 32mg • Fiber: 2g • Carbohydrates: 10g

1. Combine romaine, cauliflower, carrots, apple, and 1 cup of tea in a blender and blend until thoroughly combined.

2. Add remaining tea as needed while blending until desired consistency is achieved.

Ever Heard of Allicin?

The amazing powers of cauliflower are not enjoyed enough in the standard American diet. Packed with important nutrition that satisfies daily dietary needs, this stark white veggie is packing a powerful secret weapon, too. Cauliflower provides allicin, an important compound that actually reduces the risk of stroke and heart disease while detoxifying the blood and liver (allicin is also found in garlic). With abilities like that, cauliflower is a must-have in any disease-preventing diet.

SAVOR CELERY

To waken your senses in the early morning or even in the mid-afternoon, these antioxidant-rich ingredients work together to provide energy, renewed vitality, and overall improved health.

INGREDIENTS

1 cup arugula

1 celery stalk

1 tomato

½ red bell pepper, cored with ribs intact

1 green onion

1 garlic clove

⅛ cup parsley

2 cups purified water

Yields: 5–6 cups

Per 1 cup serving • Calories: 13 • Fat: 0g • Protein: 1g • Sodium: 13mg • Fiber: 1g • Carbohydrates: 3g

1. Combine arugula, celery, tomato, red pepper, onion, garlic, parsley, and 1 cup of water in a blender and blend until thoroughly combined.

2. Add remaining water as needed while blending until desired consistency is achieved.

The Importance of Celery for Diabetics

The sodium content in this crisp veggie plays an important role in a diabetic's diet. By consuming this delicious vegetable, the body is more efficient in regulating and maintaining water balance. Celery is rich in vitamins A, C, K, B_6, B_1, and folate as well as calcium, potassium, and fiber, and is also a natural diuretic.

A COOL BLEND

Maintaining a diet that optimizes sugar levels to ensure diabetic health is easy with this delicious blend. The combination of ingredients makes a refreshing treat that will keep you going when you need a boost.

INGREDIENTS

1 cup watercress

1 celery stalk

1 cucumber, peeled

2 pears, cored

2 tablespoons mint

1 cup Greek yogurt

Yields: 3–4 cups

Per 1 cup serving • Calories: 94 • Fat: 0g • Protein: 7g • Sodium: 38mg • Fiber: 4g • Carbohydrates: 18g

1. Combine watercress, celery, cucumber, pears, mint, and ½ cup yogurt in a blender and blend until thoroughly combined.

2. Add remaining yogurt as needed while blending until desired consistency is achieved.

COLLIDE WITH COLLARDS

Refreshing and nutritious, this blend delivers powerful vitamins and minerals that work as hard as you do. To satisfy your body's energy requirements and replenish your muscles' stores, green veggies are your best bet for complete balanced nutrition!

INGREDIENTS

1 cup collards

1 cup cauliflower

1 cup broccoli

1 carrot, peeled

2 cups purified water

Yields: 3–4 cups

Per 1 cup serving • Calories: 23 • Fat: 0g • Protein: 1g • Sodium: 30mg • Fiber: 2g • Carbohydrates: 5g

1. Combine collards, cauliflower, broccoli, carrot, and 1 cup of water in a blender and blend until thoroughly combined.

2. Add remaining water as needed while blending until desired consistency is achieved.

FANTASTIC FENNEL

Although it can be found in almost every grocery store's produce section, people rarely purchase fennel or prepare it at home. The vitamins and minerals in this veggie make it a must-have, and the taste is amazingly unique.

INGREDIENTS

1 cup romaine lettuce

2 fennel bulbs

1 cucumber, peeled

1 carrot, peeled

1 celery stalk

2 cups purified water

Yields: 3–4 cups

Per 1 cup serving • Calories: 52 • Fat: 0g • Protein: 2g • Sodium: 84mg • Fiber: 5g • Carbohydrates: 12g

1. Combine romaine, fennel, cucumber, carrot, celery, and 1 cup of purified water in a blender and blend until thoroughly combined.

2. Add remaining water while blending until desired texture is achieved.

Vitamins to the Rescue

Research shows that many antioxidants interact with and protect each other. Vitamin C, for instance, can react with a damaged vitamin E molecule and convert it back to its antioxidant form, while the antioxidant glutathione can return vitamin C to its original form. Studies also show that vitamin C enhances the protective effects of vitamin E.

FANTASTIC FRISÉE

Not too many people enjoy flavorful frisée. Take a chance on this delectable green in your smoothie, and you'll benefit from its richness in vitamins, minerals, antioxidants, and flavor.

INGREDIENTS

1 cup frisée

1 tomato

1 celery stalk

1 cucumber, peeled

1 garlic clove

2 cups purified water

Yields: 3–4 cups

Per 1 cup serving • Calories: 16 • Fat: 0g • Protein: 1g • Sodium: 16mg • Fiber: 1g • Carbohydrates: 3g

1. Combine frisée, tomato, celery, cucumber, garlic, and 1 cup water in a blender and blend until thoroughly combined.

2. Add remaining water while blending until desired texture is achieved.

What Makes a Cucumber Bitter?

As a cucumber gets older on the vine, its seeds become larger and more bitter. If you are using an old cucumber, cut it in half and scoop out the seeds with a spoon to eliminate the bitter taste. According to an old wives' tale, the more bitter the vegetable, the better it is for you. But you'll still get the nutritional benefits cucumbers have to offer without the bitter seeds.

GARLIC AND ONIONS KEEP THE DOCTOR AWAY

Although it will probably keep more people away than just the doctor, garlic and onions make for an amazing taste combination that will surprise any green-smoothie skeptic. The watercress, celery, and zucchini downplay the intense flavors of the garlic and onions.

INGREDIENTS

1 cup watercress

1 celery stalk

1 green onion

1 zucchini

1 clove garlic

2 cups purified water

Yields: 3–4 cups

Per 1 cup serving • Calories: 13 • Fat: 0g • Protein: 1g • Sodium: 19mg • Fiber: 1g • Carbohydrates: 3g

1. Combine watercress, celery, onion, zucchini, garlic, and 1 cup of water in a blender and blend until thoroughly combined.

2. Add remaining water as needed while blending until desired consistency is achieved.

GEAR UP WITH GARLIC

This savory smoothie makes a delicious meal replacement for an invigorating breakfast, satisfying lunch, or delightful dinner. The strong flavors of spinach and garlic combine with the cucumber, tomato, and celery for a taste sensation to savor.

INGREDIENTS

1 cup spinach

1 cucumber, peeled

1 celery stalk

1 tomato

2–3 garlic cloves, depending on size

2 cups purified water

Yields: 3–4 cups

Per 1 cup serving • Calories: 17 • Fat: 0g • Protein: 1g • Sodium: 19mg • Fiber: 1g • Carbohydrates: 3g

1. Combine spinach, cucumber, celery, tomato, garlic, and 1 cup water in a blender and blend until thoroughly combined.

2. Add remaining water as needed while blending until desired consistency is achieved.

Garlic Prep for Optimal Benefits

Cooking garlic for as little as 60 seconds has been shown to cause it to lose some of its anticancer properties. Packed with an abundance of vitamins, minerals, and nutrients that fight cancer and heart disease, prevent bacterial and viral infections, improve iron metabolism, control blood pressure, and act as an anti-inflammatory, garlic's abilities can be optimized by crushing or chopping it and preparing it without heat.

GREAT GARLIC

In addition to keeping vampires away, this strong addition can do wonders for your health. Just one small clove of garlic helps promote a strong heart, and makes almost anything taste absolutely delightful.

INGREDIENTS

1 cup spinach

1 celery stalk

1 tomato

3 garlic cloves

2 cups purified water

Yields: 3–4 cups

Per 1 cup serving • Calories: 12 • Fat: 0g • Protein: 1g • Sodium: 18mg • Fiber: 1g • Carbohydrates: 3g

1. Combine spinach, celery, tomato, garlic, and 1 cup water in a blender and blend until thoroughly combined.

2. Add remaining water, if needed, while blending until desired texture is achieved.

THE GREEN BLOODY MARY

The alcoholic Bloody Mary may be tempting, but the alcohol can do a load of damage to cells, skin, digestion, and your mind. This green version of the Bloody Mary has all of the necessary ingredients to repair exactly what the alcoholic version destroys!

INGREDIENTS

1 cup watercress

2 tomatoes

2 celery stalks

½ lemon, peeled

1 tablespoon horseradish

½ teaspoon cayenne pepper (optional)

1 cup purified water

Yields: 3–4 cups

Per 1 cup serving • Calories: 19 • Fat: 0g • Protein: 1g • Sodium: 36mg • Fiber: 1g • Carbohydrates: 4g

1. Combine watercress, tomatoes, celery, lemon, horseradish, and cayenne with ½ cup purified water in a blender and blend until thoroughly combined.

2. Add remaining water while blending until desired texture is achieved.

KALE CARROT COMBO

Kale is a very strong-tasting green that has many benefits. This recipe pairs it with other strong, and very sweet, vegetables and fruits that blend well with it and make it a delicious addition to any day.

INGREDIENTS

2 kale leaves

4 carrots, peeled

1 apple, cored and peeled

1 banana, peeled

2 cups purified water

Yields: 3–4 cups

Per 1 cup serving • Calories: 83 • Fat: 0g • Protein: 2g • Sodium: 52mg • Fiber: 4g • Carbohydrates: 21g

1. Combine kale leaves, carrots, apple, banana, and 1 cup purified water in a blender and blend until thoroughly combined

2. Add remaining water while blending until desired texture is achieved.

KILLER KALE KICKOFF

Packed with an abundance of vitamin K, a fat-soluble compound, kale is a healthy way to get your daily recommended amount of K in a one-stop shop that delivers important vitamins and minerals for focus and sustainable energy.

INGREDIENTS

2 kale leaves

4 carrots, peeled

1 cucumber, peeled

2 green onions

2 garlic cloves

2 cups purified water

Yields: 3–4 cups

Per 1 cup serving • Calories: 43 • Fat: 0g • Protein: 2g • Sodium: 6mg • Fiber: 3g • Carbohydrates: 9g

1. Combine kale, carrots, cucumber, onions, garlic, and 1 cup of water in a blender and blend until thoroughly combined.

2. Add remaining water as needed while blending until desired consistency is achieved.

RUNNER'S DELIGHT

Any endurance runner feels amped before and pumped following a run. After all that hard work, you're definitely entitled to enjoy a sweet reward. Instead of undoing your efforts with empty calories, indulge in the sweet taste of citrus with all its added benefits!

INGREDIENTS

1 cup watercress

3 oranges, peeled

1 cup strawberries

1 cup raspberries

1 cup Greek yogurt

Yields: 3–4 cups

Per 1 cup serving • Calories: 126 • Fat: 0g • Protein: 8g • Sodium: 28mg • Fiber: 6g • Carbohydrates: 25g

1. Combine watercress, oranges, berries, and ½ cup yogurt in a blender and blend until thoroughly combined.

2. Add remaining yogurt as needed while blending until desired consistency is achieved.

POWERFUL PARSNIPS

Full of vitamin C, parsnips make a tasty ingredient in this surprisingly sweet smoothie. Rich in important minerals for energy and stamina, root veggies are a great way to maximize your smoothie's potency potential.

INGREDIENTS

1 cup watercress

1 parsnip, peeled

3 carrots, peeled

2 cups purified water

Yields: 3–4 cups

Per 1 cup serving • Calories: 31 • Fat: 0g • Protein: 1g • Sodium: 39mg • Fiber: 2g • Carbohydrates: 7g

1. Combine watercress, parsnip, carrots, and 1 cup of water in a blender and blend until thoroughly combined.

2. Add remaining water as needed while blending until desired consistency is achieved.

"PEA" IS FOR PREVENTION

Sweetening this smoothie with sweet green peas makes it a delightful treat. This tasty blend of watercress, cucumbers, and peas delivers a refreshing and filling snack, with amazing health benefits in every ingredient.

INGREDIENTS

1 cup watercress

2 cucumbers, peeled

1 cup petite sweet green peas

2 cups purified water

Yields: 3–4 cups

Per 1 cup serving • Calories: 39 • Fat: 0g •
Protein: 3g • Sodium: 44mg • Fiber: 2g •
Carbohydrates: 7g

1. Combine watercress, cucumbers, peas, and 1 cup of water in a blender and blend until thoroughly combined.

2. Add remaining water as needed while blending until desired consistency is achieved.

The Power of a Pea

Adding just 1 cup of this sweet veggie to your daily diet will provide over 50 percent of your daily recommended intake of vitamin K, along with folate and other B vitamins, vitamin C, manganese, fiber, and protein. This results in stronger bones; heightened disease prevention; efficient metabolism of carbohydrates, fats, and proteins; improved cardiac health; and more energy.

A PEPPERY WAY TO PROMOTE HEALTH

Spicy arugula and red pepper join forces with crisp celery and spicy garlic for a drink with a bite in this smoothie rich in vitamins and antioxidants.

INGREDIENTS

1 cup arugula

2 celery stalks

½ red bell pepper, cored with ribs intact

1 garlic clove

1½ cups water

Yields: 3–4 cups

Per 1 cup serving • Calories: 14 • Fat: 0g •
Protein: 1g • Sodium: 26mg • Fiber: 1g •
Carbohydrates: 3g

1. Combine arugula, celery, red pepper, garlic, and ¾ cup of the water in a blender and blend until thoroughly combined.

2. Add remaining water as needed while blending until desired consistency is achieved.

PEPPERS AND ONIONS, HOLD THE PHILLY

The fat-laden Philly cheese steak is a yummy, but nutrient-lacking, meal. Rather than indulging in a sandwich that leaves you full but running on empty, try this smoothie that delivers the amazing flavors of onions, peppers, and garlic. Hold the guilt!

INGREDIENTS

1 cup iceberg lettuce

1 green pepper

1 red pepper

1 green onion

1 clove garlic

2 cups purified water

Yields: 3–4 cups

Per 1 cup serving • Calories: 27 • Fat: 0g • Protein: 1g • Sodium: 8mg • Fiber: 2g • Carbohydrates: 6g

1. Combine iceberg, peppers, onion, garlic, and 1 cup water in a blender and blend until thoroughly combined.

2. Add remaining water while blending until desired texture is achieved.

POWERFUL PEPPER TRIO

The vibrant colors of peppers show their powerful vitamin-rich content, which makes for a delicious and nutritious treat. This smoothie's mix of spicy arugula, peppers, and garlic combine for a savory treat you can enjoy anytime.

INGREDIENTS

1 cup arugula

1 red pepper, cored

1 green pepper, cored

1 yellow pepper, cored

1 garlic clove

2 cups purified water

Yields: 3–4 cups

Per 1 cup serving • Calories: 29 • Fat: 0g • Protein: 1g • Sodium: 6mg • Fiber: 2g • Carbohydrates: 7g

1. Combine arugula, peppers, garlic, and 1 cup of water in a blender and blend until thoroughly combined.

2. Add remaining water while blending until desired texture is achieved.

RED BELLS MAKE HEARTS RING

Delicious red peppers star in this simple savory smoothie. Packed with aromatic red bell peppers, spicy arugula, cooling cucumbers, and crisp celery, this combination is perfect for a filling meal that tastes great and makes for a strong heart.

INGREDIENTS

1 cup arugula

1 red bell pepper, top and seeds removed
   and ribs intact

2 cucumbers, peeled

2 celery stalks

2 cups chamomile tea

Yields: 3–4 cups

Per 1 cup serving • Calories: 26 • Fat: 0g •
Protein: 1g • Sodium: 23mg • Fiber: 2g •
Carbohydrates: 5g

1. Combine arugula, red pepper, cucumbers, celery, and 1 cup of tea in a blender and blend until thoroughly combined.

2. Add remaining tea as needed while blending until desired consistency is achieved.

A SAVORY CELERY CELEBRATION

Celery is a powerful ingredient in any diet needing lower sodium and less water retention. Pills and powders barely hold water in comparison to this delightfully fresh veggie.

INGREDIENTS

1 cup watercress

3 celery stalks

1 cucumber, peeled

1 garlic clove

1 cup purified water

Yields: 3–4 cups

Per 1 cup serving • Calories: 13 • Fat: 0g •
Protein: 1g • Sodium: 30mg • Fiber: 1g •
Carbohydrates: 2g

1. Combine watercress, celery, cucumber, garlic, and ½ cup water in a blender and blend until thoroughly combined.

2. Add remaining water while blending until desired texture is achieved.

SPICE IT UP!

The arugula, onion, and pepper combine in this recipe for a powerfully delicious blend. Mushrooms are a woody ingredient that tones down the peppery flavor of arugula.

INGREDIENTS

1 cup arugula

1 green onion

½ red bell pepper, cored

½ cup mushrooms, stems intact

2 cups purified water

Yields: 3–4 cups

Per 1 cup serving • Calories: 14 • Fat: 0g • Protein: 1g • Sodium: 8mg • Fiber: 1g • Carbohydrates: 3g

1. Combine arugula, onion, red pepper, mushrooms, and 1 cup of water in a blender and blend until thoroughly combined.

2. Add remaining water as needed while blending until desired consistency is achieved.

Red Bell Peppers and Vitamins C and A

This beautiful vegetable not only provides a tasty crunch to salads and entrées, it also provides a whopping dose of both vitamins A and C. Providing almost 300 percent of your RDA of vitamin C and just over 100 percent of your RDA of vitamin A, it prevents illnesses like cancer, heart disease, and influenza and protects against free radicals that can cause aged-looking skin, increased fatigue, and zapped energy and mental focus.

SAVORY SQUASH SURPRISE

When you take a look at this smoothie, you'll see the vibrant colors of the veggies, and thus their valuable nutrition. The bright-green spinach, yellow squash, and orange carrot combine to make a smoothie that pleases the eye as well as the taste buds.

INGREDIENTS

1 cup spinach

½ butternut squash, peeled, deseeded, and cubed

1 carrot, peeled

2 garlic cloves

2 cups purified water

Yields: 3–4 cups

Per 1 cup serving • Calories: 18 • Fat: 0g • Protein: 1g • Sodium: 20mg • Fiber: 1g • Carbohydrates: 4g

1. Combine spinach, squash, carrot, garlic, and 1 cup of water in a blender and blend until thoroughly combined.

2. Add remaining water while blending until desired texture is achieved.

SPICY SPINACH

The taste of spinach can be altered by including it in certain combinations with other strong vegetables and fruits. Using these specific ingredients, especially the cilantro and garlic, makes this smoothie one of a kind.

INGREDIENTS

1 cup spinach

1 tomato

1 celery stalk

1–2 tablespoons cilantro

1 garlic clove

2 cups purified water

Yields: 3–4 cups

Per 1 cup serving • Calories: 13 • Fat: 0g • Protein: 1g • Sodium: 24mg • Fiber: 1g • Carbohydrates: 3g

1. Combine spinach, tomato, celery, cilantro, garlic, and 1 cup water in a blender and blend until thoroughly combined.

2. Add remaining water while blending until desired texture is achieved.

Garlic

Garlic may be one of the healthiest vegetables you can add to your smoothies. Studies credit it with fighting bladder, skin, colon, and stomach cancer. Eating one to three cloves per day is recommended for optimal results. Including garlic in your smoothies is an easy way to meet that requirement.

A SPICY ASSORTMENT

Variety is the spice of life, right? This savory smoothie offers a salty, spicy, and amazingly delicious combination of vegetables.

INGREDIENTS

1 cup arugula

2 carrots, peeled

1 zucchini

1 celery

½ jalapeño, or to taste

1 garlic clove

1 cup purified water

Yields: 3–4 cups

Per 1 cup serving • Calories: 35 • Fat: 0g • Protein: 2g • Sodium: 49mg • Fiber: 2g • Carbohydrates: 8g

1. Combine arugula, carrots, zucchini, celery, jalapeño, garlic, and ½ cup water in a blender and blend until thoroughly combined.

2. Add remaining water while blending until desired texture is achieved.

SWEET AND SAVORY BEET

Beets and their greens are filled with antioxidants and vitamins. Paired with flavorful carrots and cucumbers, they create a sweet and delicious smoothie you're sure to enjoy!

INGREDIENTS

1 cup beet greens

2 beets

2 carrots, peeled

1 cucumber, peeled

2 cups purified water

Yields: 3–4 cups

Per 1 cup serving • Calories: 38 • Fat: 0g • Protein: 1g • Sodium: 78mg • Fiber: 3g • Carbohydrates: 8g

1. Combine beet greens, beets, carrots, cucumber, and 1 cup water in a blender and blend until thoroughly combined.

2. Add remaining water while blending until desired texture is achieved.

Beet Colors

Beets come in many colors, from deep red to orange. They also can be white. The Chioggia beet is called a candy cane beet because it has red and white rings. Small or medium beets are more tender than larger ones. Beets can be enjoyed on their own or flavored with some butter, salt, and pepper for a simple side dish.

SWEET POTATO SMOOTHIE

Even though being an avid athlete means focusing on the healthiest foods that provide ideal nutrition calorie for calorie, cravings for sweet treats creep up every once in a while. Calm those cravings with combinations like this that satisfy with sound nutrition!

INGREDIENTS

½ cup walnuts

2 cups purified water

1 cup spinach

1 sweet potato, peeled and cut for blender's ability

1 teaspoon pumpkin pie spice

Yields: 3–4 cups

Per 1 cup serving • Calories: 127 • Fat: 10g • Protein: 3g • Sodium: 19mg • Fiber: 2g • Carbohydrates: 9g

1. Combine walnuts and 1 cup of water in a blender and blend until emulsified and no walnut bits remain.

2. Add spinach, sweet potato, pumpkin pie spice, and remaining water while blending until desired consistency is achieved.

Walnuts for Athletic Performance

In just ¼ cup of walnuts, you can find almost 100 percent of your daily value of omega-3s with the richness of monounsaturated fats. Not only a tasty, protein-packed morsel, the walnut helps athletes perform at their best by improving circulation and heart health, controlling blood pressure, providing essential amino acids, and acting as a powerful antioxidant.

A BIKER'S BEST FRIEND

Nothing keeps sustained energy up like slow-releasing carbohydrates. Root vegetables are the best friend of any distance cyclist on a mission for better times and better health!

INGREDIENTS

1 cup spinach

2 yams, peeled

2 apples, peeled and cored

2 carrots, peeled

2 cups purified water

Yields: 3–4 cups

Per 1 cup serving • Calories: 110 • Fat: 0g • Protein: 2g • Sodium: 50mg • Fiber: 4g • Carbohydrates: 27g

1. Combine spinach, yams, apples, carrots, and 1 cup water in a blender and blend until thoroughly combined.

2. Add remaining water as needed while blending until desired consistency is achieved.

ROOT VEGGIE VARIETY

Root vegetables are packed with especially high levels of minerals that promote eye health and offer protection against a number of cancers. Drink up to promote the best defense against serious illnesses.

INGREDIENTS

1 cup romaine lettuce

1 turnip, peeled and cut to blender capacity

3 carrots, peeled

1 apple, peeled and cored

2 cups purified water

Yields: 3–4 cups

Per 1 cup serving • Calories: 49 • Fat: 0g • Protein: 1g • Sodium: 55mg • Fiber: 3g • Carbohydrates: 12g

1. Combine romaine, turnip, carrots, apple, and 1 cup of water in a blender and blend until thoroughly combined.

2. Add remaining water as needed while blending until desired consistency is achieved.

Maximize Your Root Veggies' Potential

One of the many reasons raw food enthusiasts adopt and adhere to the raw food diet is the dramatic drop in vitamins, minerals, and nutrients when produce is heated above a certain temperature. Most people prefer to have their root vegetables steamed, mashed, baked, or roasted. While cooked veggies taste great, the scorching heat also scorches a large percentage of the nutrient content. Blending root veggies in a green smoothie is a delicious way to enjoy these superfoods with all of the nutrition nature intended.

TURNIP TURNAROUND

Turnips are most often seen roasted with other root vegetables around the holidays; not many people would think to include them in a green smoothie. Try it: The turnip and carrots make for a surprisingly delicious taste combination.

INGREDIENTS

1 cup watercress

2 turnips, peeled and cut to fit blender

3 carrots, peeled

2 celery stalks

2 cups purified water

Yields: 3–4 cups

Per 1 cup serving • Calories: 40 • Fat: 0g • Protein: 1g • Sodium: 94mg • Fiber: 3g • Carbohydrates: 9g

1. Combine watercress, turnips, carrots, celery, and 1 cup of water in a blender and blend until thoroughly combined.

2. Add remaining water as needed while blending until desired consistency is achieved.

TANGY TOMATO

Tomatoes, celery, cilantro, and garlic blend beautifully with arugula in this recipe to deliver a vitamin-rich, tangy smoothie that's absolutely splendid.

INGREDIENTS

1 cup arugula

2 tomatoes

1 celery stalk

2 tablespoons cilantro

1 clove garlic

2 cups purified water

Yields: 3–4 cups

Per 1 cup serving • Calories: 15 • Fat: 0g • Protein: 1g • Sodium: 15mg • Fiber: 1g • Carbohydrates: 3g

1. Combine arugula, tomatoes, celery, cilantro, garlic, and 1 cup water in a blender and blend until thoroughly combined.

2. Add remaining water while blending until desired texture is achieved.

THE TEMPTATION OF TURNIPS

When was the last time you ate a turnip? Rich in nutrition, this rarely enjoyed root vegetable is a great addition to any diet.

INGREDIENTS

1 cup romaine lettuce

2 turnips, peeled and cut best for blender's ability

2 carrots, peeled

2 celery stalks

2 cups purified water

Yields: 3–4 cups

Per 1 cup serving • Calories: 35 • Fat: 0g • Protein: 1g • Sodium: 81mg • Fiber: 3g • Carbohydrates: 8g

1. Combine romaine, turnips, carrots, celery, and 1 cup water in a blender and blend until thoroughly combined.

2. Add remaining water while blending until desired texture is achieved.

Turnip Lanterns

Pumpkins aren't the only vegetable that have been carved for Halloween. The Irish started the tradition of carving lanterns on Halloween, but originally turnips were used. Turnip lanterns were left on doorsteps in order to ward off evil spirits.

Turnip lanterns are an old tradition; since inaugural Halloween festivals in Ireland and Scotland, turnips (rutabaga) have been carved out and used as candle lanterns. At Samhain, candle lanterns carved from turnips—Samhnag—were part of the traditional Celtic festival. Large turnips were hollowed out, carved with faces, and placed in windows, used to ward off harmful spirits.

VEGGIE DELIGHT Ⓥ

If you're in the mood for a refreshingly savory smoothie, this one might be just what you're looking for! The ingredients create a splendid drink that might be delicious and filling enough to take the place of dinner.

INGREDIENTS

1 cup romaine lettuce

2 tomatoes

1 zucchini

2 celery stalks

1 cucumber

½ cup green onions

2 garlic cloves

2 cups purified water

Yields: 4–6 cups

Per 1 cup serving • Calories: 28 • Fat: 0g • Protein: 1g • Sodium: 6mg • Fiber: 1g • Carbohydrates: 6g

1. Combine romaine, tomatoes, zucchini, celery, cucumber, green onions, garlic, and 1 cup water in a blender and blend until thoroughly combined.

2. Add remaining water, if needed, while blending until desired texture is achieved.

THE ZESTY ZOOMER

Spicy arugula, sweet red pepper, cilantro, and garlic team up to deliver a spicy and sweet combination in this smoothie.

INGREDIENTS

1 cup arugula

1 red pepper, cored

2 tablespoons cilantro

1 garlic clove

2 cups purified water

Yields: 3–4 cups

Per 1 cup serving • Calories: 16 • Fat: 0g • Protein: 1g • Sodium: 7mg • Fiber: 1g • Carbohydrates: 3g

1. Combine arugula, pepper, cilantro, garlic, and 1 cup water in a blender and blend until thoroughly combined.

2. Add remaining water, if needed, while blending until desired texture is achieved.

ZIPPY ZUCCHINI

As a meal option, this smoothie combines intensely flavored, filling ingredients that will provide sustainable energy and improved mental processes in a satisfying alternative to fattening, salt-laden savory entrées. Pair it with a slice of whole-grain bread.

INGREDIENTS

2 kale leaves

1 zucchini, peeled

1 cup asparagus

½ red bell pepper

1 green onion

2 garlic cloves

2 cups purified water

Yields: 3–4 cups

Per 1 cup serving • Calories: 31 • Fat: 0g • Protein: 2g • Sodium: 17mg • Fiber: 2g • Carbohydrates: 6g

1. Combine kale, zucchini, asparagus, red pepper, onion, garlic, and 1 cup water in a blender and blend until thoroughly combined.

2. Add remaining water as needed while blending until desired consistency is achieved.

ZOOM WITH ZUCCHINI

The vibrant veggies and cayenne pepper in this recipe make for a fat-burning, calorie-zapping smoothie that will fill you up and fire your engines!

INGREDIENTS

1 cup spinach

1 zucchini

1 tomato

2 celery stalks

1 green onion

2 garlic cloves

⅛ teaspoon cayenne pepper

2 cups purified water

Yields: 3–4 cups

Per 1 cup serving • Calories: 22 • Fat: 0g • Protein: 1g • Sodium: 32mg • Fiber: 2g • Carbohydrates: 5g

1. Combine spinach, zucchini, tomato, celery, onion, garlic, cayenne, and 1 cup of water in a blender and blend until thoroughly combined.

2. Add remaining water as needed while blending until desired consistency is achieved.

ZUCCHINI APPLE Ⓥ

Many people heavily season zucchini when preparing it as a side dish because of its somewhat bland taste. In this recipe, no seasonings are needed! The sweet carrots and apples blend beautifully with the spinach and zucchini to deliver maximum flavor.

INGREDIENTS

1 cup spinach

1 zucchini

3 carrots, peeled

2 red apples, cored and peeled

2 cups purified water

Yields: 3–4 cups

Per 1 cup serving • Calories: 76 • Fat: 0g • Protein: 1g • Sodium: 46mg • Fiber: 4g • Carbohydrates: 19g

1. Combine spinach, zucchini, carrots, apples, and 1 cup water in a blender and blend until thoroughly combined.

2. Add remaining water while blending until desired texture is achieved.

CHAPTER 6

GREEN SMOOTHIES

APPLES

APPLE CELERY FOR HYDRATION

The fruits and greens in this smoothie provide natural sugars and carbohydrates, and celery regulates water levels.

INGREDIENTS

1 cup romaine lettuce

3 Granny Smith apples, peeled and cored

2 celery stalks

¼" ginger, peeled

2 cups purified water

Yields: 3–4 cups

Per 1 cup serving • Calories: 64 • Fat: 0g • Protein: 1g • Sodium: 19mg • Fiber: 2g • Carbohydrates: 17g

1. Combine romaine, apples, celery, ginger, and 1 cup of water in a blender and blend until thoroughly combined.

2. Add remaining water as needed while blending until desired consistency is achieved.

APPLE PEACH ENERGY ⓥ

Apples, peaches, and almond milk create a sweet, smooth blend that complements the snappy watercress. If you're looking for a healthy snack, skip the processed sweets and energy drinks and opt for this quick and easy smoothie that will give you sustainable energy for the rest of your day.

INGREDIENTS

1 cup watercress

3 peaches, pitted

2 apples, cored and peeled

2 cups almond milk

Yields: 3–4 cups

Per 1 cup serving • Calories: 137 • Fat: 2g • Protein: 2g • Sodium: 79mg • Fiber: 4g • Carbohydrates: 32g

1. Combine watercress, peaches, apples, and 1 cup almond milk in a blender and blend until thoroughly combined.

2. Add remaining almond milk while blending until desired texture is achieved.

GINGER APPLE SOOTHER Ⓥ

The fiber from the romaine and apples offers the benefit of a digestive system tune-up, and the ginger soothes any stomach discomfort. This recipe is highly recommended for those days you may feel especially irregular or uncomfortable.

INGREDIENTS

1 cup romaine lettuce

3 apples, cored and peeled

1 tablespoon ginger, peeled

2 cups almond milk

Yields: 3–4 cups

Per 1 cup serving • Calories: 119 • Fat: 2g • Protein: 1g • Sodium: 78mg • Fiber: 4g • Carbohydrates: 28g

1. Combine romaine, apples, ginger, and 1 cup almond milk in a blender and blend until thoroughly combined.

2. Add remaining almond milk while blending until desired texture is achieved.

Fiber and Ginger Combination

Ginger is hailed as one of nature's most potent medicinal plants, with its best-known cure being for stomach ailments. Combining ginger with the fiber found in fruits and leafy greens is an effective way to clean out the digestive tract, promote the release of good digestive enzymes, and soothe the stomach.

HEALTH'S NO JOKE WITH ARTICHOKES

Although artichokes are most commonly used in dips, salads, and entrées, raw artichokes make for a tasty addition to green-smoothie recipes such as this one. Artichokes pack a protective punch against disease, inflammation, and bone loss.

INGREDIENTS

1 cup spinach

4 artichoke hearts

1 green onion

2 celery stalks

2 cups purified water

Yields: 3–4 cups

Per 1 cup serving • Calories: 59 • Fat: 0g • Protein: 4g • Sodium: 130mg • Fiber: 7g • Carbohydrates: 13g

1. Combine spinach, artichoke hearts, onion, celery, and 1 cup of water in a blender and blend until thoroughly combined.

2. Add remaining water as needed while blending until desired consistency is achieved.

APPLE PROTEIN PACKER

The tasteful creamy combination of sweet fruits and almonds blends beautifully with the crisp watercress for a protein-filled delight you're sure to enjoy after a strenuous workout.

INGREDIENTS

¼ cup almonds

¾ cup purified water

1 cup watercress

1 apple, peeled and cored

1 banana, peeled

1 cup Greek yogurt

Yields: 3–4 cups

Per 1 cup serving • Calories: 130 • Fat: 5g • Protein: 8g • Sodium: 29mg • Fiber: 2g • Carbohydrates: 16g

1. Combine almonds and water in a blender and emulsify until no almond bits remain.

2. Add watercress, apple, banana, and ½ cup yogurt and blend until thoroughly combined with almond milk.

3. Add remaining yogurt as needed while blending until desired consistency is achieved.

What Is Watercress?

This leafy green veggie is loaded with vitamin C, calcium, and potassium, all important vitamins for maintaining a healthy immune system and providing structural support for the bones of an athlete. But that's not all! Its acid-forming minerals cleanse and normalize the intestines while the chlorophyll stimulates the metabolism and the circulatory system. Higher metabolism, better blood distribution, less illness and disease, and cleaner digestion all packed in a single serving of this amazing green leafy veggie!

RED AND GREEN SMOOTHIE Ⓥ

The ingredients in this recipe offer a wide variety of health benefits. Iron, powerful vitamin C, fiber, antioxidants, and natural diuretics combine to make this a beneficial treat that packs plenty of flavor.

INGREDIENTS

1 cup spinach

1 cucumber, peeled

2 celery stalks

2 red Gala apples, cored and peeled

1 lemon, peeled

1 lime, peeled

1 cup purified water

Yields: 3–4 cups

Per 1 cup serving • Calories: 68 • Fat: 0g • Protein: 1g • Sodium: 25mg • Fiber: 4g • Carbohydrates: 18g

1. Combine spinach, cucumber, celery, apples, lemon, lime, and ½ cup water in a blender and blend until thoroughly combined.

2. Add additional water, if needed, while blending until desired texture is achieved.

SMART START

This smoothie is the perfect way to start your day! Loaded with vitamin- and mineral-rich fruits and greens, this recipe's nutrition and sustaining benefits will last throughout your day.

INGREDIENTS

1 cup spinach

2 apples, peeled and cored

2 pears, peeled and cored

2 bananas, peeled

¼" ginger, peeled

2 cups chamomile tea

Yields: 4–6 cups

Per 1 cup serving • Calories: 8 • Fat: 0g • Protein: 1g • Sodium: 6mg • Fiber: 3g • Carbohydrates: 22g

1. Combine spinach, apples, pears, bananas, ginger, and 1 cup of tea in a blender and blend until thoroughly combined.

2. Add remaining tea as needed while blending until desired consistency is achieved.

BANANA, BERRIES, AND CHERRIES

BANANA BERRY BOOST

You can't beat the taste of smooth bananas and sweet berries blended with creamy yogurt! There's no better follow-up to a satisfying workout than a dose of sweet fruits blended with powerful protein to optimize your muscles' recovery.

INGREDIENTS

1 cup watercress

2 bananas, peeled

2 cups goji berries

1 cup Greek yogurt

Yields: 3–4 cups

Per 1 cup serving • Calories: 266 • Fat: 0g • Protein: 15g • Sodium: 28mg • Fiber: 10g • Carbohydrates: 64g

1. Combine watercress, bananas, goji berries, and ½ cup yogurt in a blender and blend until thoroughly combined.

2. Add remaining yogurt as needed while blending until desired consistency is achieved.

The Goji Berry

Goji berries provide excellent health benefits for everything from cancer prevention to eye health. Although research has shown that the nutrients and phytochemicals in berries are responsible for preventing serious illnesses and diseases, the goji berry's specific effects are still under review. Including these sweet jewels makes for one delicious smoothie that will not only satisfy your sweet tooth, but also make your body a flu-fighting machine.

PEACHY ORANGE BANANA Ⓥ

Delightfully refreshing citrus paired with sweet peaches and smooth bananas make this smoothie a delicious treat for breakfast, lunch, a snack, or dessert.

INGREDIENTS

1 cup watercress

1 orange, peeled

2 peaches, pitted

1 banana, peeled

1 cup coconut milk

Yields: 3–4 cups

Per 1 cup serving • Calories: 183 • Fat: 12g • Protein: 3g • Sodium: 11mg • Fiber: 3g • Carbohydrates: 20g

1. Combine watercress, orange, peaches, banana, and ½ cup coconut milk in a blender and blend until thoroughly combined.

2. Add remaining coconut milk while blending until desired texture is achieved.

BACKWARDS BERRY

Beautiful, healthier, more hydrated skin and hair are added benefits from this smoothie. The antioxidants provided protect against free radical damage that can wreak havoc on the inside and outside of your body.

INGREDIENTS

1 cup spinach

1 pint blackberries

1 pint raspberries

¼" ginger, peeled

½ lemon, peeled

2 cups chamomile tea

Yields: 3–4 cups

Per 1 cup serving • Calories: 67 • Fat: 1g • Protein: 2g • Sodium: 10mg • Fiber: 8g • Carbohydrates: 16g

1. Combine spinach, berries, ginger, lemon, and 1 cup of tea in a blender and blend until thoroughly combined.

2. Add remaining tea as needed while blending until desired consistency is achieved.

DELICIOUS BANANAS AND BERRIES Ⓥ

While satisfying your sweet tooth with this delicious blend of bananas, blueberries, and strawberries, consider boosting your daily protein intake by adding a scoop of whey protein or soy protein powder to the mix.

INGREDIENTS

1 cup romaine lettuce

2 bananas, peeled

1 pint strawberries

1 pint blueberries

2 cups almond milk

Yields: 3–4 cups

Per 1 cup serving • Calories: 316 • Fat: 19g • Protein: 4g • Sodium: 18mg • Fiber: 12g • Carbohydrates: 39g

1. Combine romaine, bananas, berries, and 1 cup almond milk in a blender and blend until thoroughly combined.

2. Add remaining almond milk while blending until desired texture is achieved.

Soy Versus Whey

For the devout vegan who consumes absolutely no animal products, including dairy or eggs, soy protein is the way to go. Soy protein has absolutely no milk derivatives in its makeup and is acceptable for a strict dairy-free diet. For vegetarians who welcome dairy additions in their diet, whey is acceptable as well as soy. Whey is made from milk byproducts, making it suitable for those who include dairy in their diet.

BREATHE EASY WITH BLACKBERRIES

Delicious blackberries are made even more tasty with the addition of lemon and ginger in this recipe. This smoothie offers a healthy dose of much-needed vitamins and minerals, and is rich and satisfying with the addition of protein-packed yogurt.

INGREDIENTS

1 cup watercress

2 pints blackberries

1 banana, peeled

½ lemon, peeled

½" ginger, peeled

1 cup Greek yogurt

Yields: 3–4 cups

Per 1 cup serving • Calories: 125 • Fat: 1g • Protein: 8g • Sodium: 29mg • Fiber: 9g • Carbohydrates: 25g

1. Combine watercress, blackberries, banana, lemon, ginger, and ½ cup of yogurt in a blender and blend until thoroughly combined.

2. Add remaining yogurt as needed while blending until desired consistency is achieved.

Blackberries Promote Respiratory Relief

Rich blackberries are not just a tasty treat; they are also sources of a variety of vitamins and minerals that can aid in overall health. Specifically, the magnesium content in blackberries is what makes this fruit a key to promoting respiratory ease. Best known for its ability to relax the muscles and thin the mucus most commonly associated with breathing difficulties, blackberries are an important addition to those in need of breathing assistance.

BERRIES AND BANANAS FOR BONE HEALTH

The crisp taste of iceberg lettuce is beautifully balanced with the addition of citrus, blackberries, bananas, and yogurt for a flavor combination that will make you enjoy eating better for your health.

INGREDIENTS

1 cup iceberg lettuce

1 pint blackberries

1 cup pineapple, peeled and cored

2 bananas, peeled

1 cup Greek yogurt

Yields: 3–4 cups

Per 1 cup serving • Calories: 137 • Fat: 1g • Protein: 8g • Sodium: 27mg • Fiber: 6g • Carbohydrates: 29g

1. Combine iceberg, blackberries, pineapple, bananas, and ½ cup yogurt in a blender and blend until thoroughly combined.

2. Add remaining yogurt as needed while blending until desired consistency is achieved.

Magnesium for Bone Health

The magnesium in blackberries can do amazing things for respiratory relief, and can also help create stronger bones. Playing an important role in the absorption of calcium, a diet rich in this powerful mineral ensures strong bones. Diets deficient in magnesium have also been shown to prevent the body's proper use of estrogen, which can spell disaster for many of the body's cancer-fighting abilities.

BONE UP WITH BLACKBERRIES

Rich vitamins and minerals that will optimize all those steps you take for optimal health are abundant in this smoothie recipe.

INGREDIENTS

1 cup watercress

2 cups blackberries

2 bananas, peeled

2 oranges, peeled

2 cups chamomile tea

Yields: 3–4 cups

Per 1 cup serving • Calories: 128 • Fat: 1g • Protein: 3g • Sodium: 7mg • Fiber: 8g • Carbohydrates: 32g

1. Combine watercress, blackberries, bananas, oranges, and 1 cup tea in a blender and blend until thoroughly combined.

2. Add remaining tea as needed while blending until desired consistency is achieved.

CITRUS BERRY Ⓥ

Blend these delightfully fresh fruits with the refreshing taste of watercress, and the only overwhelming feeling you'll encounter is pure pleasure. Your mouth, mind, and body will all benefit from the vitamins and minerals.

INGREDIENTS

1 cup watercress

2 oranges, peeled

1 cup strawberries

1 cup blueberries

1 cup coconut milk

Yields: 3–4 cups

Per 1 cup serving • Calories: 188 • Fat: 12g • Protein: 3g • Sodium: 12mg • Fiber: 4g • Carbohydrates: 21g

1. Combine watercress, oranges, strawberries, blueberries, and ½ cup coconut milk in a blender and blend until thoroughly combined.

2. Add remaining coconut milk while blending until desired texture is achieved.

Strawberries for Disease Prevention

Strawberries are a delicious, sweet treat, and they're amazingly healthy, too. Packed with B vitamins, vitamin C, and ellagic acid (an anticancer compound), these rich berries protect against disease and cancer. Shown to help reduce the risk of Alzheimer's disease and lower bad cholesterol, strawberries are essential for any diet.

FLOWERY FRUITS Ⓥ

Although these fruits don't flower, dandelion greens do make a pretty addition to this wonderful smoothie. The dandelion greens, arugula, and pineapple create a splendidly sweet combination.

INGREDIENTS

½ cup dandelion greens

½ cup arugula

2 cups pineapple, peeled and cored

1 banana, peeled

2 cups coconut milk

Yields: 3–4 cups

Per 1 cup serving • Calories: 290 • Fat: 24g
• Protein: 3g • Sodium: 22mg • Fiber: 1g •
Carbohydrates: 20g

1. Combine dandelion greens, arugula, pineapple, banana, and 1 cup coconut milk in a blender and blend until thoroughly combined.

2. Add remaining coconut milk while blending until desired texture is achieved.

The Rich Flavors of Protein Powder

You can easily add protein powders to your green smoothies. No longer bland or chalky, protein powders are available in a wide variety of flavors and flavor combinations that will provide a healthy helping of protein while satisfying your sweet tooth. Chocolate, banana cream, and many more flavors are now available. Blend them into these recipes to increase your daily protein intake while adhering to your vegan diet.

GRAPPLEBERRY

Morning, noon, or night, you can enjoy this delightful treat packed with powerful nutrition. Promoting total health on the inside and out, this recipe provides balanced nutrition for any and all health issues.

INGREDIENTS

1 cup watercress

1 cup red grapes

2 apples, peeled and cored

1 pint raspberries

2 cups chamomile tea

Yields: 3–4 cups

Per 1 cup serving • Calories: 98 • Fat: 1g • Protein: 1g • Sodium: 7mg • Fiber: 5g • Carbohydrates: 25g

1. Combine watercress, grapes, apples, raspberries, and 1 cup of tea in a blender and blend until thoroughly combined.

2. Add remaining tea as needed while blending until desired consistency is achieved.

MANGO BERRY Ⓥ

Watercress acts as a beautiful background green for this deliciously sweet and smooth recipe. The mangos, raspberries, and coconut milk provide a healthy serving of vitamins, minerals, and strong antioxidants.

INGREDIENTS

1 cup watercress

2 mangos, pitted and peeled

2 pints raspberries

1½ cups coconut milk

Yields: 3–4 cups

Per 1 cup serving • Calories: 316 • Fat: 19g • Protein: 4g • Sodium: 18mg • Fiber: 12g • Carbohydrates: 39g

1. Combine watercress, mangos, raspberries, and half of the coconut milk in a blender and blend until thoroughly combined.

2. Add remaining coconut milk while blending until desired texture is achieved.

Mangos and Digestion

When starting on a new raw food diet, some people report having difficulty digesting the amount and type of fiber found in the healthy ingredients like greens and fresh fruits. Mangos aid in digestion by combating acidity and uncomfortable acids in the digestive system and create a more placid, balanced system capable of a smooth, regular digestive process.

ACHE AID

Reducing aches, pains, soreness, and stiffness can be as easy as blending this delicious fruit, veggie, and herb smoothie that will get you up and moving again!

INGREDIENTS

1 cup watercress

2 cups cantaloupe

1 cucumber, peeled

2 tablespoons mint leaves

¼" ginger, peeled

1 cup chamomile tea

Yields: 3–4 cups

Per 1 cup serving • Calories: 35 • Fat: 0g • Protein: 1g • Sodium: 19mg • Fiber: 1g • Carbohydrates: 8g

1. Combine watercress, cantaloupe, cucumber, mint, ginger, and ½ cup tea in a blender and blend until thoroughly combined.

2. Add remaining tea as needed while blending until desired consistency is achieved.

CHERRY VANILLA RESPIRATORY RELIEF

Move over ice cream! This delicious smoothie will have you wondering, "Where's the greens?" Although the overpowering flavors of cherry and vanilla take center stage, the vitamin and mineral content of all of the ingredients (including the spinach) will do your body a world of good.

INGREDIENTS

1 cup spinach

2 cups cherries, pitted

1 apple, peeled and cored

1 vanilla bean's pulp

½" ginger, peeled

2 cups purified water

Yields: 3–4 cups

Per 1 cup serving • Calories: 73 • Fat: 0g • Protein: 1g • Sodium: 9mg • Fiber: 2g • Carbohydrates: 18g

1. Combine spinach, cherries, apple, vanilla bean pulp, ginger, and 1 cup water in a blender and blend until thoroughly combined.

2. Add remaining water as needed while blending until desired consistency is achieved.

The Breathing Benefit of Cherries

The abundant phytochemical content in cherries lends a hand in breathing. Phytochemicals make an impact on inflammation everywhere in the body. Commonly suggested for patients suffering from inflammation of joints, cherries can also assist in reducing the inflammation of airways and respiratory-related muscles.

FIGS, GRAPES, AND CITRUS

FABULOUS FIG FUSION

Sweet figs sparkle with this spice-infused blend full of fiber and antioxidants, which combine to protect against illness while promoting regularity. All these health benefits are whirled up in a smoothie with a creamy taste that will take you by surprise!

INGREDIENTS

1 cup figs, peeled and cored

1 teaspoon cardamom

1 teaspoon ginger

1 cup almond milk

1 cup ice

Yields: 2 cups

Per 1 cup serving • Calories: 136 • Fat: 1g • Protein: 1g • Sodium: 46mg • Fiber: 3g • Carbohydrates: 36g

1. In a blender, combine the figs, cardamom, ginger, and almond milk with ½ cup ice, and blend until thoroughly combined.

2. While blending, add remaining ice until desired consistency is achieved.

A GRAPE WAY TO BONE HEALTH

The sweetness of this smoothie just can't be beat! This recipe provides abundant vitamins and minerals with the added benefit of an amazingly refreshing taste.

INGREDIENTS

1 cup watercress

2 cups red grapes

2 pears, cored

1 banana, peeled

1 cup purified water

Yields: 3–4 cups

Per 1 cup serving • Calories: 131 • Fat: 0g • Protein: 1g • Sodium: 7mg • Fiber: 4g • Carbohydrates: 34g

1. Combine watercress, grapes, pears, banana, and ½ cup of water in a blender and blend until thoroughly combined.

2. Add remaining water as needed while blending until desired consistency is achieved.

Grapes' Anthocyanins and Proanthocyanidins

You may never have heard of these two amazing compounds, but they are extremely important in promoting strong bones and optimizing bone health. Anthocyanins and proanthocyanidins are compounds found in cells, and their duty is to ensure that the bone structure is stabilized and to promote the collagen-building process that is absolutely imperative for strong bones. The two foods richest in these strong compounds are deep-red and purple grapes and blueberries.

FORTIFYING FRUCTOSE

The combination of citrus fruits in this smoothie will give you the nutrients you need after a great workout.

INGREDIENTS

1 cup romaine lettuce

½ pineapple, peeled and cored

½ red grapefruit, peeled

1 tangerine, peeled

½ lemon, peeled

½ lime, peeled

1 cup purified water

Yields: 3–4 cups

Per 1 cup serving • Calories: 88 • Fat: 0g • Protein: 1g • Sodium: 4mg • Fiber: 2g • Carbohydrates: 23g

1. Combine romaine, pineapple, grapefruit, tangerine, lemon, lime, and ½ cup water in a blender and blend until thoroughly combined.

2. Add remaining water as needed while blending until desired consistency is achieved.

Fructose: The Smart Sugar

Fructose, the natural sugar found in fruit, is the healthiest version of sugar because it's an all-natural, nonprocessed version of the table sugars and artificial sweeteners commonly used. For an athlete, fruit is important for its vitamins and minerals and because it can satisfy cravings for sweets without the unhealthy crash associated with processed sugar, or the possible health risks associated with artificial sweeteners.

VITAMIN C CANCER PREVENTION

This vitamin C–packed recipe is a delicious blend of grapefruit, pineapple, and orange, intensified by the addition of ginger and vitamin K- and iron-rich spinach.

INGREDIENTS

1 cup spinach

1 grapefruit, peeled

1 cup pineapple, peeled and cored

1 orange, peeled

½" ginger, peeled

1 cup purified water

Yields: 3–4 cups

Per 1 cup serving • Calories: 62 • Fat: 0g • Protein: 1g • Sodium: 8mg • Fiber: 2g • Carbohydrates: 16g

1. Combine spinach, grapefruit, pineapple, orange, ginger, and ½ cup water in a blender and blend until thoroughly combined.

2. Add remaining water as needed while blending until desired consistency is achieved.

The Amazing Power of C

Not only is this strong vitamin the best known for illness prevention, it works absolute wonders in many areas of promoting optimal health. In addition to being a strong supporter of bone health by aiding the collagen-making process, building and retaining quality muscle, and improving the efficiency of blood vessels, it actually aids in the body's absorption of iron. Common mineral deficiencies can be reversed by including an abundance of vitamin C with your daily intake of iron-rich foods.

GREEN CITRUS Ⓥ

Vitamin C and a wide variety of other vitamins, minerals, fiber, and antioxidants, and amazing flavor in this smoothie create a delicious way to combat illnesses in the tastiest way possible!

INGREDIENTS

1 cup watercress

1 grapefruit, peeled

2 oranges, peeled

1 banana, peeled

1 cup purified water

Yields: 3–4 cups

Per 1 cup serving • Calories: 90 • Fat: 0g • Protein: 2g • Sodium: 5mg • Fiber: 4g • Carbohydrates: 23g

1. Combine watercress, grapefruit, oranges, banana, and ½ cup water in a blender and blend until thoroughly combined.

2. Add remaining water while blending until desired texture is achieved.

GREEN SWEET CITRUS Ⓥ

This recipe is a wonderfully refreshing option for any time your body and mind may need a boost. The mildly peppery taste of watercress combines with the citrus flavors to develop a light and refreshing vitamin-packed treat.

INGREDIENTS

1 cup watercress

1 grapefruit, peeled

2 oranges, peeled

½" ginger, peeled

½ lemon, peeled

1 cup purified water

Yields: 3–4 cups

Per 1 cup serving • Calories: 67 • Fat: 0g • Protein: 2g • Sodium: 5mg • Fiber: 3g • Carbohydrates: 17g

1. Combine watercress, grapefruit, oranges, ginger, lemon, and ½ cup water in a blender and blend until thoroughly combined.

2. Add remaining water while blending until desired texture is achieved.

MANGOS AND MELONS

BRIGHT FIGHT AGAINST DISEASE

It's well known that fruits and veggies signal their potency with their vibrant colors, so imagine the powerful nutrition and antioxidant power of this delightful blend! Mangos, strawberries, lemon, sweet romaine, and soothing chamomile combine to fight illness.

INGREDIENTS

1 cup romaine lettuce

2 cups mangos

1 pint strawberries

½ lemon, peeled

2 cups chamomile tea

Yields: 3–4 cups

Per 1 cup serving • Calories: 81 • Fat: 0g • Protein: 1g • Sodium: 6mg • Fiber: 3g • Carbohydrates: 21g

1. Combine romaine, mangos, strawberries, lemon, and 1 cup of tea in a blender and blend until thoroughly combined.

2. Add remaining tea as needed while blending until desired consistency is achieved.

Food Combining for Optimal Benefits

When you're looking for the benefits from fruits and vegetables, how can you possibly decide which is the best? With the varied vitamin and mineral contents in different fruits and vegetables, there's no one "best." Your best bet would be to include as much nutrition from fruits and vegetables in as wide a variety as possible; the benefits to your immune system, major bodily functions, brain chemistry, and mental processes are innumerable!

CANTALOUPE FOR CANCER PREVENTION

The vibrant color of cantaloupe is from the abundant levels of beta-carotene, known for providing health benefits. Not only a sweet treat, this smoothie provides a wide variety of vitamins and minerals that work hard in preventing illness and disease.

INGREDIENTS

1 cup watercress

½ cantaloupe, rind and seeds removed

1 apple, peeled and cored

1 banana, peeled

¼" ginger, peeled

1 cup purified water

Yields: 3–4 cups

Per 1 cup serving • Calories: 70 • Fat: 0g • Protein: 1g • Sodium: 16mg • Fiber: 2g • Carbohydrates: 18g

1. Combine watercress, cantaloupe, apple, banana, ginger, and ½ cup water in a blender and blend until thoroughly combined.

2. Add remaining water as needed while blending until desired consistency is achieved.

Beta-Carotene's Fight Against Cancer

Among the many benefits beta-carotene offers, one of the major responsibilities of this strong antioxidant is to combat free radicals from the environment, certain foods, and unhealthy lifestyles. Free radicals can cause abnormal growth in cells, which can lead to dangerous illnesses like cancer. Studies have shown that diets rich in carotenes promote proper cell growth, thereby reducing the chances of cancers and disease.

COLORFUL COMBO FOR CANCER PREVENTION

Combined into a sweet, down-to-earth flavor, these fruits and vegetables blended with dark leafy greens and chamomile make for an intoxicating blend for your mind and body's total health.

INGREDIENTS

1 cup romaine lettuce

2 cups cantaloupe

2 carrots, peeled

1 cup pineapple

1 beet

2 cups chamomile tea

Yields: 3–4 cups

Per 1 cup serving • Calories: 68 • Fat: 0g • Protein: 2g • Sodium: 53mg • Fiber: 2g • Carbohydrates: 17g

1. Combine romaine, cantaloupe, carrots, pineapple, beet, and 1 cup of tea in a blender and blend until thoroughly combined.

2. Add remaining tea as needed while blending until desired consistency is achieved.

A YOGI'S FAVORITE

Hot, or not, yoga can be a powerful workout. Replenish your body and refresh your senses with this sweet blend of melons and citrus. A definite "Yum!" to follow your "Ohm!"

INGREDIENTS

1 cup watercress

½ honeydew, rind and seeds removed

2 tangerines, peeled

1 cucumber, peeled

1 cup Greek yogurt

Yields: 3–4 cups

Per 1 cup serving • Calories: 120 • Fat: 0g • Protein: 7g • Sodium: 58mg • Fiber: 2g • Carbohydrates: 24g

1. Combine watercress, honeydew, tangerines, cucumber, and ½ cup yogurt in a blender and blend until thoroughly combined.

2. Add remaining yogurt as needed while blending until desired consistency is achieved.

FAT-BURNING FUEL

The refreshing combination of watermelon, raspberries, lime, crisp romaine, and calming chamomile will take your life to new heights by improving metabolism and promoting healthy brain function.

INGREDIENTS

1 cup romaine lettuce

2 cups watermelon, deseeded

1 pint raspberries

½ lime, peeled

1 cup chamomile tea

Yields: 3–4 cups

Per 1 cup serving • Calories: 59 • Fat: 1g • Protein: 1g • Sodium: 4mg • Fiber: 5g • Carbohydrates: 14g

1. Combine romaine, watermelon, raspberries, lime, and ½ cup of tea in a blender and blend until thoroughly combined.

2. Add remaining tea as needed while blending until desired consistency is achieved.

OH, MY! OMEGAS

In this tasty recipe, omega-3s are plentiful without the need for salmon or rich meats. If salmon isn't your favorite food, consider smoothies that contain flaxseed for your daily value of omegas.

INGREDIENTS

1 cup watercress

½ cantaloupe, rind and seeds removed

1 banana, peeled

1 orange, peeled

1 cup raspberries

1 tablespoon flaxseed

2 cups purified water

Yields: 3–4 cups

Per 1 cup serving • Calories: 102 • Fat: 2g • Protein: 2g • Sodium: 18mg • Fiber: 5g • Carbohydrates: 23g

1. Combine watercress, cantaloupe, banana, orange, raspberries, flaxseed, and 1 cup of water in a blender and blend until thoroughly combined.

2. Add remaining water as needed while blending until desired consistency is achieved.

Flaxseed for Omega-3s!

Everybody needs omegas! Although many athletes include meats in their diets, some vegetarian and vegan athletes need to turn to alternatives to fulfill their omega needs. Flaxseed provides amazing amounts of omegas that are comparable to rich meats and fish (which are also high in undesirable fat content). Flaxseed makes a mildly nutty addition to your favorite smoothie blends.

SUNBURN SOOTHER

It's funny to think you could soothe a sunburn with a sweet green smoothie, but it can be done! The hydrating melons not only are able to calm skin discomfort, but also provide electrolytes that promote balance for the body and the mind.

INGREDIENTS

1 cup arugula

2 cups watermelon, deseeded

2 cups cantaloupe, rind and seeds removed

½ lemon, peeled

½ lime, peeled

½" ginger, peeled

2 cups chamomile tea

Yields: 3–4 cups

Per 1 cup serving • Calories: 56 • Fat: 0g • Protein: 1g • Sodium: 17mg • Fiber: 2g • Carbohydrates: 15g

1. Combine arugula, watermelon, cantaloupe, lemon, lime, ginger, and 1 cup of tea in a blender and blend until thoroughly combined.

2. Add remaining tea as needed while blending until desired consistency is achieved.

Melons for Disease Protection

Although most people enjoy these fruits for their hydrating qualities and deliciously sweet flavor, watermelons and cantaloupes are strong warriors in the fight against cancer. Enhancing the immune system with their wealth of B vitamins and vitamin C, these melons have been shown to reduce the risks of certain cancers including prostate, ovarian, cervical, oral, and pharyngeal cancers.

DOUBLE-DUTY DELIGHT

Luscious fruits like papaya, pineapple, and strawberries make for the perfect blend with delicious vitamin- and mineral-rich romaine. This smoothie's powerful antioxidants will make you look and feel younger.

INGREDIENTS

1 cup romaine lettuce

1 cup papaya

1 cup pineapple, peeled and cubed

1 pint strawberries

2 cups chamomile tea

Yields: 3–4 cups

Per 1 cup serving • Calories: 46 • Fat: 0g • Protein: 1g • Sodium: 5mg • Fiber: 2g • Carbohydrates: 11g

1. Combine romaine, papaya, pineapple, strawberries, and 1 cup tea in a blender and blend until thoroughly combined.

2. Add remaining tea as needed while blending until desired consistency is achieved.

PEARS, PINEAPPLE, AND POMEGRANATES

PEARS WITH A TART TWIST Ⓥ

Providing an amazing percentage of essential vitamins and minerals needed for the optimal functioning of your mind and body, this smoothie is a sweet, tart, and smart way to pep up your day!

INGREDIENTS

4 cups romaine lettuce

4 pears, cored

1 banana, peeled

6 tablespoons lemon juice

2 cups purified water

Yields: 4–6 cups

Per 1 cup serving • Calories: 94 • Fat: 0g • Protein: 1g • Sodium: 6mg • Fiber: 5g • Carbohydrates: 25g

1. Combine romaine, pears, banana, lemon juice, and 1 cup water in a blender and blend until thoroughly combined.

2. Add remaining water while blending until desired texture is achieved.

PEAR PREVENTION

This refreshing smoothie makes a great snack when your body and mind need a lift. The sweet pears, spicy ginger, and rich cabbage and celery combine with the cooling cucumber for an overall refreshing blend.

INGREDIENTS

1 cup green cabbage

3 pears, cored

1 cucumber, peeled

1 celery stalk

½" ginger, peeled

1 cup kefir

Yields: 3–4 cups

Per 1 cup serving • Calories: 132 • Fat: 2g • Protein: 3g • Sodium: 46mg • Fiber: 6g • Carbohydrates: 27g

1. Combine cabbage, pears, cucumber, celery, ginger, and ½ cup kefir in a blender and blend until thoroughly combined.

2. Add remaining kefir as needed while blending until desired consistency is achieved.

SPICY PEAR REFRESHMENT

Spicy arugula gets sweetened up a bit with pears, grapes, and zippy ginger to make for a wonderful smoothie. This recipe is full of vitamins, minerals, and antioxidants that provide total health, beautiful eyes, and luxurious skin.

INGREDIENTS

1 cup arugula

4 pears, peeled and cored

1 cup red grapes

½" ginger, peeled

2 cups chamomile tea

Yields: 3–4 cups

Per 1 cup serving • Calories: 131 • Fat: 0g • Protein: 1g • Sodium: 23mg • Fiber: 6g • Carbohydrates: 35g

1. Combine arugula, pears, grapes, ginger, and 1 cup of tea in a blender and blend until thoroughly combined.

2. Add remaining tea as needed while blending until desired consistency is achieved.

Balanced Diet for Better Skin

Crash dieting is a definite no-no when trying to clear up acne! Studies have shown that extreme changes in diet like the total avoidance of fats or excessive inclusion of fats as the main source of food can destabilize the amount of secretions of the pores, which is the major source of acne. So, include a variety of fresh fruits and veggies with minimal fats to promote the most balanced environment for beautiful skin!

VERY CHERRY PEARS Ⓥ

If you like cherry, vanilla, and pears, this recipe is for you! Add a scoop of soy protein powder to make the health benefits of this smoothie even greater.

INGREDIENTS

1 cup iceberg lettuce

2 pears, cored

1 banana, peeled

1 cup cherries, pitted

½ vanilla bean's pulp

2 cups almond milk

Yields: 3–4 cups

Per 1 cup serving • Calories: 150 • Fat: 2g • Protein: 2g • Sodium: 78mg • Fiber: 5g • Carbohydrates: 35g

1. Combine iceberg, pears, banana, cherries, vanilla bean pulp, and 1 cup almond milk in a blender and blend until thoroughly combined.

2. Add remaining almond milk while blending until desired texture is achieved.

AGENT PINEAPPLE AGAINST ARTHRITIS

This vitamin-packed smoothie does a world of good for preventing discomfort associated with everything from common colds to arthritis. Sweet, satisfying, and full of fruits and veggies, this is one smoothie that does it all!

INGREDIENTS

1 cup watercress

1 pint blueberries

2 cups pineapple, peeled and cored

¼" ginger, peeled

2 cups chamomile tea

Yields: 3–4 cups

Per 1 cup serving • Calories: 81 • Fat: 0g • Protein: 1g • Sodium: 7mg • Fiber: 2g • Carbohydrates: 21g

1. Combine watercress, blueberries, pineapple, ginger, and 1 cup of tea in a blender and blend until thoroughly combined.

2. Add remaining tea as needed while blending until desired consistency is achieved.

Pineapple Prevention

Did you know that every bite of pineapple has powerful protective vitamins and enzymes that can drastically reduce the discomfort associated with common ailments? The vitamin C content and the enzyme bromelain are responsible for the major health benefits offered up by this superfruit. Those suffering from asthma, arthritis, angina, and indigestion can find extra relief from indulging in one of nature's most delightfully sweet treats.

THE SWEET SENSATION OF HEALTH

If your diet and lifestyle leave you feeling in need of refreshment and vitality, this smoothie is for you. Hydrating melon and citrus combine with rich greens to provide a revitalizing lift.

INGREDIENTS

1 cup watercress

2 cups watermelon

1 cup pineapple, peeled and cored

1 cup kefir

Yields: 3–4 cups

Per 1 cup serving • Calories: 83 • Fat: 2g • Protein: 3g • Sodium: 36mg • Fiber: 1g • Carbohydrates: 14g

1. Combine watercress, watermelon, pineapple, and ¾ cup kefir in a blender and blend until thoroughly combined.

2. Add remaining kefir as needed while blending until desired consistency is achieved.

The Body's Need for Water

Cravings, fatigue, lack of focus, and derailed bodily functions can all result from not getting adequate water. The minimum recommended water intake is eight 8-ounce glasses of water daily, but those who exercise require even more. In addition to the water added while blending, the fruits and vegetable in this smoothie provide a tasty way to increase your hydration.

METABOLISM MAX-OUT

Vitamin C plays an important part in fighting illness, promoting your body's ability to function properly in every aspect, and optimizing metabolism for a fat-burning effect like no other.

INGREDIENTS

1 cup watercress

2 cups pineapple, peeled and cored

1 white grapefruit, peeled

3 tangerines, peeled

1 lemon, peeled

1 cup green tea

Yields: 3–4 cups

Per 1 cup serving • Calories: 97 • Fat: 0g • Protein: 2g • Sodium: 6mg • Fiber: 2g • Carbohydrates: 25g

1. Combine watercress, pineapple, grapefruit, tangerines, lemon, and ½ cup tea in a blender and blend until thoroughly combined.

2. Add remaining tea as needed while blending until desired consistency is achieved.

VIVACIOUS VITAMIN C

Eating a balanced diet of vibrant fruits, vegetables, and leafy greens can ensure that you're providing for your health and your athletic ability.

INGREDIENTS

1 cup watercress

½ pineapple, peeled and cored

3 oranges, peeled

1 lemon, peeled

1 cup strawberries

1 cup purified water

Yields: 3–4 cups

Per 1 cup serving • Calories: 138 • Fat: 0g • Protein: 3g • Sodium: 7mg • Fiber: 4g • Carbohydrates: 35g

1. Combine watercress, pineapple, oranges, lemon, strawberries, and ½ cup water in a blender and blend until thoroughly combined.

2. Add remaining water as needed while blending until desired consistency is achieved.

Vitamins and Minerals for Proactive Health

How important is vitamin C to an athlete? When was the last time you saw a top-performing athlete take first place hacking and heaving all the way to the finish line? Never! If you're going to keep your body in top shape, ready for anything, sound nutrition isn't the only thing requiring attention. In order to get the biggest bang for your buck out of performance nutrition, load up on vibrant fruits and veggies that do double duty.

SWIMMER'S SENSATION

Although your time is spent in a body of water, you can come out feeling dehydrated and in need of a boost of energy. A refreshing combination of pineapple, lemon, and cooling cucumbers can deliver exactly what your mind and body need.

INGREDIENTS

1 cup iceberg lettuce

2 cups pineapple, peeled and cored

2 cucumbers, peeled

½ lemon, peeled

1 cup Greek yogurt

Yields: 3–4 cups

Per 1 cup serving • Calories: 86 • Fat: 0g • Protein: 7g • Sodium: 29mg • Fiber: 1g • Carbohydrates: 15g

1. Combine iceberg, pineapple, cucumbers, lemon, and ½ cup yogurt in a blender and blend until thoroughly combined.

2. Add remaining yogurt as needed while blending until desired consistency is achieved.

POMEGRANATE PREVENTER

Packed with vitamins and minerals that promote health and fight illness, blending these delicious fruits and vegetables is a tasty way to maintain great health.

INGREDIENTS

1 cup iceberg lettuce

2 cups pomegranate pips

1 orange, peeled

1 banana, peeled

1 cup purified water

Yields: 3–4 cups

Per 1 cup serving • Calories: 123 • Fat: 1g • Protein: 2g • Sodium: 6mg • Fiber: 6g • Carbohydrates: 29g

1. Combine iceberg, pomegranate, orange, banana, and ½ cup water in a blender and blend until thoroughly combined.

2. Add remaining water as needed while blending until desired consistency is achieved.

ROMAINE AND SPINACH

AHHH, SWEET GREENS! Ⓥ

Apples and spinach in the same smoothie may seem like an unlikely pair, but one sip of this blend will have even the harshest skeptic agreeing that the duo makes a delicious treat.

INGREDIENTS

1 cup spinach

2 bananas, peeled

2 apples, cored and peeled

2 cups almond milk

Yields: 3–4 cups

Per 1 cup serving • Calories: 147 • Fat: 2g • Protein: 2g • Sodium: 82mg • Fiber: 4g • Carbohydrates: 34g

1. Combine spinach, bananas, apples, and 1 cup almond milk in a blender and blend until thoroughly combined.

2. Add remaining almond milk while blending until desired texture is achieved.

Fiber Benefits

Leafy greens, vegetables, and fruits all contain some amount of this miracle substance. Because fiber is almost completely undigestible by the human body, we benefit from its tendency to require more chewing time, make our stomachs feel full, and clear our intestinal tracts by remaining nearly intact throughout digestion. Although fiber is available in pill and powder forms, they are a far cry from a healthy bowl of spinach, broccoli, or fresh fruit.

ROMAINE TO THE RESCUE!

Crisp romaine, broccoli, carrots, garlic, and ginger combine in this recipe to make for one satisfying, savory smoothie that will promote health for your eyes, digestion, muscle repair, and mental clarity.

INGREDIENTS

2 cups romaine lettuce

½ cup broccoli

2 carrots

1 garlic clove

½" ginger, peeled

2 cups purified water

Yields: 3–4 cups

Per 1 cup serving • Calories: 22 • Fat: 0g • Protein: 1g • Sodium: 29mg • Fiber: 2g • Carbohydrates: 5g

1. Combine romaine, broccoli, carrots, garlic, ginger, and 1 cup of water in a blender and blend until thoroughly combined.

2. Add remaining water as needed while blending until desired consistency is achieved.

A SWEET STEP TO GREAT HEALTH

Vitamins K and C, beta-carotenes, potassium, folate, and protein are rich in this delicious smoothie. A one-stop shop for many of your fruit and vegetable servings, this delicious recipe satisfies your sweet tooth and dietary needs.

INGREDIENTS

1 cup romaine lettuce

1 cup pineapple, peeled and cored

1 pint strawberries

1 banana, peeled

1 cup Greek yogurt

Yields: 3–4 cups

Per 1 cup serving • Calories: 108 • Fat: 0g • Protein: 7g • Sodium: 26mg • Fiber: 3g • Carbohydrates: 21g

1. Combine romaine, pineapple, strawberries, banana, and ½ cup yogurt in a blender and blend until thoroughly combined.

2. Add remaining yogurt as needed while blending until desired consistency is achieved.

ANTIOXIDANT ASSIST

No matter how healthy your body may feel, there's always room for some assistance by antioxidants. Warding off illness and preventing degeneration of your body's processes is the main responsibility of these powerful preventers.

INGREDIENTS

½ cup arugula

½ cup spinach

½ cup asparagus

½ cup broccoli

1 clove garlic

2 cups chamomile tea

Yields: 3–4 cups

Per 1 cup serving • Calories: 13 • Fat: 0g • Protein: 1g • Sodium: 14mg • Fiber: 1g • Carbohydrates: 3g

1. Combine arugula, spinach, asparagus, broccoli, garlic, and 1 cup of tea in a blender and blend until thoroughly combined.

2. Add remaining tea as needed while blending until desired consistency is achieved.

MENTAL MAKEOVER

Hate forgetting things? Feel like you have absentmindedness a little too often? This smoothie is designed to get your brain back on track with rich sources of vitamins and minerals that stimulate and rejuvenate brain functions.

INGREDIENTS

1 cup spinach

2 cucumbers, peeled

2 celery stalks

1 tomato

2 cups chamomile tea

Yields: 3–4 cups

Per 1 cup serving • Calories: 25 • Fat: 0g • Protein: 1g • Sodium: 29mg • Fiber: 2g • Carbohydrates: 5g

1. Combine spinach, cucumbers, celery, tomato, and 1 cup of tea in a blender and blend until thoroughly combined.

2. Add remaining tea as needed while blending until desired consistency is achieved.

The Many Hats of Spinach

In addition to being a rich source of iron and folate (which actually aids in iron absorption), this amazing veggie holds a wealth of vitamins A, B, C, D, and K that provide cancer-fighting power against liver, ovarian, colon, and prostate cancers. By including just 1 cup of this powerful veggie in your daily diet (raw), you can satisfy over 180 percent of your daily value for vitamin K and almost 400 percent of your vitamin A intake!

POPEYE'S FAVORITE

Popeye had the right idea, and it showed in his powerful abilities. This recipe is filled with iron, vitamin K, folate, and fiber, and will have you feeling as strong as the Sailor Man!

INGREDIENTS

1 cup spinach

1 kale leaf

1 cup broccoli

3 apples, peeled and cored

2 cups purified water

Yields: 3–4 cups

Per 1 cup serving • Calories: 76 • Fat: 0g • Protein: 2g • Sodium: 23mg • Fiber: 3g • Carbohydrates: 19g

1. Combine spinach, kale, broccoli, apples, and 1 cup of water in a blender and blend until thoroughly combined.

2. Add remaining water as needed while blending until desired consistency is achieved.

Greens for All

When you were a kid, Popeye was one amazing example of what could happen if you ate your spinach! How many times did your parents reference Popeye when trying to get you to eat your spinach? And how often do you reference strength when trying to get your kids to eat greens now? Spinach contains loads of vitamins A, B, C, E, and K as well as iron, phosphorus, and fiber. With all that nutrition delivered in each serving, spinach should be in every athlete's daily diet . . . for strength like Popeye's!

SAVOR CANCER PREVENTION

Protect yourself by arming your body's defenses with great nutrition that will not only create energy, focus, and total health, but is strong prevention against serious cancers, too.

INGREDIENTS

½ cup romaine lettuce

½ cup spinach

½ cup broccoli

½ cup cauliflower

2 carrots, peeled

1 celery stalk

1 garlic clove

2 cups chamomile tea

Yields: 3–4 cups

Per 1 cup serving • Calories: 24 • Fat: 0g • Protein: 1g • Sodium: 42mg • Fiber: 2g • Carbohydrates: 5g

1. Combine romaine, spinach, broccoli, cauliflower, carrots, celery, garlic, and 1 cup of tea in a blender and blend until thoroughly combined.

2. Add remaining tea as needed while blending until desired consistency is achieved.

BEANY SPINACH Ⓥ

One of the most common bean dishes people enjoy is chili. The high sodium content and heat diminish the health benefits found in fiber- and protein-packed beans. This smoothie maximizes the benefits by keeping them in the raw form.

INGREDIENTS

1 cup spinach

1 cup red kidney beans, soaked and drained

1 cup northern white beans, soaked and drained

½ teaspoon cayenne

2 cups purified water

Yields: 3–4 cups

Per 1 cup serving • Calories: 311 • Fat: 1g • Protein: 21g • Sodium: 26mg • Fiber: 21g • Carbohydrates: 57g

1. Combine spinach, kidney beans, white beans, and cayenne pepper with 1 cup water in a blender and blend until thoroughly combined.

2. Add remaining water while blending until desired texture is achieved.

Cayenne for Digestive Health

You would think that such a spicy addition would cause stomach discomfort, but this pepper has amazing benefits. Cayenne has the ability to promote a digestive enzyme that works to kill bad bacteria ingested from foods while also promoting the good bacteria that optimizes the digestive process. As if that wasn't enough, these hot little items also work so hard to fight off bad bacteria, they actually prevent stomach ulcers!

SWEET SPINACH SPINNER

This sweet spin on vitamin-rich spinach makes a delightful treat you can enjoy before or after an exercise session. The low glycemic index of the ingredients makes a sustainable energy-powering blend of vitamins, minerals, and phytochemicals that will help you perform without the energy crash of caffeinated energy drinks.

INGREDIENTS

1 cup spinach

4 apples, peeled and cored

¼" ginger, peeled

2 cups purified water

Yields: 3–4 cups

Per 1 cup serving • Calories: 79 • Fat: 0g
• Protein: 1g • Sodium: 8mg • Fiber: 2g •
Carbohydrates: 21g

1. Combine spinach, apples, ginger, and 1 cup of water in a blender and blend until thoroughly combined.

2. Add remaining water as needed while blending until desired consistency is achieved.

VERY GREEN SMOOTHIE

This very green smoothie combines a variety of greens for the very best benefits! Spinach, kale, and wheatgrass are packed with vitamins and minerals that work hard to maintain your health.

INGREDIENTS

1 cup spinach

2 kale leaves

1 cup wheatgrass

1 celery stalk

½ lemon, peeled

1 garlic clove

2 cups chamomile tea

Yields: 3–4 cups

Per 1 cup serving • Calories: 16 • Fat: 0g •
Protein: 1g • Sodium: 25mg • Fiber: 1g •
Carbohydrates: 3g

1. Combine spinach, kale, wheatgrass, celery, lemon, garlic, and 1 cup of tea in a blender and blend until thoroughly combined.

2. Add remaining tea as needed while blending until desired consistency is achieved.

CHAPTER 7

KID-FRIENDLY SMOOTHIES

BLUEBERRY BURST

Even kids who say they hate blueberries love this smoothie. Tasting more like ice cream than a green smoothie, this blueberry treat is chock full of vitamins and minerals with a taste your kids will crave.

INGREDIENTS

1 cup watercress

2 pints blueberries

2 bananas, peeled

1 cup blueberry kefir

1 cup ice

Yields: 3–4 cups

Per 1 cup serving • Calories: 173 • Fat: 1g • Protein: 5g • Sodium: 38mg • Fiber: 5g • Carbohydrates: 40g

1. Combine watercress, blueberries, bananas, and kefir in a blender container and blend until thoroughly combined.

2. Add ice as needed while blending until desired consistency is achieved.

Blueberries and Bananas for Overall Health

Not only does the delicious blend of blueberries and bananas taste great, this combination makes for an amazingly nutritional treat for youngsters. The rich potassium, magnesium, B$_6$, and electrolyte stores of the bananas add to the vitamin C, saponins, and powerful antioxidants of the blueberries for a delicious way to promote heart health, mental clarity and focus, energy, and immune-fighting power!

CHERRY VANILLA MILKSHAKE

This recipe is one for the serious doubters who don't believe a child will consume greens blended in a smoothie. Vitamin-rich spinach, vibrant cherries, sweet banana, and vanilla bean combine with creamy kefir for a cherry vanilla milkshake!

INGREDIENTS

1 cup spinach

2 cups cherries, pitted

1 banana, peeled

Pulp of 1½ vanilla beans or 1½ teaspoons vanilla extract

2 cups vanilla kefir

1 cup ice

Yields: 3–4 cups

Per 1 cup serving • Calories: 146 • Fat: 0g • Protein: 7g • Sodium: 70mg • Fiber: 3g • Carbohydrates: 29g

1. Combine spinach, cherries, banana, vanilla, and 1 cup of kefir in a blender and blend until thoroughly combined.

2. Add remaining kefir and ice as needed while blending until desired consistency is achieved.

CANTALOUPE QUENCHER

Kids love fresh cantaloupe! Juice running down their little chins, they can't get enough of this vitamin-rich fruit, which makes it the perfect star of a green smoothie recipe like this one.

INGREDIENTS

1 cup iceberg lettuce

2 cups cantaloupe, rind and seeds removed

2 bananas, peeled

1 cup almond milk

1 cup ice

Yields: 3–4 cups

Per 1 cup serving • Calories: 91 • Fat: 1g • Protein: 1g • Sodium: 47mg • Fiber: 2g • Carbohydrates: 21g

1. Combine iceberg, cantaloupe, bananas, and ½ cup almond milk in a blender and blend until thoroughly combined.

2. Add remaining almond milk and ice as needed while blending until desired consistency is achieved.

Protect Your Family with Vitamins and Antioxidants

Although many people get the flu shot, exercise regularly, and try to eat a diet that will promote illness protection, when was the last time your child was guzzling vitamin C for the health benefits or finishing off his spinach because of the rich iron content? Children eat what tastes great, and when we make nutritious food delicious, they arm their own bodies with immunity-building protection.

CHOCOLATE BANANA BLITZ

Kids love chocolate! A brilliant way to transform a plain old green vegetable into pure deliciousness for a child is to add chocolatey carob for a taste sensation that will make for your kids' favorite fake-out of all!

INGREDIENTS

1 cup romaine lettuce

2 tablespoons carob powder

3 bananas, peeled

Pulp of 1 vanilla bean or 1 teaspoon vanilla extract

1 cup vanilla kefir

1 cup ice

Yields: 3–4 cups

Per 1 cup serving • Calories: 122 • Fat: 1g • Protein: 4g • Sodium: 35mg • Fiber: 3g • Carbohydrates: 26g

1. Combine romaine, carob powder, bananas, vanilla, and kefir in a blender and blend until thoroughly combined.

2. Add ice as needed while blending until desired consistency is achieved.

The Chocolate Alternatives

Powdered raw cacao and carob are two alternatives to the not-so-healthy chocolate enhanced with sugars that can bring out undesirable overstimulation in your little one. By including the flavors of the chocolate alternatives, you can provide a chocolate-flavored delight packed with rich antioxidants and vitamins and minerals from the delicious greens and fruit additions. Healthy—no sugar, no additives, no guilt!

A MONKEY'S CHOCOLATE DREAM

Your little ones and their sometimes more stubborn elders will fall for the deliciously rich flavors of this recipe, with the only questions being, "Are there seconds?"

INGREDIENTS

1 cup spinach

2 tablespoons carob powder

3 bananas, peeled

2 cups almond milk

1 cup ice

Yields: 3–4 cups

Per 1 cup serving • Calories: 153 • Fat: 2g • Protein: 2g • Sodium: 84mg • Fiber: 4g • Carbohydrates: 35g

1. Combine spinach, carob, bananas, and 1 cup almond milk in a blender and blend until thoroughly combined.

2. Add remaining almond milk and ice as needed while blending until desired consistency is achieved.

CITRUS BURST

For kids who love citrus fruits, this recipe is absolutely amazing. Blending an entire cup of greens into a deliciously sweet, tangy, and delightfully refreshing treat for any age, this is one great-tasting way to get your fiber.

INGREDIENTS

1 cup watercress

3 cups pineapple

1 tangerine, peeled

½ lemon, peeled

1 cup Greek yogurt

1 cup ice

Yields: 3–4 cups

Per 1 cup serving • Calories: 103 • Fat: 0g • Protein: 7g • Sodium: 30mg • Fiber: 1g • Carbohydrates: 21g

1. Combine watercress, pineapple, tangerine, lemon, and yogurt in a blender and blend until thoroughly combined.

2. Add ice as needed while blending until desired consistency is achieved.

GREAT GRAPE

With balanced nutrition and a great taste your kids will love, this is one sweet treat you'll never feel guilty about giving them!

INGREDIENTS

1 cup watercress

3 cups grapes

2 pears, cored and peeled

1 cup almond milk

1 cup ice

Yields: 3–4 cups

Per 1 cup serving • Calories: 153 • Fat: 1g • Protein: 2g • Sodium: 45mg • Fiber: 4g • Carbohydrates: 38g

1. Combine watercress, grapes, pears, and almond milk in a blender and blend until thoroughly combined.

2. Add ice as needed while blending until desired consistency is achieved.

Benefits of Grapes

Although many people choose grapes as a snack because they're light, low-calorie, and a sweet treat, the health benefits of grapes are another great reason to include them in your daily diet. Containing high levels of manganese, B vitamins, and vitamin C, these fruits also contain powerful polyphenols that can serve as strong antioxidants to help reduce chances of heart disease and fight multiple types of cancer!

GRAPEFRUIT TANGERINE

Grapefruit can pack a punch with tart taste, but combining it with tangerines, pineapple, and soothing green tea makes for a delicious balance of flavors for one remarkably sweet and refreshing smoothie your kids will enjoy.

INGREDIENTS

1 cup watercress

2 grapefruits, peeled

2 tangerines, peeled

1 cup pineapple

1 cup green tea

1 cup ice

Yields: 3–4 cups

Per 1 cup serving • Calories: 63 • Fat: 0g • Protein: 1g • Sodium: 6mg • Fiber: 1g • Carbohydrates: 16g

1. Combine watercress, grapefruits, tangerines, pineapple, and ½ cup tea in a blender and blend until thoroughly combined.

2. Add remaining tea and ice as needed while blending until desired consistency is achieved.

HONEYDEW FOR YOUR HONEYS

This smooth, slightly sweet treat is delicious without being overpowering. With a very cool color and a taste your kids will love, this recipe makes a fruity green milkshake that delivers loads of vitamins and minerals and only tastes like a sinful treat!

INGREDIENTS

1 cup romaine lettuce

2 cups honeydew, rind and seeds removed

2 bananas, peeled

½ cup Greek yogurt

1 cup ice

Yields: 3–4 cups

Per 1 cup serving • Calories: 101 • Fat: 0g • Protein: 4g • Sodium: 29mg • Fiber: 2g • Carbohydrates: 23g

1. Combine romaine, honeydew, bananas, and yogurt in a blender and blend until thoroughly combined.

2. Add ice as needed while blending until desired consistency is achieved.

GREEN LEMONADE

Most kids won't pass up lemonade! Revamp the old nutrition-lacking version of lemonade by blending this delicious mix of real lemons, sweet apples, raw honey or agave nectar, vitamin-rich spinach, and green tea.

INGREDIENTS

1 cup spinach

2 apples, peeled and cored

4 lemons, peeled

1 tablespoon raw honey or agave nectar

2 cups green tea

1 cup ice

Yields: 3–4 cups

Per 1 cup serving • Calories: 74 • Fat: 0g • Protein: 1g • Sodium: 7mg • Fiber: 3g • Carbohydrates: 21g

1. Combine spinach, apples, lemons, honey or agave, and 1 cup of tea in a blender and blend until thoroughly combined.

2. Add remaining tea and ice as needed while blending until desired consistency is achieved.

NUTS 'N' HONEY

Trail mixes, cereals, granola, and granola bars often turn what could be a healthy blend of nutritious ingredients into a sugar-packed, preservative-enhanced trap! Combining some of these fresh ingredients at home into a smoothie, you'll be free of unhealthy additives and know exactly where the ingredients came from.

INGREDIENTS

⅛ cup almonds

⅛ cup walnuts

1 tablespoon ground flaxseed

2 cups almond milk

1 cup romaine lettuce

2 bananas, peeled

1½ tablespoons raw honey or agave nectar

1 cup ice

Yields: 3–4 cups

Per 1 cup serving • Calories: 173 • Fat: 7g • Protein: 3g • Sodium: 78mg • Fiber: 4g • Carbohydrates: 28g

1. Combine nuts, flaxseed, and 1 cup almond milk in a blender and emulsify until no nut bits remain.

2. Add romaine, bananas, and honey or agave and blend until thoroughly combined.

3. Add remaining almond milk and ice as needed while blending until desired consistency is achieved.

Flaxseed for Kids

If your child isn't wild about salmon, or any fish for that matter, you can ensure quality omega-3s in his diet in an undetectable form. Ground flaxseed provides a mild nutty flavor without an extreme taste that would even be detectable in a smoothie with overpowering ingredients. Sold at grocery stores and mega-marts around the country, organic ground flaxseed is an inexpensive way to boost your child's omegas.

PINEAPPLE MELON

Sweet pineapple and naturally syrupy cantaloupe make for a delicious duo in this amazing recipe. Your kids will only recognize the flavors of the sweet citrus and melon.

INGREDIENTS

1 cup romaine lettuce

2 cups pineapple

2 cups cantaloupe, rind and seeds removed

1 cup green tea

1 cup ice

Yields: 3–4 cups

Per 1 cup serving • Calories: 66 • Fat: 0g • Protein: 1g • Sodium: 15mg • Fiber: 1g • Carbohydrates: 17g

1. Combine romaine, pineapple, cantaloupe, and ½ cup tea in a blender and blend until thoroughly combined.

2. Add remaining tea and ice as needed while blending until desired consistency is achieved.

SWEET PEARS

Pears have a unique flavor that blends with the crisp watercress, sweet bananas, and delicious kefir to make an amazing blend of fruits and vegetables. It provides intense vitamins and minerals in every scrumptious sip!

INGREDIENTS

1 cup watercress

4 pears, peeled and cored

2 bananas, peeled

2 cups vanilla kefir

1 cup ice

Yields: 3–4 cups

Per 1 cup serving • Calories: 192 • Fat: 1g • Protein: 4g • Sodium: 38mg • Fiber: 7g • Carbohydrates: 46g

1. Combine watercress, pears, bananas, and 1 cup of kefir in a blender and blend until thoroughly combined.

2. Add remaining kefir and ice as needed while blending until desired consistency is achieved.

PEAS, PLEASE!

This veggie-packed smoothie actually tastes sweet! If your kiddo likes peas and loves carrots, this smoothie's a sure thing; if he is antiveggie, this smoothie's probably going to get him to admit they're not half bad.

INGREDIENTS

1 cup spinach

1 cup sweet peas

2 carrots, peeled

1 apple, peeled and cored

1 cup green tea

1 cup ice

Yields: 3–4 cups

Per 1 cup serving • Calories: 60 • Fat: 0g • Protein: 2g • Sodium: 64mg • Fiber: 3g • Carbohydrates: 13g

1. Combine spinach, peas, carrots, apple, and tea in a blender and blend until thoroughly combined.

2. Add ice as needed while blending until desired consistency is achieved.

The Lonely Sweet Pea

Very rarely do kids get heaping helpings of peas on a regular basis. Providing more than 50 percent of the RDA of vitamin K and loaded with folate and other B vitamins, vitamin C, iron, zinc, manganese, and protein, peas are a great choice for a regular addition to any child's diet. Promoting brain health, bone strength, heart health, and disease-fighting protection, these sweet green morsels are worth their weight in health!

PEACHES 'N' CREAM

With fresh or frozen ingredients, sipped fireside or poolside, this smoothie is a mouthwatering way to deliver fresh ingredients, no added sugars, an entire cup of greens, and plentiful fruit servings to kids who need and deserve great-tasting nutrition.

INGREDIENTS

1 cup romaine lettuce

3 peaches, pitted

2 bananas, peeled

1 cup vanilla kefir

1 cup ice

Yields: 3–4 cups

Per 1 cup serving • Calories: 133 • Fat: 1g • Protein: 5g • Sodium: 34mg • Fiber: 3g • Carbohydrates: 30g

1. Combine romaine, peaches, bananas, and kefir in a blender and blend until thoroughly combined.

2. Add ice as needed while blending until desired consistency is achieved.

VERY VITAMIN C!

Big helpings of vitamin C–rich fruits, mineral-boasting greens, and delicious chamomile combine for a refreshing and sweet breakfast, lunch, snack, or dessert for anyone of any size.

INGREDIENTS

1 cup watercress

2 tangerines, peeled

2 cups pineapple

1 cup grapefruit

1 cup green tea

1 cup ice

Yields: 3–4 cups

Per 1 cup serving • Calories: 100 • Fat: 0g
• Protein: 2g • Sodium: 5mg • Fiber: 2g •
Carbohydrates: 26g

1. Combine watercress, tangerines, pineapple, grapefruit, and ½ cup tea in a blender and blend until thoroughly combined.

2. Add remaining tea and ice as needed while blending until desired consistency is achieved.

GREEN MACHINE

This smoothie appeals to youngsters because the overall taste is sweet and the color is very different from ordinary juices. This flavorful combination is an amazingly nutrition-packed drink.

INGREDIENTS

1 cup spinach

4 Granny Smith apples, peeled and cored

2 bananas, peeled

2 cups purified water

1 cup ice

Yields: 3–4 cups

Per 1 cup serving • Calories: 132 • Fat: 0g
• Protein: 1g • Sodium: 10mg • Fiber: 4g •
Carbohydrates: 34g

1. Combine spinach, apples, bananas, and 1 cup of water in a blender and blend until thoroughly combined.

2. Add remaining water and ice as needed while blending until desired consistency is achieved.

Lead By Example

Monkey-see, monkey-do. Kids look up to their parents for cues about what is desirable in dealing with everything from speech to behavior to food likes and dislikes. Show your child that you indulge in green smoothies and enjoy them; you'll be nurturing yourself with powerful nutrition while being a positive role model. You'll discourage your child from being a picky eater, and she'll reap the benefits of a healthy, balanced diet.

SWEET PUMPKIN PIE

Masking an entire cup of spinach in the delicious flavors of sweet pie is an excellent idea! Sweet potatoes and almond milk, along with intense aromatic spices, will never give away the star ingredient: spinach!

INGREDIENTS

1 cup spinach

2 sweet potatoes, peeled

1 teaspoon cinnamon

1 teaspoon pumpkin pie spice

2 cups almond milk

1 cup ice

Yields: 3–4 cups

Per 1 cup serving • Calories: 134 • Fat: 1g • Protein: 2g • Sodium: 88mg • Fiber: 3g • Carbohydrates: 29g

1. Combine spinach, sweet potatoes, cinnamon, pumpkin pie spice, and 1 cup almond milk in a blender and blend until thoroughly combined.

2. Add remaining almond milk and ice as needed while blending until desired consistency is achieved.

STRAWBERRY BREAKFAST SMOOTHIE

This deliciously rich strawberry banana smoothie will be your kids' favorite breakfast after just one taste.

INGREDIENTS

1 cup romaine lettuce

2 pints strawberries

2 bananas, peeled

1 cup strawberry kefir

1 cup ice

Yields: 3–4 cups

Per 1 cup serving • Calories: 136 • Fat: 1g • Protein: 5g • Sodium: 35mg • Fiber: 5g • Carbohydrates: 30g

1. Combine romaine, strawberries, bananas, and kefir in a blender and blend until thoroughly combined.

2. Add ice as needed while blending until desired consistency is achieved.

WATERMELON WONDER

Watermelon's super powers don't end with its amazing hydrating effects, which make it one of the top go-to summer fruits. This delicious smoothie with the hidden taste of romaine will make a veggie eater of your pickiest eater!

INGREDIENTS

1 cup romaine lettuce

2 cups watermelon, rind and seeds removed

2 bananas, peeled

½ cup Greek yogurt

1 cup ice

Yields: 3–4 cups

Per 1 cup serving • Calories: 82 • Fat: 0g • Protein: 4g • Sodium: 15mg • Fiber: 2g • Carbohydrates: 18g

1. Combine romaine, watermelon, bananas, and yogurt in a blender and blend until thoroughly combined.

2. Add ice as needed while blending until desired consistency is achieved.

A Great Gatorade Alternative

Packed with delicious flavor and hydrating power, watermelon offers up the added benefit of much-needed electrolytes for active kids. Most commercial drinks that promise a boost of balancing electrolytes are packed with sugars and not nutrition! Sweet homemade green smoothies are a smarter choice for your youngster following any high-endurance activity.

VANILLA BANANA BONKERS

At least if your child does go bonkers, you know it's from the intensely rich vitamin, mineral, antioxidant, and probiotic power of these amazing ingredients.

INGREDIENTS

1 cup romaine lettuce

4 bananas, peeled

Pulp of 1½ vanilla beans or 1½ teaspoons vanilla extract

2 cups vanilla kefir

1 cup ice

Yields: 3–4 cups

Per 1 cup serving • Calories: 98 • Fat: 1g • Protein: 6g • Sodium: 65mg • Fiber: 1g • Carbohydrates: 17g

1. Combine romaine, bananas, vanilla bean pulp, and 1 cup kefir in a blender and blend until thoroughly combined.

2. Add remaining kefir and ice as needed while blending until desired consistency is achieved.

CHAPTER 8

SMOOTHIES FOR HEALTHY LIVING

ALCOHOL RECOVERY RECIPE

Although this smoothie may not relieve that pounding headache, it will definitely assist your liver in flushing out the toxins provided by alcohol consumption. This delightful blend will get your body back on track!

INGREDIENTS

1 cup spinach

3 carrots, peeled

2 apples, peeled and cored

1 beet

2½ cups purified water

Yields: 3–4 cups

Per 1 cup serving • Calories: 68 • Fat: 0g • Protein: 1g • Sodium: 56mg • Fiber: 3g • Carbohydrates: 17g

1. Combine spinach, carrots, apples, beet, and half of the water in a blender and blend until thoroughly combined.

2. Add remaining water while blending, as needed, until desired texture is achieved.

Combating the Effects of Alcohol

Because alcohol can really do a number on your liver, it is important to supply your body with the best foods to maintain your liver's optimal functioning following heavy alcohol consumption. Spinach, carrots, apples, beets, lemon, wheatgrass, and grapefruit have been shown to be true superfoods when it comes to purging the liver of harmful toxins. In addition, they are also high in vitamin C and promote health while minimizing feelings of moodiness and depression.

ALMOND PEAR WITH CHERRIES

The sweet flavor of almonds gets even sweeter with cherries and frosty pears. Being healthy and eating healthy by staying away from processed sugar–packed foods is easy with smoothies like this one!

INGREDIENTS

¼ cup almonds

2 cups purified water

1 cup romaine lettuce

2 pears, cored and peeled

½ cup cherries, pitted

½ vanilla bean's pulp

Yields: 3–4 cups

Per 1 cup serving • Calories: 117 • Fat: 5g • Protein: 3g • Sodium: 4mg • Fiber: 5g • Carbohydrates: 19g

1. Combine almonds with 1 cup of water in a blender and emulsify until no nut pieces remain.

2. Add romaine, pears, cherries, and vanilla bean and blend until thoroughly combined.

3. Add remaining water as needed while blending until desired consistency is achieved.

AMAZING APPLES FOR DIGESTION

Apples star in this delightful recipe because of their high fiber content. With the added benefits from pineapple's vitamin C stores, this combination of deep greens, vibrant fruits, and chamomile tea will make for a digestive system that performs at peak functioning!

INGREDIENTS

1 cup watercress

3 apples, peeled and cored

1 cup pineapple

¼" ginger, peeled

2 cups chamomile tea

Yields: 3–4 cups

Per 1 cup serving • Calories: 78 • Fat: 0g • Protein: 1g • Sodium: 6mg • Fiber: 2g • Carbohydrates: 20g

1. Combine watercress, apples, pineapple, ginger, and 1 cup of tea in a blender and blend until thoroughly combined.

2. Add remaining tea as needed while blending until desired consistency is achieved.

APRICOT-BANANA WONDER

Sweet fruits make for delicious smoothies, and bananas act as a natural thickening agent as opposed to lactose-packed milk alternatives.

INGREDIENTS

1 cup romaine lettuce

3 apricots

2 bananas, peeled

¼" ginger, peeled

2 cups purified water

Yields: 3–4 cups

Per 1 cup serving • Calories: 68 • Fat: 0g • Protein: 1g • Sodium: 4mg • Fiber: 2g • Carbohydrates: 17g

1. Combine romaine, apricots, bananas, ginger, and 1 cup of water in a blender and blend until thoroughly combined.

2. Add remaining water as needed while blending until desired consistency is achieved.

BERRY CITRUS BANANA

The refreshing blend of berries, citrus, and banana makes for a delicious flavor sensation that delivers plentiful antioxidants with a healthy dose of vitamin C.

INGREDIENTS

1 cup romaine lettuce

1 banana, peeled

1 cup strawberries

1 cup blueberries

1 cup blackberries

2 tangerines, peeled

1 cup purified water

Yields: 3–4 cups

Per 1 cup serving • Calories: 100 • Fat: 1g • Protein: 2g • Sodium: 4mg • Fiber: 5g • Carbohydrates: 25g

1. Combine romaine, banana, berries, tangerines, and ½ cup water in a blender and blend until thoroughly combined.

2. Add remaining water as needed while blending until desired consistency is achieved.

A Natural Thickening Agent?

Because bananas have such low water content, they can be used to thicken a liquefied smoothie. They make a great natural alternative to common artificial thickening agents. You can experiment with this smoothie and watch the banana thicken it before your very eyes!

A BITTER-SWEET TREAT

The watercress, carrots, and sweet fruits in this recipe make for a tantalizing smoothie you won't soon forget!

INGREDIENTS

1 cup watercress

3 carrots, peeled

2 apples, cored and peeled

1 banana, peeled

1 cup coconut milk

Yields: 3–4 cups

Per 1 cup serving • Calories: 205 • Fat: 12g • Protein: 2g • Sodium: 44mg • Fiber: 4g • Carbohydrates: 25g

1. Combine watercress, carrots, apples, banana, and ½ cup coconut milk in a blender and blend until thoroughly combined.

2. If needed, add remaining coconut milk while blending until desired texture is achieved.

Watercress

You may have heard of watercress, but never actually tried it. If that's the case, you'll be pleasantly surprised by this smoothie. With a delicious taste, this green (not a lettuce, but a green) is rich in disease- and cancer-fighting properties that will keep your immune system, brain, blood, bones, and even your sex drive running at optimal levels.

CABBAGE CALMS INDIGESTION

This delightful combination of cabbage and cruciferous veggies packs a punch in providing rich vitamins and minerals, and aids digestion with its rich sources of vitamin K and carotenes that combine to act as an anti-inflammatory.

INGREDIENTS

1 cup cabbage

1 cup broccoli

1 cup cauliflower

1 garlic clove (optional)

2 cups chamomile tea

Yields: 3–4 cups

Per 1 cup serving • Calories: 20 • Fat: 0g • Protein: 1g • Sodium: 21mg • Fiber: 2g • Carbohydrates: 4g

1. Combine cabbage, broccoli, cauliflower, garlic, and 1 cup of tea in a blender and blend until thoroughly combined.

2. Add remaining tea as needed while blending until desired consistency is achieved.

CANDIDA CLEANSER 💚

The discomforts of pregnancy aren't limited to nausea. Bacterial infections resulting from hormonal fluctuations can be worsened with diet and make for an uncomfortable time. Find relief by combating the culprit with smoothies like this one!

INGREDIENTS

1 cup cabbage

½ cup broccoli

½ cup cauliflower

1 celery stalk

2 cups red raspberry tea

Yields: 3–4 cups

Per 1 cup serving • Calories: 19 • Fat: 0g • Protein: 1g • Sodium: 29mg • Fiber: 2g • Carbohydrates: 4g

1. Combine cabbage, broccoli, cauliflower, celery, and 1 cup of tea in a blender and blend until thoroughly combined.

2. Add remaining tea as needed while blending until desired consistency is achieved.

Candida Infections

Candida infections result from an overgrowth of the yeast candida, occurring when organisms kill off the protecting beneficial bacteria found in the digestive system. Sufferers experience headaches, bladder infections, indigestion, diarrhea, constipation, and moodiness. Candida infections can be avoided by changes in diet. Avoiding sugar-laden fruit juices and starchy vegetables like carrots, potatoes, and corn while implementing a probiotic drink like kefir can starve candida while promoting beneficial bacteria growth.

CARROT TOP OF THE MORNING TO YOU

Rich in beta-carotene, this smoothie blends romaine lettuce with tasty carrots and apples to give you a sweet start that can help you stay focused, provide lasting energy, and maintain the health of your eyes and metabolism.

INGREDIENTS

2 cups romaine lettuce

3 carrots, peeled

1 apple, peeled and cored

1 cup purified water

Yields: 1 quart

Per 1 cup serving • Calories: 42 • Fat: 0g • Protein: 1g • Sodium: 35mg • Fiber: 2g • Carbohydrates: 10g

1. Combine first three ingredients in the order listed into a blender.

2. Add water slowly while blending until desired texture is achieved.

Carrots Can Save the Day!

With the ability to protect your body from cancer, heart attacks, premature aging, and poor vision, this vegetable is a must-have in your daily diet. Its deep orange color is the tell-tale sign that it is rich in beta-carotene (vitamin A), but it's also packed with B vitamins, biotin, vitamin K, and potassium. Talk about a multitasker!

CHOCOLATEY ALMOND TREAT

Although puréed dates lend a chocolatey sweetness to smoothies all by themselves, this recipe combines sweet dates, raw cacao powder, and cayenne pepper for a delightful, slightly spicy chocolate smoothie.

INGREDIENTS

2 cups purified water

¼ cup almonds

1 cup watercress

1 banana, peeled

2 dates, pitted

1 tablespoon powdered cacao

¼ teaspoon cayenne

½ vanilla bean's pulp

Yields: 3–4 cups

Per 1 cup serving • Calories: 117 • Fat: 5g • Protein: 3g • Sodium: 7mg • Fiber: 3g • Carbohydrates: 18g

1. Combine 1 cup water and almonds in a blender and emulsify until no nut pieces remain.

2. Add watercress, banana, dates, cacao, cayenne, and vanilla bean pulp and blend until thoroughly combined.

3. Add remaining water as needed while blending until desired consistency is achieved.

CHERRY-BANANA BLISS

This delicious, thick fruit blend also has a mild sweet nuttiness from the almond milk. This is a filling smoothie with no guilt and tons of flavor.

INGREDIENTS

1 cup spinach

2 cups cherries, pitted

2 bananas, peeled

½ lemon, peeled

2 cups almond milk

Yields: 3–4 cups

Per 1 cup serving • Calories: 150 • Fat: 2g • Protein: 2g • Sodium: 82mg • Fiber: 4g • Carbohydrates: 35g

1. Combine spinach, cherries, bananas, lemon, and 1 cup of almond milk in a blender and blend until thoroughly combined.

2. Add remaining almond milk as needed while blending until desired consistency is achieved.

CITRUS BERRY BLAST

There is nothing more refreshing and uplifting than sweet citrus! Mind in a fog? Stress levels high? Smoothie combinations like this one are a delightful remedy to what ails the mind and body.

INGREDIENTS

1 cup watercress

3 oranges, peeled

½ grapefruit, peeled

1 cup strawberries

1 cup blueberries

1 cup purified water

Yields: 3–4 cups

Per 1 cup serving • Calories: 103 • Fat: 0g • Protein: 2g • Sodium: 5mg • Fiber: 5g • Carbohydrates: 26g

1. Combine watercress, oranges, grapefruit, berries, and ½ cup of water in a blender and blend until thoroughly combined.

2. Add remaining water as needed while blending until desired consistency is achieved.

CINCH POUNDS WITH CITRUS

This sweet combination of greens and citrus makes for a refreshing snack for your body and mind. This smoothie stimulates your brain for improved mental clarity and focus, your body for more efficient metabolism, and your overall health with the abundance of vitamins and minerals.

INGREDIENTS

1 cup watercress

1 grapefruit, peeled

½ pineapple, peeled and cored

1 orange, peeled

½ lemon, peeled

½ lime, peeled

2 cups green tea

Yields: 3–4 cups

Per 1 cup serving • Calories: 104 • Fat: 0g • Protein: 2g • Sodium: 5mg • Fiber: 2g • Carbohydrates: 27g

1. Combine watercress, grapefruit, pineapple, orange, lemon, lime, and 1 cup of tea in a blender and blend until thoroughly combined.

2. Add remaining tea as needed while blending until desired consistency is achieved.

Vitamin C

Some restrictive diets can leave your body feeling fatigued and your mind fuzzy. With those side effects, no wonder so many people abandon their diet plans! With an increase in vitamin C in your daily diet, your body's metabolism of proteins, fats, and carbohydrates improves, making for wonderful effects in mental clarity, improved energy and stamina, and a better feeling of fullness from your foods. It also improves the body's ability to remove toxins and waste.

CLEANSE YOUR BODY WITH SWEET CITRUS

Vitamin C does more than prevent illness—it also promotes great health. This delicious combination of citrus fruits, watercress, and ginger makes for a tasty way to detoxify your body and promote health in one tasty treat.

INGREDIENTS

1 cup watercress

2 cups pineapple, peeled and cored

1 orange, peeled

2 apples, peeled and cored

½" ginger, peeled

2 cups purified water

Yields: 4–6 cups

Per 1 cup serving • Calories: 99 • Fat: 0g • Protein: 1g • Sodium: 7mg • Fiber: 3g • Carbohydrates: 26g

1. Combine watercress, pineapple, orange, apples, ginger, and 1 cup of water in a blender and blend until thoroughly combined.

2. Add remaining water while blending, as needed, until desired texture is achieved.

SMOOTH CITRUS FOR SMOOTH DIGESTION

A delicious remedy for stomach discomfort, this banana blend is a much sweeter and more nutritious alternative to the over-the-counter antacid.

INGREDIENTS

1 cup watercress

2 cups pineapple

1 peach, pitted and peeled

1 orange, peeled

2 bananas, peeled

2 cups chamomile tea

Yields: 3–4 cups

Per 1 cup serving • Calories: 124 • Fat: 0g • Protein: 2g • Sodium: 9mg • Fiber: 3g • Carbohydrates: 32g

1. Combine watercress, pineapple, peach, orange, bananas, and 1 cup of tea in a blender and blend until thoroughly combined.

2. Add remaining tea as needed while blending until desired consistency is achieved.

COCO-NANA

Coconuts and bananas make for an exciting pair in this recipe! The tropical flavor of the coconut and a hint of cinnamon are wonderful first thing in the morning or as a delicious dessert.

INGREDIENTS

1 cup watercress

Flesh of ½ coconut

2 bananas, peeled

¼ teaspoon cinnamon

2 cups purified water

Yields: 3–4 cups

Per 1 cup serving • Calories: 230 • Fat: 17g • Protein: 2g • Sodium: 15mg • Fiber: 6g • Carbohydrates: 21g

1. Combine watercress, coconut flesh, bananas, cinnamon, and 1 cup of water in a blender and blend until thoroughly combined.

2. Add remaining water as needed while blending until desired consistency is achieved.

Get Crazy for Coconuts!

In addition to being a staple in the diets of many countries around the world, the coconut is held in very high regard for its medicinal abilities. Thought to cure and relieve the symptoms associated with many illnesses, the coconut's flesh, milk, water, and oil are all used for their intense health benefits.

THE CONSTIPATION CURE

Cure constipation and other uncomfortable indigestion symptoms with delicious smoothies like this one, which features a tasty blend of sweet and crisp vegetables.

INGREDIENTS

1 cup romaine

1 cup asparagus

1 cup broccoli

2 carrots, peeled

2 cups chamomile tea

Yields: 3–4 cups

Per 1 cup serving • Calories: 29 • Fat: 0g • Protein: 1g • Sodium: 33mg • Fiber: 2g • Carbohydrates: 6g

1. Combine romaine, asparagus, broccoli, carrots, and 1 cup of tea in a blender and blend until thoroughly combined.

2. Add remaining tea as needed while blending until desired consistency is achieved.

COOL OFF COLITIS

Remedy this terrible digestive disorder with vegetables rich in vitamin E. Spinach, asparagus, carrots, tomato, and light chamomile make for a savory, yet slightly sweet, smoothie.

INGREDIENTS

1 cup spinach

1 cup asparagus

3 carrots, peeled

1 tomato

2 cups chamomile tea

Yields: 3–4 cups

Per 1 cup serving • Calories: 33 • Fat: 0g • Protein: 2g • Sodium: 42mg • Fiber: 3g • Carbohydrates: 7g

1. Combine spinach, asparagus, carrots, tomato, and 1 cup of tea in a blender and blend until thoroughly combined.

2. Add remaining tea as needed while blending until desired consistency is achieved.

CUCUMBER COOLER

The refreshing combination of sweet citrus, crisp greens, zippy ginger, and cooling cucumbers will perk you up while calming your tummy. Indigestion stands no chance against the chilling effects of this cool combo.

INGREDIENTS

1 cup watercress

1 pink grapefruit, peeled

1 orange, peeled

2 cucumbers, peeled

¼" ginger, peeled

2 cups chamomile tea

Yields: 3–4 cups

Per 1 cup serving • Calories: 61 • Fat: 0g • Protein: 2g • Sodium: 8mg • Fiber: 3g • Carbohydrates: 14g

1. Combine watercress, grapefruit, orange, cucumbers, ginger, and 1 cup of tea in a blender and blend until thoroughly combined.

2. Add remaining tea as needed while blending until desired consistency is achieved.

Cucumbers Aren't Just Water

Even though a cucumber is mostly water (and fiber), it is far more than a tasty, hydrating, and filling snack option. These green veggies are a great addition to a diet in need of moisture and clarity . . . for the skin! A clear complexion is the aesthetic benefit of consuming cucumbers. By consuming 1 serving of cucumbers per day, you'll enjoy clearer, more hydrated skin.

DREAMY DIGESTION

On the uncomfortable nights that indigestion creeps up, turn to your blender for quick relief. This delightfully sweet fruit and veggie combination provides indigestion relief in one sweet treat you can enjoy as dessert or right when the burn hits!

INGREDIENTS

1 cup romaine lettuce

2 apples, cored and peeled

2 carrots, peeled

1 cucumber, peeled

½ lemon, peeled

2 cups chamomile tea

Yields: 3–4 cups

Per 1 cup serving • Calories: 61 • Fat: 0g • Protein: 1g • Sodium: 26mg • Fiber: 3g • Carbohydrates: 15g

1. Combine romaine, apples, carrots, cucumber, lemon, and 1 cup of tea in a blender and blend until thoroughly combined.

2. Add remaining tea as needed while blending until desired consistency is achieved.

A Recipe for Sweet Dreams

Indigestion can strike at any time of day, but can be especially uncomfortable at night and can lead to painful discomfort, interrupted sleep, and moodiness. Taking a two-step approach to relieving your indigestion may help: (1) Use fruit and vegetable combinations shown to regulate stomach acid and promote more alkaline levels of the digestive tract, and (2) drink chamomile tea before bed. Chamomile tea has been shown to relieve indigestion by soothing the esophageal muscles and those of the large and small intestine.

FABULOUS FERTILITY ℗

This delicious blend of crisp watercress, refreshing melons, and zippy ginger delivers a taste combination that will refresh your body and mind while satisfying your sweet tooth.

INGREDIENTS

1 cup watercress

2 cups watermelon, deseeded

½ cantaloupe, rind and seeds removed

½" ginger, peeled

1 cup red raspberry tea

Yields: 3–4 cups

Per 1 cup serving • Calories: 38 • Fat: 0g • Protein: 1g • Sodium: 20mg • Fiber: 1g • Carbohydrates: 9g

1. Combine watercress, watermelon, cantaloupe, ginger, and ½ cup tea in a blender and blend until thoroughly combined.

2. Add remaining tea as needed while blending until desired consistency is achieved.

Clean Eating for Fertility

Whole health from the inside out is the best place to start when you're trying to conceive. Consuming a diet of fruits and vegetables enables your body to function at optimal efficiency. Start by including bright produce in your daily diet. By providing your body with vibrant nutrition following conception, you're providing your baby with the best chance of survival, health, and immunity.

FERTILITY FOUND! ⓟ

A blend of berries, melon, and vanilla downplay the taste of spinach for a deliciously sweet and tart smoothie that provides vitamins, minerals, and phytochemicals for better health for mom and baby!

INGREDIENTS

1 cup spinach

2 cups cranberries

1 cup cantaloupe, rind and seeds removed

½ vanilla bean's pulp

1 cup kefir

Yields: 3–4 cups

Per 1 cup serving • Calories: 78 • Fat: 2g • Protein: 3g • Sodium: 44mg • Fiber: 4g • Carbohydrates: 14g

1. Combine spinach, cranberries, cantaloupe, vanilla bean pulp, and ½ cup kefir in a blender and blend until thoroughly combined.

2. Add remaining kefir as needed while blending until desired consistency is achieved.

Copper for Fertility

Alternative and holistic medicine promotes the use of herbs, vitamins, minerals, and herbal teas to remedy infertility in both men and women. Among a variety of other responsibilities of copper in the human body, proper iron absorption and reproductive health are enhanced with proper copper levels. Copper is abundant in deep leafy greens, so add more to your diet to increase copper consumption.

FABULOUS FIBER FLUSH

Kale provides an abundance of vitamins A and K. Combined with the iron- and folate-rich broccoli, pectin-providing apples, and beta-carotene-filled carrot, the kale makes this smoothie a completely fiber-filled one.

INGREDIENTS

2 large kale leaves

1 cup broccoli

2 apples, peeled and cored

1 carrot, peeled

½ lemon, peeled

2 cups purified water

Yields: 3–4 cups

Per 1 cup serving • Calories: 71 • Fat: 0g • Protein: 2g • Sodium: 35mg • Fiber: 3g • Carbohydrates: 17g

1. Combine kale, broccoli, apples, carrot, lemon, and 1 cup of water in a blender and blend until thoroughly combined.

2. Add remaining water while blending, as needed, until desired texture is achieved.

SWEET FIBER

Apricots, apples, and bananas blend with sweet romaine for a delicious, fiber-rich treat that will keep you clear and promote optimal digestion. Uncomfortable symptoms of indigestion can also be alleviated with deep greens like romaine.

INGREDIENTS

1 cup romaine lettuce

4 apricots, peeled

2 apples, peeled and cored

1 banana, peeled

2 cups chamomile tea

Yields: 3–4 cups

Per 1 cup serving • Calories: 84 • Fat: 0g • Protein: 1g • Sodium: 4mg • Fiber: 6g • Carbohydrates: 21g

1. Combine romaine, apricots, apples, banana, and 1 cup of tea in a blender and blend until thoroughly combined.

2. Add remaining tea as needed while blending until desired consistency is achieved.

Fabulous Fiber

Fiber is absolutely necessary to promote the most efficient digestive system free of toxins, waste, and buildup that may have accrued over the years. Stock up on fiber-rich foods and blend them in delicious smoothies. Not only does blending the fiber-packed fruits and veggies make for delicious meal and snack options, blending them breaks down the indigestible fiber for the best possible absorption.

FOLATE FOR FINE SPINES

A sweet blend of fruits and vibrant vegetables makes for one splendid recipe that satisfies a variety of vitamin and mineral requirements.

INGREDIENTS

1 cup spinach

2 carrots, peeled

2 red Gala apples, peeled and cored

1 banana, peeled

2 cups red raspberry tea

Yields: 3–4 cups

Per 1 cup serving • Calories: 79 • Fat: 0g • Protein: 1g • Sodium: 30mg • Fiber: 3g • Carbohydrates: 20g

1. Combine spinach, carrots, apples, banana, and 1 cup of tea in a blender and blend until thoroughly combined.

2. Add remaining tea as needed while blending until desired consistency is achieved.

Importance of Folate in Pregnancy

Among the important vitamins and minerals found to prevent birth defects, one of the best-known is folate. Studies have shown that ideal levels of folate in pregnancy reduce or remedy the chance of neural and spinal-tube defects. You can take a prenatal vitamin that includes folate, but what about natural sources? Eating a diet rich in deep leafy greens and vibrant-green vegetables can provide a great amount of folate naturally.

GARLIC GETS IT DONE

Garlic provides an amazing amount of protection against illness, including strong vitamins and minerals, excellent antioxidants, and health benefits for your heart.

INGREDIENTS

1 cup romaine lettuce

1 cup broccoli

1 celery stalk

1 tomato

1 green onion

2 garlic cloves

2 cups purified water

Yields: 3–4 cups

Per 1 cup serving • Calories: 20 • Fat: 0g • Protein: 1g • Sodium: 21mg • Fiber: 1g • Carbohydrates: 4g

1. Combine romaine, broccoli, celery, tomato, onion, and garlic with 1 cup of water in a blender and blend until thoroughly combined.

2. Add remaining water as needed while blending until desired consistency is achieved.

GET RID OF GAS!

Gas is one of the most embarrassing symptoms associated with indigestion and digestive disorders. Gas-fighting foods are combined in this delicious smoothie.

INGREDIENTS

1 cup spinach

2 carrots, peeled

3 celery stalks, leaves intact

¾ cup petite sweet peas

2 cups chamomile tea

Yields: 3–4 cups

Per 1 cup serving • Calories: 38 • Fat: 0g • Protein: 2g • Sodium: 80mg • Fiber: 3g • Carbohydrates: 8g

1. Combine spinach, carrots, celery, peas, and 1 cup of tea in a blender and blend until thoroughly combined.

2. Add remaining tea as needed while blending until desired consistency is achieved.

GINGER ALE SMOOTHIE

Ginger ale is the most common remedy for any type of stomach ailment. This natural version of ginger ale provides all of the powerful nutrition without the sometimes uncomfortable and problematic carbonation.

INGREDIENTS

1 cup watercress

4 apples, peeled and cored

¼" ginger, peeled

2 cups chamomile tea

Yields: 3–4 cups

Per 1 cup serving • Calories: 79 • Fat: 0g • Protein: 1g • Sodium: 6mg • Fiber: 2g • Carbohydrates: 21g

1. Combine watercress, apples, ginger, and 1 cup of tea in a blender and blend until thoroughly combined.

2. Add remaining tea as needed while blending until desired consistency is achieved.

GINGER APPLE DELIGHT

Delicious fiber-rich apples star in this quick and easy recipe. Romaine provides a crisp background for the sweet apples and smooth banana, and the ginger adds a hint of spice.

INGREDIENTS

1 cup romaine lettuce

2 apples, cored and peeled

1 banana, peeled

¼" ginger, peeled

2 cups purified water

Yields: 3–4 cups

Per 1 cup serving • Calories: 67 • Fat: 0g • Protein: 1g • Sodium: 4mg • Fiber: 2g • Carbohydrates: 17g

1. Combine romaine, apples, banana, ginger, and 1 cup of water in a blender and blend until thoroughly combined.

2. Add remaining water as needed while blending until desired consistency is achieved.

GINGER CITRUS

The tang of sweet citrus and the zing of ginger make for a stimulating blend that will get your senses and taste buds on high alert. Delicious and rejuvenating, it can turn any stressful day around in no time!

INGREDIENTS

1 cup watercress

2 cups pineapple, peeled and cored

2 bananas, peeled

¼" ginger, peeled

1 cup purified water

Yields: 3–4 cups

Per 1 cup serving • Calories: 91 • Fat: 0g • Protein: 1g • Sodium: 6mg • Fiber: 2g • Carbohydrates: 23g

1. Combine watercress, pineapple, bananas, ginger, and ½ cup water in a blender and blend until thoroughly combined.

2. Add remaining water as needed while blending until desired consistency is achieved.

GORGEOUS GREENS FOR A GORGEOUS BODY

These gorgeous green fruits and veggies make a wonderfully refreshing treat. Not only is this a filling smoothie option, but the ingredients offer up balanced nutrition, vitamins, minerals, and strong antioxidants that will keep you moving throughout your day.

INGREDIENTS

1 cup spinach

2 Granny Smith apples, peeled and cored

2 celery stalks

1 cucumber, peeled

½ lime, peeled

2 cups green tea

Yields: 3–4 cups

Per 1 cup serving • Calories: 53 • Fat: 0g • Protein: 1g • Sodium: 23mg • Fiber: 2g • Carbohydrates: 14g

1. Combine spinach, apples, celery, cucumber, lime, and 1 cup of tea in a blender and blend until thoroughly combined.

2. Add remaining tea as needed while blending until desired consistency is achieved.

Total Health Inside and Out

The natural nutrition found in greens and fruits can do wonders for your body on the inside and out! Consuming deep greens and vibrant fruits and veggies, hydrating with purified water, and exercising daily combine for health benefits you can see and feel. Improved energy to help you run faster and farther, mental clarity to keep you focused on your goals, faster metabolism, improved recovery time, and beautiful skin, hair, and nails are all benefits of sound nutrition.

THE GREEN GO-GETTER

Packed with green spinach and apples, this creamy green smoothie will kick your morning off with a boost of essential amino acids, vitamins, minerals, and an absolutely amazing taste.

INGREDIENTS

1 cup spinach

2 green apples, peeled and cored

1 banana, peeled

1 cup purified water

Yields: 3–4 cups

Per 1 cup serving • Calories: 89 • Fat: 0g • Protein: 1g • Sodium: 10mg • Fiber: 3g • Carbohydrates: 23g

1. Combine spinach, apples, and banana with ½ cup of water in a blender and blend until thoroughly combined.

2. Continue adding remaining water while blending until desired texture is achieved.

A Smoothie for Even the Greenest Green Smoothie Maker!

Some people who are new to creating green smoothies can have a hard time enjoying the powerful taste of the greens. The combination of bananas, apples, and spinach with more fruit than greens provides an appetizing taste that is sweet and lessens the intensity of the spinach. This smoothie is a great starter for anyone who is turned off by the overpowering taste of greens.

GREEN TEA GREEN SMOOTHIE

With all the intense nutrition packed into a green smoothie, how could it get any better? Add powerful antioxidant-rich green tea to the vitamins and minerals provided by the greens and citrus!

INGREDIENTS

1 cup spinach

2 lemons, peeled

½" ginger, peeled

1 tablespoon raw honey

2 cups green tea

Yields: 3–4 cups

Per 1 cup serving • Calories: 37 • Fat: 0g • Protein: 1g • Sodium: 9mg • Fiber: 1g • Carbohydrates: 10g

1. Combine spinach, lemons, ginger, honey, and 1 cup of tea in a blender and blend until thoroughly combined.

2. Add remaining tea as needed while blending until desired consistency is achieved.

THE HANGOVER HELPER

When you realize certain lifestyle choices may not make for the best days following, this smoothie is the perfect pick-me-up to calm your head and your stomach while pleasing your taste buds.

INGREDIENTS

1 cup iceberg lettuce

1 apple, cored and peeled

1 banana, peeled

½"–1" ginger, peeled and sliced or chopped

1 cup vanilla almond milk

Yields: 3–4 cups

Per 1 cup serving • Calories: 103 • Fat: 1g • Protein: 1g • Sodium: 54mg • Fiber: 3g • Carbohydrates: 24g

1. Combine iceberg, apple, banana, ginger, and half of the almond milk in a blender and blend until thoroughly combined.

2. If needed, add remaining almond milk while blending until desired texture is achieved.

Ginger and Hangovers

Because the ginger root's capabilities include alleviating symptoms associated with indigestion, nausea, and fever as well as promoting optimal blood circulation and maintaining clear sinuses, this is one ingredient that can help ease many of the symptoms resulting from an evening of too much of anything. This smoothie is a must for any of those not-so-healthy days!

HEARTBURN, BE GONE

A tasty way to combat heartburn and provide fast-acting relief, this smoothie combines flavorful veggies that will soothe your esophagus and relieve the pain associated with acid indigestion.

INGREDIENTS

1 cup spinach

2 tomatoes

3 celery stalks, leaves intact

1½ cups chamomile tea

Yields: 3–4 cups

Per 1 cup serving • Calories: 18 • Fat: 0g • Protein: 1g • Sodium: mg • Fiber: 1g • Carbohydrates: 4g

1. Combine spinach, tomatoes, celery, and ¾ cup of tea in a blender and blend until thoroughly combined.

2. Add remaining tea as needed while blending until desired consistency is achieved.

Lifestyle Changes for Heartburn Relief

Not much can compare to the potentially disabling condition of acid reflux, which can make days and nights unbearable. Many people find themselves popping antacids and heartburn relievers numerous times throughout the day just to make the discomfort subside. A great way to combat this debilitating condition is to change your diet to include a wide variety of fruits and vegetables while cutting out caffeine, cigarettes, alcohol, fatty and acidic foods, and carbonation.

ILLNESS PREVENTER

Protect your body from illness by packing in the vitamin C. Not only does this amazing vitamin promote health and immunity, it can alleviate stress and improve mental stability and happiness.

INGREDIENTS

1 cup watercress

2 oranges, peeled

½ pineapple, peeled and cored

½ lemon, peeled

½ lime, peeled

1 cup red raspberry tea

Yields: 3–4 cups

Per 1 cup serving • Calories: 105 • Fat: 0g • Protein: 2g • Sodium: 6mg • Fiber: 3g • Carbohydrates: 27g

1. Combine watercress, oranges, pineapple, lemon, and lime in a blender and blend until thoroughly combined.

2. Add 1 cup of tea as needed while blending until desired consistency is achieved.

IMPERATIVE IRON 🅟

Skip the chips and go for this savory, satisfying smoothie, packed with important iron!

INGREDIENTS

1 cup spinach

2 carrots, peeled

½ cup broccoli spears

½ cup asparagus spears

1 garlic clove

2 cups red raspberry tea

Yields: 3–4 cups

Per 1 cup serving • Calories: 23 • Fat: 0g • Protein: 1g • Sodium: 34mg • Fiber: 2g • Carbohydrates: 5g

1. Combine spinach, carrots, broccoli, asparagus, garlic, and 1 cup of tea in a blender and blend until thoroughly combined.

2. Add remaining tea as needed while blending until desired consistency is achieved.

Why Iron Needs Increase in Pregnancy

Pregnant women require 27mg of iron per day (as opposed to 18mg when not pregnant). Because many women are iron deficient prior to becoming pregnant, their needs are even higher and the risks associated with iron deficiency are more severe. Preterm delivery, low birth weight, and infant mortality are all risks of iron deficiency in pregnancy. Ensure that your body is provided with sufficient nonheme iron—the vitamin C from the broccoli will help improve the absorption of the nonheme iron.

INDIGESTION INHIBITOR

Digestion discomfort can be painful, and the resulting gassy symptoms can be downright embarrassing. This delightful blend of sweet fruits and veggies combines with chamomile tea for a wonderfully soothing effect on indigestion.

INGREDIENTS

1 cup watercress

1 carrot, peeled

1 apple, peeled and cored

1 pear, peeled and cored

¼" ginger, peeled

2 cups chamomile tea

Yields: 3–4 cups

Per 1 cup serving • Calories: 53 • Fat: 0g • Protein: 1g • Sodium: 15mg • Fiber: 2g • Carbohydrates: 14g

1. Combine watercress, carrot, apple, pear, ginger, and 1 cup of tea in a blender and blend until thoroughly combined.

2. Add remaining tea as needed while blending until desired consistency is achieved.

Why Fruits and Vegetables Aid Digestion

Research shows that diets high in fiber and complex carbohydrates, both found in abundance in fruits and vegetables, promote healthy digestive systems and can reduce many digestive disorders. Indigestion, ulcers, low stomach acid, constipation, diarrhea, motion sickness, colitis, and many more conditions can be relieved or reversed with the power of produce.

KEEP IT MOVING

Flavorful spinach and zucchini make for a splendid blend with fresh, lightly flavored zucchini. Wonderfully light and delicious, this is a smoothie that tastes great but relieves constipation and the uncomfortable symptoms that result.

INGREDIENTS

1 cup spinach

2 zucchini, peeled

3 celery stalks, leaves intact

2 cups chamomile tea

Yields: 3–4 cups

Per 1 cup serving • Calories: 22 • Fat: 0g • Protein: 2g • Sodium: 42mg • Fiber: 2g • Carbohydrates: 5g

1. Combine spinach, zucchini, celery, and 1 cup of tea in a blender and blend until thoroughly combined.

2. Add remaining tea as needed while blending until desired consistency is achieved.

Produce for Constipation Relief

Constipation can really slow you down! The irritating condition can make you feel lethargic, uncomfortable, and irritable. Stay regular by including the recommended five servings of fruits and veggies daily. All of this produce contains lots of fiber, which relieves constipation.

KIWI-MANGO COMBO

Tropical kiwifruit takes a star presence in this deliciously sweet treat that will provide tons of fruit servings without weighing you down.

INGREDIENTS

1 cup watercress

2 cups mango, peeled and pitted

2 tangerines, peeled

4 kiwis, peeled

½ lemon, peeled

2 cups purified water

Yields: 3–4 cups

Per 1 cup serving • Calories: 126 • Fat: 1g • Protein: 2g • Sodium: 11mg • Fiber: 5g • Carbohydrates: 32g

1. Combine watercress, mango, tangerines, kiwis, lemon, and 1 cup of water in a blender and blend until thoroughly combined.

2. Add remaining water as needed while blending until desired consistency is achieved.

LIVEN UP THE LIVER

The liver is a powerful organ responsible for removing unhealthy toxins from the body. Beet greens, beets, and apples are known to optimize liver functioning, and the addition of the banana's smooth texture makes this a healthy and tasty liver-purifying blend.

INGREDIENTS

1 cup beet greens

1 beet

3 apples, peeled and cored

1 banana, peeled

2 cups purified water

Yields: 3–4 cups

Per 1 cup serving • Calories: 86 • Fat: 0g • Protein: 1g • Sodium: 24mg • Fiber: 3g • Carbohydrates: 23g

1. Combine beet greens, beet, apples, banana, and 1 cup of water in a blender and blend until thoroughly combined.

2. Add remaining water while blending, as needed, until desired texture is achieved.

LUSCIOUS LEGS IN PREGNANCY ℗

One beautiful benefit of this blend is better circulation and reduced swelling in the legs—bye-bye, cankles!

INGREDIENTS

1 cup watercress

1 grapefruit, peeled

½ cantaloupe, rind and seeds removed

½ pineapple, peeled and cored

1 cup strawberries

1 cup red raspberry tea

Yields: 3–4 cups

Per 1 cup serving • Calories: 112 • Fat: 0g • Protein: 2g • Sodium: 17mg • Fiber: 2g • Carbohydrates: 29g

1. Combine watercress, grapefruit, cantaloupe, pineapple, strawberries, and ½ cup tea in a blender and blend until thoroughly combined.

2. Add remaining tea as needed while blending until desired consistency is achieved.

MANAGE YOUR WEIGHT WITH MANGOS

Delicious and nutritious, mangos are a sweet fruit that provides loads of vitamin C and helps optimize your fat-burning metabolism. This easy recipe combines only a few ingredients but delivers an amazing amount of nutrition for weight loss and total health.

INGREDIENTS

1 cup watercress

2 cups mangos, pitted

½ lemon, peeled

¼" ginger, peeled

1½ cups green tea

Yields: 3–4 cups

Per 1 cup serving • Calories: 72 • Fat: 0g • Protein: 1g • Sodium: 6mg • Fiber: 2g • Carbohydrates: 19g

1. Combine watercress, mangos, lemon, ginger, and ¾ cup of the tea in a blender and blend until thoroughly combined.

2. Add remaining tea as needed while blending until desired consistency is achieved.

Weight Loss Versus Total Health

Fad diets may help you lose those stubborn pounds fast, but can also make for an unhealthy body and mind when those lost pounds are regained following the return to "normal" foods. Eating a clean diet rich in vitamins and nutrients like those found in deep greens, fruits, veggies, and unprocessed foods can deliver healthy benefits for your body and mind now and years down the road! Improving all of your body's functions can make a huge difference daily and promote a longer, healthier, happier life!

MATERNITY MEDLEY ℗

This delicious smoothie recipe combines sweet fruits and luscious watercress with the zing of ginger to provide an abundance of important vitamins and minerals for your pregnancy. It will also sweeten your day!

INGREDIENTS

1 cup watercress

½ mango, peeled and deseeded

½ pineapple, peeled and cored

2 tangerines, peeled

¼" ginger, peeled

1 cup red raspberry tea

Yields: 3–4 cups

Per 1 cup serving • Calories: 98 • Fat: 0g • Protein: 1g • Sodium: 7mg • Fiber: 1g • Carbohydrates: 25g

1. Combine watercress, mango, pineapple, tangerines, ginger, and ½ cup of tea in a blender and blend until thoroughly combined.

2. Add remaining tea as needed while blending until desired consistency is achieved.

Make Calories Count in Pregnancy

Although many women strive for complete nutrition while also appreciating the increase in caloric requirements suggested in pregnancy, some fear excess troublesome weight gain. In order to ensure that your nutrition and your weight gain are ideal for your pregnancy, make every calorie count! Empty-calorie foods like fried foods and sugary treats deliver empty nutrition for your body and your baby, and lead to excessive sodium, sugar, and fat intake, which will result in stubborn post-baby pounds.

MEGA MAGNESIUM

With powerful stores of minerals, especially magnesium, the veggies in this recipe promote easier digestion along with overall health for your entire body and mind.

INGREDIENTS

1 cup cabbage

1 cup broccoli

1 cup cauliflower

2 celery stalks, leaves intact

2 cups chamomile tea

Yields: 3–4 cups

Per 1 cup serving • Calories: 23 • Fat: 0g • Protein: 2g • Sodium: 37mg • Fiber: 2g • Carbohydrates: 5g

1. Combine cabbage, broccoli, cauliflower, celery, and 1 cup of tea in a blender and blend until thoroughly combined.

2. Add remaining tea as needed while blending until desired consistency is achieved.

Magnesium Benefits

This powerful mineral is responsible for the proper functioning of our muscles and nerves, so it is very important to men and women at any age with any lifestyle. Deficiencies in magnesium can lead to debilitating conditions like diabetes, hypertension, osteoporosis, and irritable bowel syndrome. Deficiency can also negatively affect digestion by reducing its natural calming effect on muscle spasms and impairing the strength of the muscles associated with digestion.

MINTY PEARS

Sweet pears are made even sweeter by the addition of fresh lemon. Combined with romaine and refreshing mint, this unique blend of flavors makes for a wonderfully tasty treat that will satisfy sweet cravings without added sugar.

INGREDIENTS

1 cup romaine lettuce

1 tablespoon mint leaves

4 pears, cored and peeled

½ lemon, peeled

2 cups purified water

Yields: 3–4 cups

Per 1 cup serving • Calories: 108 • Fat: 0g • Protein: 1g • Sodium: 6mg • Fiber: 6g • Carbohydrates: 29g

1. Combine romaine, mint, pears, lemon, and 1 cup of water in a blender and blend until thoroughly combined.

2. Add remaining water as needed while blending until desired consistency is achieved.

MOODINESS MANIPULATOR ⓟ

Forget all the naysayers who call pregnancy moodiness "crazy." Forty weeks is a long time, and the hormone fluctuations don't help you maintain a cool, calm, and collected composure all the time. Indulge in this delicious treat that will lift your mood!

INGREDIENTS

1 cup watercress

½ cantaloupe, rind and seeds removed

½ lemon, peeled

½" ginger, peeled

1½ cups red raspberry tea

Yields: 3–4 cups

Per 1 cup serving • Calories: 27 • Fat: 0g • Protein: 1g • Sodium: 17mg • Fiber: 1g • Carbohydrates: 7g

1. Combine watercress, cantaloupe, lemon, ginger, and ¾ cup of the tea in a blender and blend until thoroughly combined.

2. Add remaining tea as needed while blending until desired consistency is achieved.

Nutrition for Stability

Creating life requires a lot of energy, and because your growing baby is depending on you for vitamins and minerals, deficiencies can leave you fatigued. Provide your body with all of the necessary vitamins and minerals in amounts that satisfy your needs and your baby's to prevent common symptoms associated with deficiencies. Improve your pregnancy experience with a diet rich in leafy greens and vibrant fruits and veggies to improve the amount of vitamins and minerals for mom and baby.

MORNING SICKNESS SAVIOR ⓟ

One of the major discomforts of pregnancy can be morning sickness—queasiness, nausea, and vomiting brought on by almost anything imaginable. This smoothie recipe is perfect for occasional or constant sufferers.

INGREDIENTS

1 cup watercress

1 grapefruit, peeled

½ lemon, peeled

½" ginger, peeled

1 cup red raspberry tea

Yields: 3–4 cups

Per 1 cup serving • Calories: 31 • Fat: 0g • Protein: 1g • Sodium: 7mg • Fiber: 1g • Carbohydrates: 8g

1. Combine watercress, grapefruit, lemon, ginger, and ½ cup tea in a blender and blend until thoroughly combined.

2. Add remaining tea as needed while blending until desired consistency is achieved.

MOVE OVER, MOTION SICKNESS!

Cabbage is a little-known weapon against motion sickness. Blending the green leafy veggie with bananas, apples, and ginger makes for a delicious remedy to this day-wrecking condition!

INGREDIENTS

1 cup cabbage

3 bananas, peeled

2 apples, cored and peeled

¼" ginger, peeled

2 cups chamomile tea

Yields: 3–4 cups

Per 1 cup serving • Calories: 71 • Fat: 0g • Protein: 1g • Sodium: 7mg • Fiber: 2g • Carbohydrates: 18g

1. Combine cabbage, bananas, apples, ginger, and 1 cup of tea in a blender and blend until thoroughly combined.

2. Add remaining tea as needed while blending until desired consistency is achieved.

NUTS AND BERRIES

Sounding like a true tree-hugger's dream smoothie, this recipe appeals to anyone in search of better health from the best nutrition. The omega-3 content of this smoothie comes from the smart addition of flaxseed, which also adds even more nutty flavor.

INGREDIENTS

2 cups almond milk

¼ cup almonds

1 tablespoon flaxseed

1 cup spinach

2 cups strawberries

3 rhubarb stalks

Yields: 3–4 cups

Per 1 cup serving • Calories: 131 • Fat: 7g • Protein: 4g • Sodium: 84mg • Fiber: 4g • Carbohydrates: 15g

1. Combine 1 cup almond milk with the almonds and flaxseed in a blender and emulsify completely until no nut pieces remain.

2. Add spinach, strawberries, and rhubarb and blend until thoroughly combined.

3. Add remaining almond milk as needed while blending until desired consistency is achieved.

OH, SWEET CABBAGE

As a delightfully sweet morning starter or equally enjoyable afternoon pick-me-up, this smoothie's combination of cabbage, sweet carrots, and apples will have you wondering why you never considered cabbage a treat before.

INGREDIENTS

1 cup cabbage

3 carrots, peeled

1 apple, cored and peeled

1 cup purified water

Yields: 3–4 cups

Per 1 cup serving • Calories: 48 • Fat: 0g • Protein: 1g • Sodium: 37mg • Fiber: 3g • Carbohydrates: 12g

1. Combine cabbage, carrots, and apple with ½ cup water in a blender and blend until thoroughly combined.

2. Add remaining water slowly while blending until desired texture is achieved.

Cancer-Fighting Cabbage

Although some green leafy vegetables don't top the list of those liked enough to be included in your daily diet, cabbage is one that certainly deserves some room near the top. Full of antioxidants that fight cancer-causing free radical damage against cells, even the lightest white cabbage (the most consumed of all cabbages) is rich enough to help stop cancer in its tracks!

ONE SUPERB HERB

Although basil has become more and more common as a main ingredient in things like pesto and pasta sauce, this herb still doesn't get the attention it deserves for the health benefits it offers.

INGREDIENTS

1 cup iceberg lettuce

½ cup basil

1 cucumber, peeled

1 garlic clove

½ cup purified water

Yields: 3–4 cups

Per 1 cup serving • Calories: 14 • Fat: 0g
• Protein: 1g • Sodium: 5mg • Fiber: 1g •
Carbohydrates: 3g

1. Combine the iceberg, basil, cucumber, and garlic in a blender with half of the water and blend until combined thoroughly.

2. If needed, continue adding remaining water while blending until desired texture is achieved.

Basil and Vitamin K

Although the greens blended into green smoothies offer vitamin K, the added benefit of using basil can be quite astounding. While many greens' servings may offer a healthy helping of vitamin K, just 2 teaspoons (or 3 grams) of basil can account for 60 percent of your RDA of vitamin K. You might fulfill, or even surpass, your RDA of vitamin K by just mixing the greens and basil in one smoothie!

ORANGE-MANGO TANGO

Beta-carotene-rich fruits add much-needed health benefits to this vitamin-packed green smoothie.

INGREDIENTS

1 cup watercress

2 cups mango, peeled and pitted

2 oranges, peeled

¼" ginger, peeled (optional)

2 cups purified water

Yields: 3–4 cups

Per 1 cup serving • Calories: 98 • Fat: 0g • Protein: 1g • Sodium: 8mg • Fiber: 4g • Carbohydrates: 25g

1. Combine watercress, mango, oranges, ginger, and 1 cup water in a blender and blend until thoroughly combined.

2. Add remaining water as needed while blending until desired consistency is achieved.

PAPAYA PROTEIN

The delicious flavors of papaya, banana, date, vanilla, and sweet almond milk virtually dance on your tongue while satisfying your body's needs and your cravings for sweets.

INGREDIENTS

1 cup watercress

2 cups papaya

1 banana, peeled

1 date, pitted

1 vanilla bean's pulp

1 tablespoon raw hemp seed protein

2 cups almond milk

Yields: 3–4 cups

Per 1 cup serving • Calories: 124 • Fat: 2g • Protein: 2g • Sodium: 82mg • Fiber: 3g • Carbohydrates: 27g

1. Combine watercress, papaya, banana, date, vanilla bean pulp, hemp protein, and 1 cup almond milk in a blender and blend until thoroughly combined.

2. Add remaining almond milk as needed while blending until desired consistency is achieved.

HERBAL PEACH

Green tea is the ingredient responsible for loading antioxidants into this flavorful smoothie! It's easy to combat illnesses and promote health and wellness for your body and mind with this quick and easy recipe.

INGREDIENTS

1 cup spinach

⅛ cup parsley

2 peaches, pitted

½ lemon, peeled

2 cups green tea

Yields: 2–3 cups

Per 1 cup serving • Calories: 35 • Fat: 0g • Protein: 1g • Sodium: 7mg • Fiber: 2g • Carbohydrates: 9g

1. Combine spinach, parsley, peaches, lemon, and 1 cup of tea in a blender and blend until thoroughly combined.

2. Add remaining tea as needed while blending until desired consistency is achieved.

Green Tea's Power

The importance of herbal tea can be seen in its use in Eastern medicinal culture. Used as a remedy for many illnesses and to promote natural health, green tea's amazing health benefits come from its rich concentration of powerful antioxidants. Antioxidants combat serious illnesses and disease and cleanse the body of toxins and waste, all while providing improved immunity, optimal functioning of the body's processes, and a great-tasting substitute to water.

PEAS FOR A PERFECT PREGNANCY Ⓟ

Although probably not the veggie that comes to mind when you think "superfood," peas are an excellent source of iron and folate—both important vitamins and minerals for promoting the best health in mom and baby!

INGREDIENTS

1 cup arugula

1 cup sweet peas

2 celery stalks

1 cucumber, peeled

1 cup red raspberry tea

Yields: 3–4 cups

Per 1 cup serving • Calories: 36 • Fat: 0g • Protein: 2g • Sodium: 56mg • Fiber: 2g • Carbohydrates: 7g

1. Combine arugula, sweet peas, celery, cucumber, and ½ cup tea in a blender and blend until thoroughly combined.

2. Add remaining tea as needed while blending until desired consistency is achieved.

BERRY PEACHY

Providing a wealth of nutrition in every sip, this smoothie makes for a delicious way to meet important fruit and veggie serving requirements with the added benefits of ginger.

INGREDIENTS

1 cup watercress

3 peaches, pitted

1 cup strawberries

1 orange, peeled

¼" ginger, peeled

2 cups purified water

Yields: 3–4 cups

Per 1 cup serving • Calories: 78 • Fat: 0g • Protein: 2g • Sodium: 6mg • Fiber: 4g • Carbohydrates: 19g

1. Combine watercress, peaches, strawberries, orange, and ginger with 1 cup of water in a blender and blend until thoroughly combined.

2. Add remaining water as needed while blending until desired consistency is achieved.

PEARS, APPLES, AND GINGER

There's not much that can compare to the sweet combination of pears, apples, and ginger. This scrumptious blend comforts your stomach with balanced nutrition in every glass.

INGREDIENTS

1 cup watercress

3 apples, cored and peeled

3 pears, cored and peeled

¼" ginger, peeled

2 cups chamomile tea

Yields: 3–4 cups

Per 1 cup serving • Calories: 137 • Fat: 0g • Protein: 1g • Sodium: 7mg • Fiber: 6g • Carbohydrates: 36g

1. Combine watercress, apples, pears, ginger, and 1 cup of tea in a blender and blend until thoroughly combined.

2. Add remaining tea as needed while blending until desired consistency is achieved.

PERFECT PEARS AND PINEAPPLES

The amazing flavors of pineapples and pears are enhanced by the addition of lemon in this recipe. With strong vitamins and minerals that act to aid in digestion and prevent discomfort, this is a splendid blend for any indigestion sufferer.

INGREDIENTS

1 cup romaine lettuce

2 cups pineapple

2 pears, peeled and cored

1 lemon, peeled

2 cups chamomile tea

Yields: 3–4 cups

Per 1 cup serving • Calories: 95 • Fat: 0g • Protein: 1g • Sodium: 5mg • Fiber: 3g • Carbohydrates: 25g

1. Combine romaine, pineapple, pears, lemon, and 1 cup of tea in a blender and blend until thoroughly combined.

2. Add remaining tea as needed while blending until desired consistency is achieved.

PLEASURABLE PREGNANCY SMOOTHIE 🅿

Pregnancy is an opportunity to give your body the pristine treatment it deserves. Treat yourself to this delicious smoothie throughout your nine months and savor the feeling of optimal health!

INGREDIENTS

1 cup watercress

2 red Gala apples, peeled and cored

1 cup cranberries

¼" ginger, peeled

2 cups red raspberry tea

Yields: 3–4 cups

Per 1 cup serving • Calories: 51 • Fat: 0g • Protein: 1g • Sodium: 6mg • Fiber: 2g • Carbohydrates: 14g

1. Combine watercress, apples, cranberries, ginger, and 1 cup of tea in a blender and blend until thoroughly combined.

2. Add remaining tea as needed while blending until desired consistency is achieved.

Pamper Yourself

Whether this is your first pregnancy or the next in a long line of lovable little ones, your pregnancy is a time that requires special attention. The hustle and bustle of everyday life can leave you run down and overwhelmed, and being pregnant can add to exhaustion and lack of focus on yourself. Be sure to spend quiet and quality time on yourself without distraction or stress. Meditation, light exercise, and quality nutrition can be the keys to a pampered pregnancy and provide happiness for all!

PINEAPPLE BERRY

The important vitamins, minerals, and antioxidants in this smoothie will provide your body with the boost it needs with a more sustainable effect than the store-bought, chemically enhanced energy drinks.

INGREDIENTS

1 cup watercress

2 cups pineapple

1 cup strawberries

1 cup blackberries

1 cup purified water

Yields: 3–4 cups

Per 1 cup serving • Calories: 65 • Fat: 0g • Protein: 1g • Sodium: 6mg • Fiber: 3g • Carbohydrates: 16g

1. Combine watercress, pineapple, strawberries, blackberries, and ½ cup of water in a blender and blend until thoroughly combined.

2. Add remaining water as needed while blending until desired consistency is achieved.

PINEAPPLE-PAPAYA PROTECTION

Although an important ingredient, the romaine's taste is almost completely masked by the flavorful fruit combination in this recipe. This smoothie not only protects the stomach lining, it is an amazing treat to be enjoyed whenever the craving for fruit strikes!

INGREDIENTS

1 cup romaine lettuce

2 cups pineapple

2 cups papaya

½ lemon, peeled

¼" ginger, peeled

2 cups chamomile tea

Yields: 3–4 cups

Per 1 cup serving • Calories: 69 • Fat: 0g • Protein: 1g • Sodium: 6mg • Fiber: 2g • Carbohydrates: 18g

1. Combine romaine, pineapple, papaya, lemon, ginger, and 1 cup of tea in a blender and blend until thoroughly combined.

2. Add remaining tea as needed while blending until desired consistency is achieved.

POMEGRANATE AND PROTEIN

Adding raw hemp seed protein powder to any of your favorite green smoothies is a delicious way to increase your protein intake.

INGREDIENTS

1 cup spinach

4 tablespoons raw hemp seed protein powder

Pips of 2 pomegranates

1 cup strawberries

1 cup raspberries

1 banana, peeled

2 cups almond milk

Yields: 3–4 cups

Per 1 cup serving • Calories: 225 • Fat: 4g • Protein: 8g • Sodium: 52mg • Fiber: 11g • Carbohydrates: 46g

1. Combine spinach, hemp protein, pomegranate pips, berries, banana, and 1 cup almond milk in a blender and blend until thoroughly combined.

2. Add remaining almond milk as needed while blending until desired consistency is achieved.

RED PEPPER RELIEF

Rich in beta-carotene, a powerful antioxidant, this veggie acts to protect your digestive tract from dangerous cancers while also providing rich vitamins and minerals that make for happy digestion.

INGREDIENTS

1 cup romaine lettuce

1 red bell pepper, top and seeds removed, ribs intact

2 celery stalks, leaves intact

½ lemon, peeled

1½ cups chamomile tea

Yields: 3–4 cups

Per 1 cup serving • Calories: 22 • Fat: 0g • Protein: 1g • Sodium: 27mg • Fiber: 2g • Carbohydrates: 5g

1. Combine romaine, red pepper, celery, lemon, and ¾ cup of tea in a blender and blend until thoroughly combined.

2. Add remaining tea as needed while blending until desired consistency is achieved.

REFRESHING RASPBERRY BLEND ♥

Raspberries offer a tangy sweet taste that is heightened by the sweet pineapple and sour lemon in this recipe. Simple, quick, and delicious, this smoothie will be a favorite go-to when you're in need of a delicious snack in little time.

INGREDIENTS

1 cup watercress

1 cup raspberries

½ pineapple, peeled and cored

½ lemon, peeled

1½ cups kefir

Yields: 3–4 cups

Per 1 cup serving • Calories: 136 • Fat: 3g • Protein: 4g • Sodium: 52mg • Fiber: 3g • Carbohydrates: 25g

1. Combine watercress, raspberries, pineapple, lemon, and ¾ cup of kefir in a blender and blend until thoroughly combined.

2. Add remaining kefir as needed while blending until desired consistency is achieved.

RICE MILK FOR REPRODUCTIVE HEALTH ♥

This sensational recipe delivers a delightfully creamy smoothie packed with protein, potassium, and omega-3s. It can satisfy your craving for sweets, creaminess, or nutty flavors!

INGREDIENTS

¼ cup almonds

1 tablespoon flaxseed

2 cups rice milk

1 cup watercress

2 bananas, peeled

Yields: 3–4 cups

Per 1 cup serving • Calories: 149 • Fat: 6g • Protein: 3g • Sodium: 30mg • Fiber: 3g • Carbohydrates: 22g

1. Combine almonds, flaxseed, and ½ cup rice milk in a blender and blend until completely emulsified and no bits of almonds remain.

2. Add watercress, bananas, and 1 cup of rice milk and blend until thoroughly combined.

3. Add remaining rice milk as needed while blending until desired consistency is achieved.

SAVORY SPINACH

The benefits of iron are outstanding, and are even greater in pregnancy. Satisfy nutritional needs and daily requirements with this smoothie recipe that combines the important green leafy veggie with sweet red peppers, vitamin-packed broccoli, and spicy garlic.

INGREDIENTS

1 cup spinach

½ red bell pepper, cored, ribs intact

½ cup broccoli spears

1 garlic clove

2 cups red raspberry tea

Yields: 3–4 cups

Per 1 cup serving • Calories: 15 • Fat: 0g • Protein: 1g • Sodium: 17mg • Fiber: 1g • Carbohydrates: 3g

1. Combine spinach, red pepper, broccoli, garlic, and 1 cup of tea in a blender and blend until thoroughly combined.

2. Add remaining tea as needed while blending until desired consistency is achieved.

SAVOY SMOOTHIE

The strong beta-carotenes in this smoothie will help keep you energized and focused throughout the day. Whether you're looking for a great morning start or a quick and healthy lunch idea, this smoothie is a great go-to!

INGREDIENTS

1 cup savoy cabbage

1 beet

1 carrot, peeled

1 apple, cored and peeled

1 banana, peeled

1 cup vanilla soymilk

Yields: 3–4 cups

Per 1 cup serving • Calories: 95 • Fat: 1g • Protein: 3g • Sodium: 56mg • Fiber: 4g • Carbohydrates: 20g

1. Combine the cabbage, beet, carrot, apple, and banana with ½ cup of the soymilk in a blender and blend until thoroughly combined.

2. Add remaining soymilk while blending until desired texture is achieved.

Savoy and Vitamin K

Cabbage is packed with vitamin K, whose most well-known benefit is its large responsibility in blood clotting. By consuming just 1 cup of savoy cabbage, you'll be getting more than 90 percent of your RDA of vitamin K.

THE SLUMP BUMPER

With the energizing effects of natural sugars (fructose) found in sweet fruits and vegetables, there's no comparison to energy drinks or junk foods that give you quick but short-lived energy.

INGREDIENTS

1 cup spinach

2 pears, cored and peeled

1 cup cherries, pitted

1 banana, peeled

2 cups almond milk

Yields: 3–4 cups

Per 1 cup serving • Calories: 149 • Fat: 2g • Protein: 2g • Sodium: 82mg • Fiber: 5g • Carbohydrates: 35g

1. Combine spinach, pears, cherries, banana, and 1 cup of almond milk in a blender and blend until thoroughly combined.

2. Add remaining almond milk while blending until desired texture is achieved.

Benefits of Cherries

Packed with an assortment of vitamins and minerals, an obvious sign from their intense red color, cherries help mental functions such as memory. Cherries also improve mental clarity and promote focus and attention.

SPICY COCOA

This recipe takes sweet and spicy to the next level by providing the flavorful combination of sweet chocolate and hot pepper with the added health benefits found in every ingredient in this powerful recipe.

INGREDIENTS

1 cup spinach

2 bananas, peeled

1 tablespoon powdered cacao

1 tablespoon raw honey

1 teaspoon cinnamon

⅛ teaspoon cayenne

2 cups almond milk

Yields: 3–4 cups

Per 1 cup serving • Calories: 121 • Fat: 2g • Protein: 2g • Sodium: 82mg • Fiber: 3g • Carbohydrates: 27g

1. Combine spinach, bananas, cacao, honey, cinnamon, cayenne, and 1 cup almond milk in a blender and blend until thoroughly combined.

2. Add remaining almond milk as needed while blending until desired consistency is achieved.

SPICY STOMACH SOOTHER

Spicy arugula and crisp veggies with a bite offer up a deliciously savory taste combination that will soothe your stomach while calming cravings for harsh spicy foods that could aggravate indigestion and lead to discomfort.

INGREDIENTS

1 cup arugula

1 green onion

3 celery stalks

1 garlic clove (optional)

2 cups chamomile tea

Yields: 3–4 cups

Per 1 cup serving • Calories: 10 • Fat: 0g • Protein: 1g • Sodium: 38mg • Fiber: 1g • Carbohydrates: 2g

1. Combine arugula, onion, celery, garlic, and 1 cup of chamomile in a blender and blend until thoroughly combined.

2. Add remaining tea as needed while blending until desired consistency is achieved.

STOMACH SOOTHER ⓟ

Digestive problems can be easily remedied with smoothies like this one. The comforting ginger will soothe your stomach while satisfying your taste buds.

INGREDIENTS

1 cup watercress

3 apples, peeled and cored

1 banana, peeled

½" ginger, peeled

2 cups red raspberry tea

Yields: 3–4 cups

Per 1 cup serving • Calories: 86 • Fat: 0g • Protein: 1g • Sodium: 6mg • Fiber: 2g • Carbohydrates: 22g

1. Combine watercress, apples, banana, ginger, and 1 cup of tea in a blender and blend until thoroughly combined.

2. Add remaining tea as needed while blending until desired consistency is achieved.

SWEET VEGGIE SURPRISE

With this smoothie, you can savor the delicious flavor of red peppers, vibrant beets, lycopene-rich tomatoes, beta-carotene-packed carrots, and spicy cilantro.

INGREDIENTS

1 cup spinach

1 tomato

4 carrots, peeled

1 beet, greens removed

½ red bell pepper, cored with ribs intact

⅛ cup cilantro

2½ cups purified water

Yields: 3–4 cups

Per 1 cup serving • Calories: 46 • Fat: 0g • Protein: 2g • Sodium: 69mg • Fiber: 3g • Carbohydrates: 10g

1. Combine spinach, tomato, carrots, beet, red pepper, cilantro, and 1¼ cups of water in a blender and blend until thoroughly combined.

2. Add the remaining water as needed while blending until desired consistency is achieved.

TUMMY PROTECTOR

A savory way to coat your sensitive stomach is with delicious vegetables like these. Romaine, celery, green onion, tomatoes, and comforting mild chamomile tea deliver comfort and protection in every delicious sip.

INGREDIENTS

1 cup romaine lettuce

3 celery stalks, leaves intact

1 green onion

2 tomatoes

2 cups chamomile tea

Yields: 3–4 cups

Per 1 cup serving • Calories: 19 • Fat: 0g • Protein: 1g • Sodium: 31mg • Fiber: 2g • Carbohydrates: 4g

1. Combine romaine, celery, onion, tomatoes, and 1 cup of tea in a blender and blend until thoroughly combined.

2. Add remaining tea as needed while blending until desired consistency is achieved.

VEGGIES FOR VITAMINS ℗

This delicious savory blend of spicy arugula, tomato, onion, cucumber, celery, and garlic combine with natural tea to give your body an amazing amount of vitamins and minerals.

INGREDIENTS

1 cup arugula

1 tomato

1 cucumber, peeled

1 celery stalk

1 green onion

1 garlic clove

2 cups red raspberry tea

Yields: 3–4 cups

Per 1 cup serving • Calories: 17 • Fat: 0g • Protein: 1g • Sodium: 15mg • Fiber: 1g • Carbohydrates: 3g

1. Combine arugula, tomato, cucumber, celery, onion, garlic, and 1 cup of tea in a blender and blend until thoroughly combined.

2. Add remaining tea as needed while blending until desired consistency is achieved.

VERY IMPORTANT VITAMIN C ℗

Immunity and health are never as important as when you're pregnant. Caring for your little one starts long before the birth, and building your body's defenses against illness makes for a healthier mom and a healthier baby.

INGREDIENTS

1 cup watercress

2 tangerines, peeled

½ grapefruit, peeled

½ pineapple, peeled and cored

½ cantaloupe, rind and seeds removed

1 cup red raspberry tea

Yields: 3–4 cups

Per 1 cup serving • Calories: 114 • Fat: 0g • Protein: 2g • Sodium: 18mg • Fiber: 2g • Carbohydrates: 29g

1. Combine watercress, tangerines, grapefruit, pineapple, and cantaloupe in a blender and blend until thoroughly combined.

2. Add 1 cup of tea as needed while blending until desired consistency is achieved.

Vitamin C Double Duty

Not only does vitamin C make for an important addition to your diet for its strong immunity-building power, this vitamin also benefits the expectant mom by providing optimal brain functioning, which means better mental clarity, improved focus, and an overall feeling of awareness that is far superior to the mental fuzziness commonly referred to as "pregnancy brain."

PART II
JUICES

CHAPTER 9

THE BASICS OF JUICING

People talk about the so-called juicing revolution, but the fact is, juicing has been around for a long, long time. In a way, we're not so much discovering the health benefits of consuming greater amounts of fruits and vegetables as we're rediscovering them. Back when family farms were the norm rather than the exception, people ate well because they ate what they grew. Today's movements for sustainability, reduced use of pesticides and fertilizers, and relying more on local food supplies have all revealed the wisdom of a better diet.

At the same time, modern technology makes juicing accessible to more people than ever before. When fresh produce meets a modern juicer, it constitutes a true evolution in the way we think about nutrition. It's fast, easy, delicious, and good for you, too!

Juices in Your Life

Modern FDA guidelines recommend four to five servings of vegetables and fruits per day. Modern foodies are embracing healthier living amid concern over how commercially produced foods may be contaminated by a variety of environmental factors and farming practices. Going organic and buying local are both on the rise, and these factors have, in turn, led to a renewed interest in how to get the most nutritional bang for your food buck and maintain optimal health at the same time.

Going Raw

Many food experts maintain that raw foods are the healthiest for the body, because heating foods above 110 degrees is thought to denature enzymes that are naturally present. Those enzymes are considered the life force of foods, helping the body to digest and absorb nutrients. Vitamin C, for example, is destroyed by heat, and the cancer-fighting sulforaphanes found in broccoli are diminished by heating.

In other cases, though, cooking can actually increase nutritional value. The lycopenes in tomatoes, for example, increase when the fruit is cooked, but that's because the fibrous portions are broken down. Kale, garlic, spinach, and onions have also been shown to be more nutritious cooked, as light cooking releases compounds that might otherwise go undigested. Whether or not you're a raw foods advocate, it's important to do your homework—and, as always, balance is the key in any diet.

Whatever your food choices, regular juicing offers the best of both worlds. Juicing gives you all the benefits of raw foods, breaking down the fibrous portions of fruits and vegetables at the cellular level to maximize their nutritive value. More than any other dietary practice, juicing puts the "whole" back in whole foods and offers great economy, digestibility, and nutrition without a huge adjustment in lifestyle.

Juicing Versus Blending

While it's true that a good high-speed blender can give you many of the same benefits as a juicer, blending doesn't break down fibers of fruits and vegetables at the cellular level. Thus, you may not derive the same nutritional punch as with a juicer.

Some newer technology claims to have narrowed the gap between juicers and blenders with higher speeds and greater cellular breakdown, especially in "bullet" type machines, but it's important to keep in mind that even the best blender will result in liquids with greater amounts of pulp and fiber, which may be harder to digest and absorb than juice products. Some juicing proponents claim that higher speeds and the resulting heat from powerful motors destroy valuable nutrients, but so far, there's not a lot of evidence to support that claim. If any machine is running so hot that it's heating your juice, it's best to put it in retirement and look for something new.

Fresh Is Best

Unless you're growing your own, it's often difficult to determine where produce comes from or how long it's been in your supermarket aisle. If you're concerned about food pedigree, be sure to check for labels. Often they will indicate whether the produce was grown outside the United States or in a country where laws governing the use of pesticides or chemical fertilizers aren't as stringent as they are here.

Local farmers' markets are a great source for fresh produce, as are food cooperatives. Food "rescue" organizations are also springing up all over the country, purchasing fresh produce in bulk from farmers, restaurant, and grocery chains and selling them to members at significantly reduced prices. Members report that for a contribution of as little as ten dollars they can receive up to sixty pounds of fresh produce.

Drink Brighter!

The more vibrant the color, the more powerful the juice. Flavonoids are the plant pigments responsible for the colors in fruits and vegetables. But they also have anti-allergic, anti-inflammatory, anti-carcinogenic, and antiviral properties. What pleases the eye is also likely to please the palate, so drink up!

When shopping for and selecting the best produce for your juicer, a good rule to follow is the G-R-O-W rule (greens, reds, oranges, and whites). It's perhaps not such a coincidence that the fruits and veggies with the most eye appeal and the deepest, most vivid colors are also likely to be the most nutritious. Greens include lettuces, spinach, broccoli, Swiss chard, and kale. Reds include beets, red cabbage, raspberries, strawberries, and red peppers. The orange group includes carrots, sweet potatoes, cantaloupe, oranges, and pumpkins. Last but not least, the "w" stands for white—cabbage, parsnips, and cauliflower.

Storage

Whether it's organic, nonorganic, or so fresh you picked it off the tree yourself, always wash your fruits and vegetables before you juice. Store your produce in the refrigerator whenever possible, and if you have a humidity setting in your vegetable drawer, keep it on the high side, in dryer, more arid zones such as Arizona, parts of California, Utah and other Western states, as higher humidity makes for longer keeping, If you live in a moister environment such as the Pacific Northwest or along the Eastern seaboard, lower humidity settings are appropriate. The more water content the produce has, the greater the yield of juice. Most produce for juicing can be safely kept for a week or more in the refrigerator, depending on what it is. Lettuces and leafy greens like spinach will begin to deteriorate after a week, but root vegetables like carrots or beets will keep much longer. And while it may seem obvious to point it out, any bruises, spots or blemishes should be trimmed away before juicing. Pick over berries and discard any that may have become overripe or wrinkled.

The Organic Controversy

An "organic" label doesn't necessarily guarantee consumer quality. Because the movement has become so popular, many companies have jumped on the bandwagon. Check your labels carefully. There's a difference between a "certified" organic label and a "transitional" organic label. The "transitional" label means that the grower may have used pesticides and chemicals in the past; while they have applied for certification, they may not get it.

Even if you do choose organic produce, be especially aware that there are some fruits and veggies that are more susceptible to environmental factors than others. E coli, for example, occurs naturally, as does anthrax, even under organically raised conditions. So rinse, rinse, rinse before juicing.

You should also be aware that some fruits and vegetables are more susceptible to absorbing chemicals and pesticides than others. The Environmental Working Group, which, among other things, analyzes produce and identifies susceptibility to pesticide and chemical residue, has identified the "Dirty Dozen" and stresses the importance of buying them from a reliable organic source. They are:

- Apples
- Blueberries
- Celery
- Cucumbers
- Grapes
- Lettuce
- Nectarines
- Peaches
- Potatoes
- Spinach
- Strawberries
- Sweet bell peppers

Their list of fruits and veggies where an organic label might not be so important includes:

- Asparagus
- Avocado
- Cabbage
- Cantaloupe
- Corn
- Eggplant
- Grapefruit
- Kiwi
- Mangos
- Onions
- Pineapple
- Sweet peas

In the best of all possible worlds, of course, you have your own garden and can exercise quality control from your own backyard. For those fortunate enough to have a garden or orchard, juicing is a great way to utilize excess yields without resorting to canning or sugar-laden preserving methods. Best of all, leftover pulp from your juicers makes excellent compost material—you can return the gift back to the soil that produced it.

To Peel or Not to Peel?

The best guide to deciding which fruits and vegetables should be peeled or cored before juicing is your own common sense. You wouldn't, for example, eat an unpeeled orange, so chances are that orange peel isn't going to make for great juice, either. Same holds true for the majority of citrus fruits. When you eat an apple, a pear, or a mango, you throw away the core, don't you? So there's no need to include it. On the other hand, you can lose significant amounts of nutrients should you peel a cucumber before juicing. Those peels are rich in chlorophyll and provide a significant amount of vitamins. If the cucumber has been waxed though, it's better peeled.

What to Juice First

If you're using a centrifugal-style juicer, it's a good idea to juice denser fruits and vegetables like carrots, sweet potatoes, and beets first, followed by softer, juicier fruits and veggies. Denser produce will pass more easily through the clean shredding filter, and the juicier produce will help to "rinse" it to avoid clogs!

Some other peels do more harm than good, no matter what their nutritive value. Consider that including the peel of a yam or sweet potato may add nutrients, but they won't be much help if the resulting juice tastes like dirt! Perhaps the best advice, though, is to consider the power and the efficiency of the juicer itself and respect your equipment. Don't feed it more than it can comfortably handle. The extra teaspoon of juice you get from including a core is harder on the machine. Woody stems on broccoli or asparagus should definitely be removed. They may damage the machine, and they don't contain much juice anyhow! So use your head, use your palate, and let your senses be your guide. You'll be a master juicer in no time.

Which Juicer Is Right for You?

With the wealth of information available to you through the Internet, television advertising, and other sources, people interested in juicing are faced with what can seem like a bewildering array of choices when it comes to the "best" juicers out there. While it's important to do your homework before investing in any kitchen appliance, it's also important to keep in mind that most of the information is designed to get you to choose one product over another. We've simplified the process by identifying the three basic types of juicers and the benefits (and drawbacks) of each. But whatever you choose, remember, the best juicer is always the one that fits your needs.

Centrifugal Juicers

Centrifugal juicers are by far the most popular because of their low-to-moderate pricing, and they can be the right choice if you're new to juicing. Using a simple design, they operate by a spinning basket that shreds the produce and forces the juice through a strainer while the pulp is usually ejected into a container. The process adds oxygen to the juice and some models can produce a fair amount of froth or foam. Many of the newer machines come with celebrity endorsements and some attractive high-tech features. But at the low end, they can be loud, difficult to clean, and without enough power to handle the demands of a two-week juice fast. Of particular note is a tendency to "walk" during operation, making some models hazardous for kids and even some adults to operate. After all, you don't want fresh juice all over the kitchen floor!

Some juice enthusiasts maintain that the higher speeds of centrifugal models can lead to oxidation and destruction of phytochemicals and enzymes through overheating, but it's doubtful than any machine will heat the juice to the point where it loses significant nutritional value. High speeds do produce more foam, though, so be sure to mix your juice thoroughly before drinking it.

Masticating Juicers

Single-gear or "masticating" juicers are more expensive, but their slower process delivers higher quality nutrition. Using a "cold press" method, juicers compress fruit and vegetables to "squeeze" out their juice. Rugged and long lasting, they are also terrific for creating healthy kitchen concoctions like gourmet nut butters, pestos, mustards, herb blends, and other delights. They can be quite heavy, however, and the less compact models take up a fair amount of real estate on your countertop. So if you're short on space or ready outlet access, consider one of the more "portable" models.

Triturating Juicers

Double-gear or "triturating" machines tend to be the most expensive and proponents insist they deliver the highest quality juice. Twin-gear triturating juicers are built to provide you the best in terms of yield and nutrition. The twin or dual gears slowly draw the produce into and through the gears, breaking down the produce into a megadose of nutrition-packed juice. Perhaps the greatest recommendation is that they don't just make juice. They can also make salsas, ice creams, and even baby food. Their slower process takes more time, and in some models cleanup can be more complicated. Still, they remain the optimal choice for hard-core juice aficionados, due to the superior efficiency at juicing things such as wheatgrass and sprouts.

Look at the Feed Tube

The size of the feed tube in a juicer is usually an excellent indicator of the machine's overall efficiency. Some models have smaller feed tubes to ensure that fruits and veggies are fed into the machine at slower speed. Though slower speeds tend to be favored in terms of nutrition, a small feed tube adds to preparation time and can be an indicator of a less powerful motor.

Ultimately, your choice of juicers depends on a number of factors—budget, space, time, and ease and efficiency of operation and cleaning. Do look for a juicer with multiple speeds, an adequately sized feed tube so you don't waste time pre-chopping, and at least 400 watts of power to start.

Where to Buy Juicers

Whatever variety of juicer you choose, most models are widely available through large retailers. Online outlets such as Overstock.com can also be a good shopping source. Expect to pay between $50 and $300 for a quality machine at retail. Some of the most recommended models are the Breville Juice Fountain, 800JEXL, Hamilton Beach Big Mouth Pro 67650, The Green Star GS-2000, the Jack LaLanne Power Juicer Pro E-1189, and the Omega 4000. Consider any brand that has served you well in other appliances like food processors, blenders, and the like. Black & Decker, for example, launched its line of small kitchen appliances only after decades of manufacturing power tools. While they may not be top of the line, the motors are rugged and reliable.

Budget-minded? You might also consider a used model. A juicer, like so many small kitchen appliances, is one of those things people either use regularly or they don't. So it's not unusual to come across a "still in the box" model at your local thrift store, or a store return up for auction on eBay. Bargain hunters can find some great values, but just make sure these secondhand machines are clean and in good condition before you buy.

CHAPTER 10

FRUIT JUICES

APPLES AND APRICOTS

APPLE CELERY CINNAMON

The addition of cinnamon in this recipe is useful for controlling blood pressure.

INGREDIENTS

2 apples

8 stalks celery

Dash of cinnamon

Yields: 1½ cups

Per 1 cup serving • Calories: 132 • Fat: 0.5g
• Protein: 1.6g • Sodium: 109mg • Sugar:
24g • Carbohydrates: 33g

1. Process the apples through an electronic juicer according to the manufacturer's directions.

2. Add the celery and cinnamon.

3. Whisk the juice to combine and serve immediately.

APPLE CELERY CUCUMBER COCKTAIL

Take this one at bedtime to ease inflammation, prevent stiff joints, and promote a good night's sleep.

INGREDIENTS

2 medium apples, cored

4 stalks celery, with leaves

1 cucumber, cut into chunks

Yields: 2 cups (2 servings)

Per 1 cup serving • Calories: 168 • Fat: 1g •
Protein: 3.3g • Sodium: 95mg • Sugar: 29g •
Carbohydrates: 42g

1. Slice the apples and process through the feed tube of an electronic juicer according to the manufacturer's directions.

2. Add the celery stalks, one or two at a time.

3. Add the cucumber chunks.

4. Whisk the juice to blend and serve immediately.

Make the Connection

Cucumber juice is rich in silica, which strengthens connective tissue such as muscles, tendons, ligaments, cartilage, and bone.

APPLE CUCUMBER COCKTAIL

When it comes to body cleansing, sometimes the simplest combinations are the best. Cucumbers are not only a good diuretic, which helps flush the kidneys, but they also help to control arthritis and eczema, and remove toxins from the blood.

INGREDIENTS

1 medium cucumber

1 medium apple, cored

Water to make 1 cup juice

Yields: 1 cup

Per 1 cup serving • Calories: 122 • Fat: 0.5g • Protein: 2.4g • Sodium: 6mg • Sugar: 21g • Carbohydrates: 31g

1. Process the cucumber and the apple through your electronic juicer according to the manufacturer's directions.

2. Add the water to make 1 cup and mix thoroughly. Drink and enjoy!

How Much to Buy?

In juicing, a good rule of thumb to follow when calculating how much produce you need to buy is: 1 pound produce will yield approximately 1 cup of juice.

APPLE BEET MINT

Filling and flavorful. The surprise is that the addition of mint enhances the sweetness and flavor of this recipe.

INGREDIENTS

2 small sugar beets, trimmed, with greens

1 large Granny Smith apple, cored

¼ cup fresh mint

Yields: 1 cup

Per 1 cup serving • Calories: 158 • Fat: 0.6g • Protein: 4g • Sodium: 136mg • Sugar: 26g • Carbohydrates: 38g

1. Process the beets and the apple through an electronic juicer according to the manufacturer's directions.

2. Add the mint.

3. Stir or shake the juice together with some ice and enjoy!

APPLE BLUEBERRY

If you prefer, you can add spring water or serve over ice to dilute this one a bit.

INGREDIENTS

2 cups fresh or frozen blueberries

1 apple, cored

1 wedge lemon or lime, peeled

Yields: 1 cup

Per 1 cup serving • Calories: 248 • Fat: 1.2g
• Protein: 2.7g • Sodium: 3mg • Sugar: 45g
• Carbohydrates: 64g

1. Process the berries through your electronic juicer according to the manufacturer's directions.

2. Add the apple, followed by the lemon or lime.

3. Stir or shake the juice thoroughly to combine the ingredients and serve.

APPLE GRAPE COCKTAIL

Many lines of creams and cosmetics are using grapeseed oils and extracts for their benefits to the skin, so if you happen to have seeded grapes on hand, don't hesitate to use them in your juices!

INGREDIENTS

2 red Gala or Fuji apples, cored

1 cup grapes, any variety

Yields: 1 cup

Per 1 cup serving • Calories: 209 • Fat: 0.5g
• Protein: 1.5g • Sodium: 3mg • Sugar: 45g
• Carbohydrates: 55g

1. Process the apples through your electronic juicer according to the manufacturer's directions.

2. Add the grapes.

3. Mix the juice thoroughly to combine and serve alone or over ice.

APPLE-MELON COOLER

Wonderfully refreshing, and fills you up, fast!

INGREDIENTS

2 apples, cored

3 (1") slices of watermelon

Yields: 1½ cups

Per 1 cup serving • Calories: 172 • Fat: 0.6g
• Protein: 1.6g • Sodium: 4mg • Sugar:
34.6g • Carbohydrates: 45g

1. Process the apples through an electronic juicer according to the manufacturer's directions.

2. Add the watermelon slices.

3. Serve the juice alone or over ice.

APPLE PLUM JUICE

The soluble fiber in this juice is terrific for occasional constipation problems, and is rich in vitamins and phyto-nutrients, too.

INGREDIENTS

2 large apples, cored

4 black plums, pitted

Yields: 1 cup

Per 1 cup serving • Calories: 227 • Fat: 1g •
Protein: 2.4g • Sodium: 0g • Sugar: 58g •
Carbohydrates: 58g

1. Process the fruits in any order through an electronic juicer according to the manufacturer's directions.

2. Serve alone or over ice.

APPLE STRAWBERRY TEMPTATION

Strawberries are known for their ability to fight free radicals and the environmental damage that comes from pollutants in the air and water.

INGREDIENTS

2 Gala apples, cored

2 Granny Smith apples, cored

1 cup strawberries

¼ lemon, rind intact

Yields: 1½ cups

Per 1 cup serving • Calories: 266 • Fat: 0.7g • Protein: 1g • Sodium: 4mg • Sugar: 51g • Carbohydrates: 71g

1. Process the apples through your electronic juicer according to the manufacturer's directions.

2. Add the strawberries, followed by the lemon wedge.

3. Mix the juice thoroughly to combine and serve alone or over ice.

KALE APPLE SPINACH

This drink will help keep your skin clear of acne. Reducing junk foods and drinking healthy juice will be steps in the right direction, too.

INGREDIENTS

2 red apples, cored

2 carrots, peeled

4 large kale leaves

1 cup spinach leaves

Yields: 1¼ cups

Per 1 cup serving • Calories: 246 • Fat: 1g • Protein: 5.3g • Sodium: 114mg • Sugar: 38g • Carbohydrates: 60g

1. Process the apples through your electronic juicer according to the manufacturer's directions, followed by the carrots.

2. Add the kale and spinach.

3. Stir or shake the juice thoroughly to combine and serve alone or over ice.

Some C and E for Your DNA

According to *The Journal of Investigative Dermatology*, people who consumed vitamins C and E saw a reduction in sunburns caused by exposure to UVB radiation, as well as a reduction of factors linked to DNA damage within skin cells. Scientists believe these two antioxidant vitamins may help protect against DNA damage.

KIWI APPLE JUICE

Kiwis have the added benefit of removing excess sodium from the body.

INGREDIENTS

2 medium red apples, cored

3 kiwis

Yield: 1 cup

Per 1 cup serving • Calories: 244 • Fat: 1.2g
• Protein: 2.8g • Sodium: 11mg • Sugar: 22g
• Carbohydrates: 61g

1. Process the apples through an electronic juicer according to manufacturer's directions.

2. Add the kiwis.

3. Mix the juice and serve immediately.

RED VELVET

This vibrantly colored juice is not exactly a piece of cake, but sweet and satisfying all the same!

INGREDIENTS

3 carrots, trimmed

2 large Granny Smith apples, cored

1 orange, peeled and segmented

¼ sugar beet, tailed and trimmed

Yields: 1½ cups

Per 1 cup serving • Calories: 290 • Fat: 0g •
Protein: 4g • Sodium: 90mg • Sugar: 52g •
Carbohydrates: 72.9g

1. Process the carrots and apples through an electronic juicer according to the manufacturer's directions.

2. Add the orange segments, followed by the beet.

3. Mix the juice thoroughly to combine the ingredients and serve alone or over ice.

Sugar in the Morning

When fasting, it's best to consume sweet fruit juices in the morning, go to green juices at lunch, and confine yourself to simple, one- or two-fruit combinations in the late afternoon for a quick pick-me-up.

APRICOT COOLER

This makes a perfect choice when you're craving something sweet.

INGREDIENTS

4 fresh apricots, pitted

1 slice honeydew melon

1 pear, cored

½ cup raspberries

Yields: 1 cup

Per 1 cup serving • Calories: 246 • Fat: 1.3g
• Protein: 4g • Sodium: 34mg • Sugar: 43g
• Carbohydrates: 61g

1. Process the apricots and melon through an electronic juicer according to the manufacturer's directions.

2. Add the pear, followed by the raspberries.

3. Mix the juice to combine the ingredients and serve over ice.

BERRIES

BERRY REFRESHING

Summer is the best time of all to juice to lose weight. Not only does appetite decrease in the heat, but a huge variety of fruits and vegetables come into season, making for an abundance of great tasting, low-cal treats!

INGREDIENTS

½ cup strawberries

1 cup raspberries

1 medium orange, peeled

Yields: 1 cup

Per 1 cup serving • Calories: 132 • Fat: 1g • Protein: 3g • Sodium: 2mg • Sugar: 17g • Carbohydrates: 31g

1. Process the fruit in any order you wish through an electronic juicer according to the manufacturer's directions.

2. Using a cocktail shaker or covered jar, shake the juice together with some ice and enjoy!

Raspberry Ketones

Raspberries have been shown to contain a natural substance called ketones, which are similar to capsaicin, the compound that gives hot peppers their fire. Animal studies have found that raspberry ketones prevent an increase in overall body fat and are a great metabolism booster.

BLACK AND BLUE

Two great berries combine in one fine juice that, in addition to its antioxidant benefits, is believed to have a beneficial effect on mood.

INGREDIENTS

1 cup blueberries

1 cup blackberries

¼ lemon, peeled

Yields: 1 cup

Per 1 cup serving • Calories: 150 • Fat: 1.2g • Protein: 3.2g • Sodium: 3.2mg • Sugar: 22g • Carbohydrates: 36g

1. Process the berries and lemon though your juicer according to the manufacturer's directions.

2. Serve the juice alone or over ice.

BLACKBERRY BOOSTER

Blackberries are rich in anti-inflammatory agents, which are great for conditions such as arthritis. They also help reduce puffy eyes and skin.

INGREDIENTS

2 cups blackberries

1 cup blueberries

½ cup raspberries

Yields: 1½ cups

Per 1 cup serving • Calories: 155 • Fat: 1.2g • Protein: 3.7g • Sodium: 3mg • Sugar: 18g • Carbohydrates: 38g

1. Process the blackberries through an electronic juicer according to the manufacturer's directions.

2. Add the blueberries and raspberries.

3. Stir or shake the juice to combine the ingredients and enjoy!

Blackberry Benefits

The high tannin content of blackberries helps tighten tissue, relieve intestinal inflammation, and reduce hemorrhoids and stomach disorders.

BLUEBERRY BLAST

Food scientists agree that blueberries are packed with antioxidants, phytoflavonoids, potassium, and vitamin C. Not only can they lower your risk of heart disease and cancer, but they are also anti-inflammatory. Many doctors believe inflammation is the underlying cause for many diseases, so it only makes sense to stop them before they start!

INGREDIENTS

1 cup blueberries

2 large carrots, trimmed

½ cup fresh pineapple chunks

Yields: 1½ cups

Per 1 cup serving • Calories: 130 • Fat: 0.4g • Protein: 2.4g • Sodium: 55mg • Sugar: 22g • Carbohydrates: 32g

1. Following the juicer manufacturer's instructions, process the blueberries, carrots, and pineapple in any order you wish.

2. Stir or shake the juice to blend completely, adding ice as desired.

3. Drink as soon as possible after blending.

Out of Season?

Are blueberries not in season where you live? Not a problem. Frozen blueberries pack the same nutritional punch as fresh.

BLUEBERRY RASPBERRY BLEND

As is true for many other areas of health, when it comes to reducing high blood pressure, it's the berries! In addition to their high levels of antioxidants, berries contain flavonoids, which have been found to decrease the risk of hypertension by as much as 25 percent.

INGREDIENTS

1 cup blueberries

1 cup raspberries

Yields: 1 cup

Per 1 cup serving • Calories: 148 • Fat: 1.2g • Protein: 2.5g • Sodium: 2.7mg • Sugar: 20g • Carbohydrates: 36g

Process the berries through your juicer according to the manufacturer's directions. Serve immediately and enjoy!

CITRUS BLUEBERRY BLEND

If you prefer a less tart juice and want more of the blueberry flavor to come through, use another orange and only half the grapefruit. If you prefer a more tart juice, use white grapefruit.

INGREDIENTS

1 cup blueberries

2 oranges, peeled

1 pink grapefruit, peeled

Yields: 1 cup

Per 1 cup serving • Calories: 238 • Fat: 1g • Protein: 4g • Sodium: 1.5mg • Sugar: 46g • Carbohydrates: 60g

1. Process the fruits through the feed tube of an electronic juicer according to the manufacturer's directions, in any order you wish.

2. Drink as soon as possible after preparation.

Grapefruit and Dieters

Adding grapefruit to your diet is believed to assist in weight loss through an enzyme that acts with protein to regulate insulin levels and control hunger pangs. One study funded by the Florida Department of Citrus found that the addition of a half grapefruit or 4 ounces of juice with meals resulted in an average weight loss of more than three pounds in twelve weeks, with some participants losing as much as ten pounds.

THE OTHER BERRIES

Mulberries are an excellent source of iron, which is a rare feature among berries, while the gooseberry, like its cousin the currant, has significantly high amounts of the phenolic phytochemicals that have been found to have beneficial effects against cancer, aging, inflammation, and neurological diseases.

INGREDIENTS

2 cups mulberries

2 cups gooseberries

Yields: 1½ cups

Per 1 cup serving • Calories: 168 • Fat: 1.9g • Protein: 4.4g • Sodium: 20mg • Sugar: 15g • Carbohydrates: 39g

1. Process the berries through an electronic juicer according to the manufacturer's directions.

2. Mix the juice to combine the ingredients and serve alone or over ice.

Mulberries

Scientific studies have shown that consumption of mulberries has potential health effects against cancer, aging and neurological diseases, inflammation, diabetes, and bacterial infections. Although more than 100 species of mulberries exist, the top three are the white mulberry, native to eastern and central China; the red or American mulberry, native to the eastern United States; and the black mulberry, native to western Asia.

CHERRIES, CRANBERRIES, AND GRAPES

CHERRY CUCUMBER COOLER

In addition to being terrific for encouraging longer, stronger hair and nails, cherries hold a number of benefits for the eyes, including helping to prevent cataracts and macular degeneration.

INGREDIENTS

1 cucumber, peeled

2 cups sweet cherries, pitted

2 celery stalks, with leaves

Yields: 1½ cups

Per 1 cup serving • Calories: 162 • Fat: 0.2g • Protein: 2.8g • Sodium: 70mg • Sugar: 23g • Carbohydrates: 40g

1. Process the cucumber through your electronic juicer according to the manufacturer's directions.

2. Add the cherries.

3. Add the celery.

4. Stir or shake the juice thoroughly to combine and serve over ice.

All about Lutein

Cherries are rich in lutein, which is known to promote cardiovascular and eye health, and it's also a powerful antioxidant. A great nonfruit source of lutein is eggs, and some researchers believe that it is best absorbed with a meal that contains some fats. So have this one for breakfast with a little extra butter on your toast!

CHERRY PEACH SHAKE

Be sure to use "cling free" varieties of white or yellow peaches for easier pitting and more juice.

INGREDIENTS

½ cup sweet cherries

1 orange, peeled

1 peach, pitted

1 nectarine, pitted

Yields: 1 cup

Per 1 cup serving • Calories: 201 • Fat: 1g • Protein: 4g • Sodium: 0g • Sugar: 39g • Carbohydrates: 49g

1. Process the fruits through an electronic juicer in any order you wish.

2. Mix the juice thoroughly and drink immediately after preparation.

Popular Peaches

These fruits have been a summertime favorite ever since the Spaniards first brought them to North America. Today, California, Georgia, and South Carolina are the biggest peach producers in the United States. They are rich in niacin, vitamin C, vitamin A, and lutein.

CHERRY WATERMELON COMBO

Sour cherries can be used in this recipe as well, but do add a spoonful of raw honey for sweetness.

INGREDIENTS

1 cup watermelon chunks

1 cup pitted cherries

½ lime, peeled

Yields: 1 cup

Per 1 cup serving • Calories: 152 • Fat: 0.6g • Protein: 2.7g • Sodium: 2mg • Sugar: 29g • Carbohydrates: 39g

Process the fruits in any order through an electronic juicer according to the manufacturer's directions. Serve juice immediately.

Life's a Bowl of Cherries?

When it comes to powerful superfoods, cherries are chock-full of life-giving elements. They are loaded with antioxidants, vitamins, and compounds that help with weight loss. Nutritionists claim they can even prevent heart disease and improve mental functioning, too. The melatonin they contain plays a big role in protecting skin from the effects of the sun and helps prevent aging.

CRANBERRY CITRUS PUNCH

If this one's too tart for your taste buds, try sweetening it with a little raw honey.

INGREDIENTS

3 cups cranberries, fresh or frozen

3 oranges, peeled

2 pink grapefruits, peeled

2 limes, peeled

Yields: 1½ cups

Per 1 cup serving • Calories: 363 • Fat: 1.0g
• Protein: 5.5g • Sodium: 9mg • Sugar: 34g
• Carbohydrates: 96g

1. Process the cranberries through an electronic juicer according to the manufacturer's directions.

2. Add the orange sections, followed by the grapefruits and limes.

3. Mix the juice thoroughly and enjoy over ice if desired.

Cranberry Facts

Cranberries contain some specific phytonutrients that just can't be found anywhere else. Plus, researchers have discovered that isolated phytonutrients in cranberries do not account for the same degree of health benefit as the same phytonutrients taken as a group. What it means is that the whole cranberry best supports your health, especially the urinary tract, as an anti-inflammatory and for help in the prevention of kidney and gallstones.

CRANAPPLE MAGIC

Why buy bottled when you can make this yourself?

INGREDIENTS

¾ cup cranberries

3 medium carrots, trimmed

2 apples, cored

Yields: 1½ cups

Per 1 cup serving • Calories: 219 • Fat: 0.5g
• Protein: 2.8g • Sodium: 83mg • Sugar: 37g
• Carbohydrates: 56g

1. Process the cranberries through an electronic juicer according to the manufacturer's directions.

2. Add the carrots and the apples.

3. Mix the juice thoroughly and serve.

Craving Cranberries?

Scientists have discovered that cranberries contain an amazing array of phytonutrients that include flavonoids, phenolic acids, and anthocyanins, all powerful antioxidants that help prevent cancer and infections, and may help to prevent ailments such as stomach ulcers.

CRANBERRY PEAR COCKTAIL

Delish! Tart cranberries are perfectly offset by the mild sweetness of pears, while ginger adds a spicy note.

INGREDIENTS

3 Anjou pears, cored

1 cup fresh or frozen cranberries

½" ginger, peeled

Dash of cinnamon

Yields: 1 cup

Per 1 cup serving • Calories: 322 • Fat: 1g •
Protein: 2.5g • Sodium: 8mg • Sugar: 47g •
Carbohydrates: 84g

1. Process the pears through an electronic juicer according to the manufacturer's directions.

2. Add the cranberries, followed by the ginger and the cinnamon.

3. Whisk or shake the juice to combine the ingredients and serve alone or over ice.

CRASBERRY JUICE

Apples, raspberries, and cranberries combine in this tart and tempting refresher.

INGREDIENTS

2 apples, cored

1 cup raspberries

1 cup fresh cranberries

Raw honey to taste, if desired

Yields: 1 cup

Per 1 cup serving • Calories: 264 • Fat: 1.3g
• Protein: 2.7g • Sodium: 3mg • Sugar: 41g
• Carbohydrates: 67g

1. Process the apples through an electronic juicer according to the manufacturer's directions.

2. Add the raspberries and cranberries. Taste the juice and add the honey if desired.

3. Whisk or shake the juice to combine the ingredients and serve alone or over ice.

Cranberries—Not Just for Thanksgiving Anymore

Though they make their appearance in markets right around Thanksgiving, fresh cranberries are available throughout the autumn. Indulge in a few bags and freeze them, with no loss of nutritional value.

THREE-GRAPE JUICE

When it comes to fruit juicing, little can compare with plain old grapes! This trio provides a nice balance of flavor, as the white and red grapes balance the more intense Concords.

INGREDIENTS

1 cup Concord grapes

1 cup red globe grapes

1 cup white or green seedless grapes

Yields: 1½ cups

Per 1 cup serving • Calories: 180 • Fat: 0.5g
• Protein: 1.8g • Sodium: 5mg • Sugar: 41g
• Carbohydrates: 47g

1. Process the grapes in any order through an electronic juicer according to the manufacturer's directions.

2. Serve alone or over ice.

Great Grapes

Regarded in many cultures as "the queen of fruits," grapes are incredibly rich in phytonutrients, antioxidants, vitamins, and minerals and are a rich source of micronutrient minerals like copper, iron, and manganese.

GRAPEBERRY COCKTAIL

Grapes are rich in the phytochemical resveratrol, a powerful antioxidant, which has been found to play a protective role against cancers of the colon and prostate, heart disease, degenerative nerve disease, Alzheimer's disease, and viral/fungal infections. Not only that, but it has marvelous benefits for aging skin and is a key ingredient in many anti-aging cosmetics.

INGREDIENTS

3 cups Concord grapes

1 medium apple, cored

½ cup blackberries

Yields: 1 cup

Per 1 cup serving • Calories: 420 • Fat: 1.2g • Protein: 4.5g • Sodium: 10mg • Sugar: 89g • Carbohydrates: 109g

1. Process the grapes through an electronic juicer according to the manufacturer's directions.

2. Add the apple, followed by the blackberries.

3. Mix the juice thoroughly and enjoy!

All about Blackberries

Blackberries help to lower your risk of heart disease and stroke, and they may lower your risk of certain cancers. Blackberries may also help to prevent diabetes and age-related cognitive decline. When choosing blackberries, be sure they don't have the hulls or green leaves attached. If they do, it means they were picked too early and they will not ripen after they have been picked.

CITRUS

TWIN CITRUS

One story of the clementine's origin is that it was an accidental hybrid said to have been discovered by Father Clément Rodier in the garden of his orphanage in Algeria around 1900, but there is evidence that these fruits were grown in China centuries earlier.

INGREDIENTS

3 large Valencia oranges, peeled

4–5 clementines, peeled

Yields: 1½ cups

Per 1 cup serving • Calories: 234 • Fat: 1.1g • Protein: 4.6g • Sodium: 2mg • Sugar: 22g • Carbohydrates: 58g

1. Process the fruit in any order through an electronic juice processor according to the manufacturer's directions.

2. Serve immediately.

What's the Difference?

Tangerines tend to be tarter than clementines and have seeds, while clementines do not. The smaller clementines also have less acid and so might be the better choice for those who are sensitive to the acids in citrus fruits.

GRAPPLE JUICE

Grapefruit, apple, and pineapple combine with watermelon for scrumptious results!

INGREDIENTS

1 large grapefruit, peeled

1 apple, cored

2 cups fresh pineapple chunks

1 large slice watermelon, or 1½ cups watermelon chunks

Yields: 2 cups

Per 1 cup serving • Calories: 217 • Fat: 0.7g • Protein: 2.9g • Sodium: 3.7mg • Sugar: 44g • Carbohydrates: 56g

1. Process the grapefruit through an electronic juicer according to the manufacturer's directions.

2. Add the apple, followed by the pineapple and the watermelon.

3. Mix or shake ingredients to blend and serve over ice.

Juice Yields

Yields for fresh juices can vary by as much as 4–5 ounces, depending on the efficiency of your juicer.

CITRUS SURPRISE

The surprise is that citrus pairs amazingly well with the bit of ginger in this recipe. It's best to peel larger limes, but when using smaller, thin-skinned Mexican limes, peeling isn't necessary.

INGREDIENTS

1 pink grapefruit, peeled

2 large oranges, peeled

2 medium limes, or 6 Mexican limes

1½" ginger, peeled

Yields: 1½ cups

Per 1 cup serving • Calories: 172 • Fat: 0.7g • Protein: 2.1g • Sodium: 4.8mg • Sugar: 17g • Carbohydrates: 47g

1. Process the grapefruit through an electronic juicer according to the manufacturer's directions.

2. Add the orange segments, followed by the limes and the ginger.

3. Serve immediately over ice if desired.

Mexican Limes

There's a lot of overlap in the world of limes. Mexican limes are, like key limes, smaller and somewhat tarter in flavor than regular limes. Traditional key limes were grown in Florida, but are now also grown in Mexico! If you're using larger limes for this recipe, do peel them to avoid adding any bitterness to the flavor. Smaller limes have thin peels and little of the bitter pith, so peeling is not necessary.

LEMON-LIME ADE

A classic that will have you wanting to set up your own sidewalk stand!

INGREDIENTS

3 lemons, peeled

6 Mexican limes

1 tablespoon raw honey

6 ounces water

Yields: 1½ cups

Per 1 cup serving • Calories: 119 • Fat: 0.4g
• Protein: 1.3g • Sodium: 7mg • Sugar: 13.6g
• Carbohydrates: 36g

1. Process the lemons and limes through an electronic juicer according to the manufacturer's directions.

2. Add the honey and the water to the juice and stir to combine.

3. Serve over ice.

HONEY ORANGE DEW

This juice is a great source of vitamin C. Honeydew melons are available year-round. When they are perfectly ripe, the skin is wrinkled.

INGREDIENTS

½ honeydew melon, peeled

½ cup watermelon, peeled

½ orange, peeled

Yields: 1½ cups

Per 1 cup serving • Calories: 189 • Fat: 0.7g
• Protein: 3g • Sodium: 77mg • Sugar: 42g •
Carbohydrates: 47.7g

1. Process the melons and orange through an electronic juicer according to the manufacturer's directions.

2. Serve the juice alone or over ice.

OJ TANGO

Orange juice is packed full of vitamins and antioxidants, but it's given an extra kick of nutrition when it's paired with tangerines.

INGREDIENTS

3 large Valencia oranges, peeled

3 tangerines, peeled

Yields: 1½ cups

Per 1 cup serving • Calories: 219 • Fat: 1.7g
• Protein: 4.5g • Sodium: 0mg • Sugar: 24g
• Carbohydrates: 59g

1. Process the fruit in any order through an electronic juice processor according to the manufacturer's directions.

2. Serve immediately.

ORANGE BONANZA

This juice will help lower your blood pressure, improve your mood, and sweep out toxins while shedding those pounds.

INGREDIENTS

2 small sugar beets, trimmed and tailed

2 large oranges, peeled

½ lemon, peeled

1 large carrot, trimmed

2 cups spinach

2 celery stalks with leaves

1" ginger, peeled

Yields: 2 cups

Per 1 cup serving • Calories: 134 • Fat: 0.6g
• Protein: 4.4g • Sodium: 162mg • Sugar:
20g • Carbohydrates: 32g

1. Process the beets through an electronic juicer according to the manufacturer's directions.

2. Add the orange segments, followed by the lemon.

3. Process the carrot, then add the spinach and celery. Add the ginger.

4. Whisk the juice to combine ingredients. Serve immediately.

ORANGE GINGER ALE

Add sparkling water or seltzer to this one for that bubbly, festive feeling!

INGREDIENTS

3 oranges, peeled

1" ginger, or to taste, peeled

¾ cup seltzer or sparkling water

Yields: 1½ cups

Per 1 cup serving • Calories: 186 • Fat: 0.4g
• Protein: 3.7g • Sodium: 0.3mg • Sugar: 37g
• Carbohydrates: 46g

1. Process the oranges and the ginger through an electronic juicer according to the manufacturer's directions.

2. Add the seltzer or sparkling water and serve over ice.

ORANGE SPINACH DELIGHT

Definitely a delightful combo, the greens take a back seat to the lively fresh taste of the orange in this recipe.

INGREDIENTS

4 oranges, peeled

2 cups fresh spinach

1 cup parsley

Yields: 1½ cups

Per 1 cup serving • Calories: 188 • Fat: 0.9g
• Protein: 5.6g • Sodium: 54mg • Sugar: 33g
• Carbohydrates: 45g

1. Process the oranges through an electronic juicer according to the manufacturer's directions.

2. Add the spinach and parsley.

3. Mix the juice to combine the ingredients and serve over ice.

Ask an Athlete
Many professional athletes praise the power of parsley to boost performance. So if your juice fast has left you feeling a little low on energy, be sure to throw a handful into your fasting favorites.

SATSUMA FENNEL TREAT

Satsuma, or honey citrus, is a small mandarin orange that becomes widely available from October through Christmas.

INGREDIENTS

3 satsuma, peeled

½ fennel bulb

¼ lemon or lime, peeled

Yields: 1 cup

Per 1 cup serving • Calories: 161 • Fat: 1g • Protein: 3.5g • Sodium: 65mg • Sugar: 24g • Carbohydrates: 40g

1. Process the satsuma segments through an electronic juicer according to the manufacturer's directions.

2. Add the fennel bulb, followed by the lemon or lime.

3. Mix the juice thoroughly to combine the ingredients and serve alone or over ice.

How to Choose the Best Satsuma

Choose fruit that is small but heavy for its size for the greatest juice yield. Satsuma is prone to mold, so store in the refrigerator.

TANGERINE TANGO

It's called the tango because it only takes two—tangerines and oranges—to make this spectacular juice.

INGREDIENTS

2–3 tangerines, peeled

1 large orange, peeled

Yields: 1 cup

Per 1 cup serving • Calories: 125 • Fat: 0.5g • Protein: 2g • Sodium: 3mg • Sugar: 25g • Carbohydrates: 31g

1. Process the fruits through an electronic juicer according to the manufacturer's directions.

2. Serve immediately.

Tangerine Temptation

Tangerines are in the mandarin family. They're easy to peel, wonderfully sweet and highly nutritious. People who have a difficult time digesting oranges can find tangerines easier on the system, too. One small tangerine can have more vitamin C than a large orange, and they help to prevent heart disease, are anti-inflammatory, improve eyesight, help relieve arthritis, and can be an aid in preventing certain cancers such as breast cancer and melanoma.

TROPICAL SUNRISE

Beautiful color and fabulous flavor will have you dreaming of the islands . . .

INGREDIENTS

2 oranges, peeled

1 Ruby Red grapefruit, peeled

¾ cup pineapple chunks

¾ cup strawberries

Yields: 2 cups

Per 1 cup serving • Calories: 155 • Fat: 0.5g
• Protein: 2.5g • Sodium: 2.4mg • Sugar: 21g
• Carbohydrates: 40g

1. Process the oranges and the grapefruit through an electronic juicer according to the manufacturer's directions.

2. Add the pineapple, followed by the strawberries.

3. Whisk or shake the juice to combine the ingredients and serve alone or over ice.

Strawberry Facts

In a recent study, researchers ranked strawberries third among all U.S. foods—including spices, seasonings, fruits, and vegetables—for their antioxidant qualities.

UGLI FRUIT JUICE

Ugli fruit, native to Jamaica, gets its name from the unattractive, pockmarked, thick skin. Ugli fruits range in color from pale green to dark orange. They are similar in size to a grapefruit and shaped like a pear. The citrusy flavor lends itself to juicing and has been a Jamaican favorite for hundreds of years.

INGREDIENTS

2 ugli fruit, peeled and segmented

Yields: 2 cups

Per 1 cup serving • Calories: 180 • Fat: 0g •
Protein: 4g • Sodium: 0mg • Sugar: 32g •
Carbohydrates: 44g

1. Process the fruits through an electronic juicer according to the manufacturer's directions.

2. Serve immediately.

Ugli Fruit

Ugli fruit can be cultivated or grown wild. It is said that this fruit comes from the accidental crossing of a Seville orange, a tangerine, and a grapefruit, so be careful where you spit your seeds! An excellent source of vitamin C, ugli fruit also promotes oral health and fights cardiovascular disease. Some sources indicate it also protects against kidney stone formation.

MELONS, PEACHES, AND PINEAPPLES

CANTALOUPE CINNAMON COOLER

On a juice fast, you can treat yourself to a whole melon without guilt!

INGREDIENTS

1 whole cantaloupe

½ teaspoon cinnamon

Yields: 2 cups

Per 1 cup serving • Calories: 140 • Fat: 0.8g
• Protein: 3.4g • Sodium: 65mg • Sugar: 30g
• Carbohydrates: 34g

1. Peel and seed the melon, then cut it into chunks.

2. Process the melon chunks through an electronic juicer according to the manufacturer's directions.

3. Add the cinnamon and mix. Serve the juice alone or over ice.

MELLOW MELON JUICE

Watermelon and cantaloupe, or muskmelon, have been shown to significantly reduce problem blood pressure when consumed regularly.

INGREDIENTS

1 cup watermelon chunks

1 cup cantaloupe chunks

4–5 strawberries

Yields: 1 cup

Per 1 cup serving • Calories: 114 • Fat: 0.6g
• Protein: 2.5g • Sodium: 26mg • Sugar: 24g
• Carbohydrates: 27g

1. Process the fruits in any order through an electronic juicer according to the manufacturer's directions.

2. Serve the juice immediately over ice.

MINTY MELON CLEANSER

All melons are good for a cleanse, because of their high water content. Cantaloupe is especially good with its high carotene content.

INGREDIENTS

½ cantaloupe, peeled and seeded

¼ cup fresh mint leaves

¼ cup parsley

1 cup blueberries

Yields: 1½ cups

Per 1 cup serving • Calories: 159 • Fat: 1g • Protein: 3.8g • Sodium: 55mg • Sugar: 30g • Carbohydrates: 38g

1. Cut the melon into chunks and process through an electronic juicer according to the manufacturer's directions.

2. Roll the mint and parsley into balls to compress and add to the juicer.

3. Add the blueberries.

4. Whisk the juice together to combine ingredients and enjoy!

Always Use Alkaline

Juice from alkaline vegetables including carrots, tomatoes, parsley, spinach, kale, and celery helps detoxify the liver, kidneys, blood, and muscle tissue of toxins that have been accumulating for years.

NECTARINE COOLER

Like its close cousin the peach, nectarines originated in China and from there spread to Central Asia, Persia, and Europe via the ancient silk routes.

INGREDIENTS

4 nectarines, pitted

1 carrot, trimmed

1 orange, peeled

Yields: 1 cup

Per 1 cup serving • Calories: 318 • Fat: 1.9g • Protein: 7g • Sodium: 49mg • Sugar: 56g • Carbohydrates: 76g

1. Process the nectarines through your electronic juicer according to the manufacturer's directions.

2. Add the carrot, followed by the orange segments.

3. Stir or shake the juice thoroughly to combine the ingredients and serve.

PEACH PERFECTION

Peaches are a wonderful source of vitamin E, which is especially beneficial for the skin.

INGREDIENTS

2 peaches, pitted

2 apricots, pitted

½ cup green grapes

Yields: 1 cup

Per 1 cup serving • Calories: 187 • Fat: 1g • Protein: 3.8g • Sodium: 2mg • Sugar: 39g • Carbohydrates: 46g

1. Process the peaches through your electronic juicer according to the manufacturer's directions.

2. Add the apricots, followed by the grapes.

3. Stir or shake the juice thoroughly to combine the ingredients and serve.

All about Apricots

These much-prized fruits were first brought to Europe by Greeks, who called them "golden eggs of the sun." Sun-dried organic fruits have more concentrated nutrient values than fresh ones, although they have less vitamin C content.

PEACHY KEEN

Peaches, honeydew melon, and kiwi combine in this cool summer refresher.

INGREDIENTS

3 large peaches, pitted

4 kiwis

2 cups honeydew melon chunks, peeled and seeded

Yields: 2 cups

Per 1 cup serving • Calories: 241 • Fat: 2g • Protein: 3.4g • Sodium: 31mg • Sugar: 46g • Carbohydrates: 58g

1. Process the peaches through an electronic juicer according to the manufacturer's directions.

2. Add the kiwis, followed by the melon.

3. Whisk or shake the juice to combine the ingredients and serve alone or over ice.

A Honey of a Melon

Though not as rich in nutrients as cantaloupe, honeydew melon supplies thiamine, niacin, pantothenic acid, folate, and vitamin B_6, all of which are important for metabolism. Their high water content and subtle flavor make them an excellent choice for combining with other fruits for juicing.

PINEAPPLE CELERY COCKTAIL

Pineapple is not only rich in vitamin C, it contains powerful anti-inflammatory ingredients. That coupled with celery's excellent hydration make this an ideal après workout treat.

INGREDIENTS

3 (1") slices fresh pineapple, peeled

3 stalks celery, with leaves

Yields: 1 cup

Per 1 cup serving • Calories: 145 • Fat: 0.5g • Protein: 2g • Sodium: 98mg • Sugar: 27g • Carbohydrates: 36g

1. Process the pineapple chunks and celery through your juicer.

2. Serve the juice immediately.

More Than Meets the Eye

Although celery doesn't seem like a superfood, its health benefits are almost too lengthy to describe. The effects of celery on the body are diuretic, expectorant, carminative (gas-expelling), and anti-asthmatic, and celery also aids in digestion, lowers blood pressure, is calmative, and is believed to strengthen a weak sex drive.

PINEAPPLE CUCUMBER COMBO

Pineapple and cucumber are two of the best choices for juice to benefit skin, hair, and nails. If the cucumber flavor seems too strong, use an English cucumber, which has a less pronounced flavor.

INGREDIENTS

1 cup pineapple chunks

1 medium cucumber

Yields: 1 cup

Per 1 cup serving • Calories: 127 • Fat: 0.5g • Protein: 3g • Sodium: 8mg • Sugar: 21g • Carbohydrates: 32g

Process the pineapple and cucumber through an electronic juicer according to the manufacturer's directions. Serve immediately.

PINEAPPLE GRAPE JUICE

Sweet and satisfying, this recipe contains nutrients that are believed to especially benefit the skin and can even help prevent sunburn!

INGREDIENTS

1 cup pineapple chunks

1 bunch red grapes

Yields: 1½ cups

Per 1 cup serving • Calories: 175 • Fat: 1.4g
• Protein: 1.9g • Sodium: 1.1mg • Sugar: 41g
• Carbohydrates: 46g

1. Process the pineapple and the grapes through an electronic juicer according to the manufacturer's directions.

2. Stir the juice to combine the ingredients and serve over ice.

PINEAPPLE MANGO

This tropical refresher is great for the skin!

INGREDIENTS

1 mango, peeled

1 cup pineapple chunks

Yields: 1 ½ cups

Per 1 cup serving • Calories: 111 • Fat: 0.6g
• Protein: 0.5g • Sodium: 0.8mg • Sugar:
9.6g • Carbohydrates: 28g

1. Process the fruits through an electronic juicer in any order according to the manufacturer's directions.

2. Stir the juice to combine the ingredients and serve alone or over ice.

How to Choose a Pineapple

Choose a pineapple that is a bit soft to the touch. The leaves should be green with no brown spots. If overripe, it will have soft spots on the skin; if underripe, it will ripen at room temperature over a few days' time.

PINEAPPLE PAPAYA POTION

For a delicious complexion, use the leftover fruit pulp from this juice as a face mask. Leave it on for 10 minutes or until slightly sticky, rinse well, and pat dry.

INGREDIENTS

1 cup pineapple, peeled

½ cup strawberries

½ papaya, seeds removed

Yields: 1 cup

Per 1 cup serving • Calories: 135 • Fat: 0.5g • Protein: 1.8g • Sodium: 4.6mg • Sugar: 24g • Carbohydrates: 34g

1. Process the pineapple chunks through your electronic juicer according to the manufacturer's directions.

2. Add the strawberries.

3. Add the papaya.

4. Stir or shake the juice thoroughly to combine and serve alone or over ice.

Papaya

Papaya contains many of the same enzymes found in pineapple, and hold many of the same benefits for the skin, so this recipe packs a double punch!

WATERMELON FAST

Some juicers swear by the effectiveness of single-ingredient, one-day fasts for cleansing the system, losing weight, and restoring the body's alkaline balance. Many favor watermelon for its ability to hydrate, and keep you feeling full while at the same time flushing away toxins.

INGREDIENTS

5–6-pound watermelon, divided into thirds

Yields: 6¾ cups (3 servings)

Per 1 cup serving • Calories: 121 • Fat: 0.6g • Protein: 2.5g • Sodium: 4mg • Sugar: 25g • Carbohydrates: 30g

Juice only one third of the watermelon for breakfast, lunch, and dinner. Consume each portion immediately after juicing.

WATERMELON ORANGE JUICE

This delicious juice reduces cravings for sugary snacks and is great for dumping excess water weight.

INGREDIENTS

2 cups watermelon chunks

1 large orange, peeled

Yield: 1½ cups

Per 1 cup serving • Calories: 102 • Fat: 0.4g • Protein: 2g • Sodium: 2mg • Sugar: 21g • Carbohydrates: 26g

1. Process the fruits through an electronic juicer according to the manufacturer's directions.

2. Serve alone or over ice.

WATERMELON PEAR COCKTAIL

Beautifully refreshing, this juice is the perfect choice for a lazy summer afternoon. For added nutrition, you could throw in a handful of blackberries.

INGREDIENTS

2 Anjou or Comice pears, cored

4 cups watermelon chunks

Yields: 2½ cups (2 servings)

Per 1¼ cup serving • Calories: 191 • Fat: 0.5g • Protein: 2.8g • Sodium: 3mg • Sugar: 35g • Carbohydrates: 49g

1. Process the fruits in any order through an electronic juicer according to the manufacturer's directions.

2. Serve alone or over ice.

Strapped for Space?

Small, seedless "personal-sized" watermelons are becoming increasingly available in produce markets for those of you with smaller households or limited refrigerator space.

RASPBERRIES AND STRAWBERRIES

RASPBERRY APPLE SNACK

Though red raspberries are the most common variety, raspberries can be either red, purple, gold, or black, with the golden variety ranking as the sweetest of all!

INGREDIENTS

2 cups raspberries

2 apples, cored

1 lime, peeled

Yields: 1½ cups

Per 1 cup serving • Calories: 225 • Fat: 1.5g • Protein: 2.6g • Sodium: 4mg • Sugar: 32.5g • Carbohydrates: 58g

1. Process the berries through an electronic juicer according to the manufacturer's directions.

2. Add the apples, followed by the lime.

3. Whisk or shake the juice to combine ingredients and serve alone or over ice.

RASPBERRY PEACH PASSION

So good-tasting, you'll want some every day! Passion fruit is rich in fiber, potassium, and vitamins A and C.

INGREDIENTS

2 large peaches, pitted

1 cup raspberries

1 cup passion fruit pulp

Yields: 1½ cups

Per 1 cup serving • Calories: 249 • Fat: 1.6g • Protein: 5.8g • Sodium: 45mg • Sugar: 21g • Carbohydrates: 60g

1. Process the peaches through your electronic juicer according to the manufacturer's directions.

2. Add the raspberries, followed by the passion fruit.

3. Stir or shake the juice thoroughly to combine ingredients and serve over ice.

A Passion for Passion Fruit

Choose fruits that are well ripened, plump, and heavy for their size. Fruits with a lightly wrinkled skin are actually more flavorful. Scoop out the pulp and discard the tough shell.

ORANGE STRAWBERRY BANANA JUICE

Yum! Once you've made it yourself, you'll find there's just no comparison to the store-bought brand.

INGREDIENTS

1 large orange, peeled

1 cup strawberries

1 banana, peeled

Yields: 1½ cups

Per 1 cup serving • Calories: 142 • Fat: 0.7g • Protein: 2.3g • Sodium: 1.8mg • Sugar: 22.5g • Carbohydrates: 35.6g

1. Process the orange and the strawberries through an electronic juicer according to the manufacturer's directions.

2. Add the banana and transfer to a blender until the mixture is smooth. Serve immediately.

PAPAYA STRAWBERRY CLEANSE

Papaya is a great cleansing fruit and is good for people with liver problems, constipation, and urinary disorders.

INGREDIENTS

2 papayas

1 cup strawberries, hull intact

Yields: 1¼ cups

Per 1¼ cup serving • Calories: 261 • Fat: 0.4g • Protein: 0.8g • Sodium: 33mg • Sugar: 34g • Carbohydrates: 70g

1. Process the papayas and strawberries through your electronic juicer according to the manufacturer's directions.

2. Stir together and enjoy!

What Is Papain?

Papayas contain papain, a digestive enzyme that is used in meat tenderizers to break down tough meat fibers. South Americans have used papain to tenderize meat for centuries, and it is now available in powdered meat tenderizers all over the world. Papaya is a very good source of vitamins A and C.

STRAWBERRY TOMATO TEMPTATION

This one may seem like an unusual combination of flavors, but it's terrific!

INGREDIENTS

1 cup strawberries

3 medium tomatoes

¼ cup fresh basil leaves

Yields: 1 cup

Per 1 cup serving • Calories: 97 • Fat: 1g • Protein: 3.5g • Sodium: 15mg • Sugar: 14g • Carbohydrates: 22g

1. Process the berries through an electronic juicer according to the manufacturer's directions.

2. Add the tomatoes, followed by the basil leaves.

3. Serve in a chilled glass, or over ice as desired.

Lycopene

Tomatoes are among the richest natural sources of lycopene, a powerful antioxidant that not only is useful in fighting cancer, but is believed to help prevent hardening of the arteries.

ASSORTED FRUIT JUICES

CACTUS JUICE

The aloe vera plant is widely known for its topical benefits for the skin, but it has internal benefits as well. Egyptian papyrus writings told of Egyptian queens who associated aloe with their physical beauty, while Greek and Roman doctors routinely used it in their practices to heal a wide range of ailments.

INGREDIENTS

2 large fronds aloe vera

2 prickly pears, spines removed

1 orange, peeled

Yields: 1 cup

Per 1 cup serving • Calories: 198 • Fat: 1g • Protein: 3g • Sodium: 18mg • Sugar: 6g • Carbohydrates: 41g

1. Process the aloe through your electronic juicer according to the manufacturer's directions.

2. Add the prickly pears.

3. Add the orange segments.

4. Stir or shake the juice thoroughly to combine and serve immediately.

More about Aloe

Choose the largest fronds available when juicing aloe and be sure to consume your juice immediately. Even when stabilized by additional vitamin C as in the recipe here, it will go rancid fast. Dog owners should also use caution, as the plant can be toxic for dogs.

FIG HEAVEN

Fresh figs are valuable for controlling hypertension and lowering blood sugar. And of course, the ancient Romans always included them at their banquets as essential to good digestion!

INGREDIENTS

10 fresh figs, halved

½ cup pomegranate pips, white pith removed

1 cup honeydew melon chunks

Yields: 1½ cups

Per 1 cup serving • Calories: 405 • Fat: 2.1g • Protein: 4.8g • Sodium: 26mg • Sugar: 86.5g • Carbohydrates: 103g

1. Process the figs through an electronic juicer according to the manufacturer's directions.

2. Add the pomegranate pips, followed by the melon.

3. Whisk or shake the juice to combine the ingredients and serve alone or over ice.

More about Figs

Fresh figs are rich in polyphenolic flavonoid antioxidants such as carotenes, lutein, tannins, and chlorogenic acid. Their antioxidant value is comparable to that of apples.

GRAPEFRUIT WATERCRESS DELIGHT

Watercress was discovered in a recent study to be of special benefit to smokers in reducing DNA damage to white blood cells.

INGREDIENTS

2 grapefruits, peeled

½ cup watercress

3 to 4 sprigs of parsley

Yields: 1½ cups

Per 1 cup serving • Calories: 162 • Fat: 0.03g • Protein: 3g • Sodium: 6mg • Sugar: 27g • Carbohydrates: 43g

1. Process the grapefruits through an electronic juicer according to the manufacturer's directions.

2. Add the watercress and parsley.

3. Serve the juice alone or over ice.

GUAVA JIVE

The more you eat of the ripened guava or its freshly extracted juice, the more health benefits you gain. Experts know the reddish-fleshed guava contains more nutrients than the white, so extract your juice from the pinkish or reddish-fleshed guava.

INGREDIENTS

2 guavas, peeled

1 cup watermelon chunks

2 cups pineapple chunks

Yields: 1½ cups

Per 1 cup serving • Calories: 190 • Fat: 1.1g • Protein: 3.7g • Sodium: 5mg • Sugar: 34g • Carbohydrates: 47g

1. Process the guava through an electronic juicer according to the manufacturer's directions.

2. Add the watermelon, followed by the pineapple.

3. Mix the juice to combine the ingredients and serve over ice.

Choosing Guava

Guavas, like melons, smell fresh and fruity when they are ripe. Choose fruit that is heavy for its size.

JICAMA JUICE

Jicama, or yam bean, is an excellent source of oligofructose inulin, a soluble dietary fiber. Inulin is a zero-calorie, sweet inert carbohydrate and does not metabolize in the human body, which makes this juice an ideal sweet snack for diabetics and dieters, because it helps you feel fuller, longer.

INGREDIENTS

1 whole jicama

2 cups spinach

½ medium beet

½ lemon, peeled

1 medium orange, peeled

Yields: 1 cup

Per 1 cup serving • Calories: 223 • Fat: 0.8g • Protein: 6g • Sodium: 94mg • Sugar: 19g • Carbohydrates: 52g

1. Process the jicama through an electronic juicer according to the manufacturer's directions.

2. Add the spinach.

3. Add the beet, followed by the lemon and orange segments.

4. Whisk or shake the juice to combine ingredients and serve over ice, if desired.

MANGO TEA

The fresh juice of mango mixed with an herbal tea of your choice provides a really great tasting tea that's good for detoxing.

INGREDIENTS

½ mango, peeled and seeded

1 cup hot water

1 herbal tea bag

Yields: 1¼ cups

Per 1 cup serving • Calories: 50 • Fat: 0.3g • Protein: 0.7g • Sodium: 6mg • Sugar: 11g • Carbohydrates: 12.5g

1. Process the mango through an electronic juicer according to the manufacturer's directions.

2. Pour water over the tea bag and let steep for 2 minutes.

3. Add ¼ cup mango juice to the tea and stir.

Herbal Teas

Herbal teas have been around for many years and have been used to treat a variety of health problems. They are also known for their earthy taste and soothing effect. There is a wide variety of herbal teas available on the market, some especially recommended for the detoxification process. As well as being delicious and nutritious, herbal teas are often caffeine-free.

PLUM DELICIOUS

This juice is rich in selenium, silica, and resveratrol—all essentials for beautiful skin.

INGREDIENTS

2 cups red seedless grapes

2 red or black plums, pitted

½ large cucumber

Yields: 1½ cups

Per 1 cup serving • Calories: 194 • Fat: 0.7g • Protein: 2.7g • Sodium: 6mg • Sugar: 41g • Carbohydrates: 50g

1. Process the grapes through an electronic juicer according to the manufacturer's directions.

2. Add the plums, followed by the cucumber.

3. Stir or shake the juice to combine ingredients and enjoy!

PRICKLY PEAR COCKTAIL

Prickly pears are also known as cactus pears. These small, egg-shaped fruits contain edible seeds and are rich in a wide variety of phytonutrients and vitamin C. Be sure to peel your pears before you use them, as the rind is not digestible.

INGREDIENTS

2 prickly pears, peeled

3 medium carrots, trimmed

1 cup red grapes

Yields: 1 cup

Per 1 cup serving • Calories: 250 • Fat: 1.5g • Protein: 4g • Sodium: 116mg • Sugar: 30g • Carbohydrates: 61g

1. Process the prickly pears through your electronic juicer according to the manufacturer's directions.

2. Add the carrots, followed by the grapes.

3. Stir or shake the juice thoroughly to combine and serve immediately.

Beautiful Beta-Carotene

Vitamin A in the form of beta-carotene is a pigment that protects the health of your eyes and skin.

POMEGRANATE POWER

Some scholars believe Eve actually ate a pomegranate she plucked from the tree of knowledge in the Garden of Eden, not an apple. Ancient Egyptians buried the dead with pomegranates because they believed that those who ate the fruit would be blessed with eternal life.

INGREDIENTS

4 pomegranates, peeled

½ lemon, peeled

2 tablespoons raw honey

Yields: 1 cup

Per 1 cup serving • Calories: 426 • Fat: 4g • Protein: 6g • Sodium: 12mg • Sugar: 83g • Carbohydrates: 101g

1. Process the peeled pomegranates through an electronic juicer according to the manufacturer's directions.

2. Add the lemon.

3. Add the honey to the resulting juice.

4. Whisk the juice until the honey is completely dissolved and enjoy!

Pomegranate Powers

Pomegranates are full of antioxidants, believed to prevent blood clots, and can lower levels of bad cholesterol. They're also good for the heart, and help fight prostate cancer and erectile dysfunction. When juicing, it's best to peel the fruits, taking care to remove the white portions, which can be bitter. Be sure to include the seeds, though, where some powerful nutrients are stored. If they seem tough to peel, score the rind and soak for 10 minutes in plain water.

CHAPTER 11

VEGETABLE JUICES

ARTICHOKE CILANTRO COCKTAIL

This juice uses Jerusalem artichokes, a root vegetable related to the sunflower family. Sometimes called sun chokes or earth apples, they can be found in organic and specialty markets. This is an intensely flavored juice, so add distilled water as desired.

INGREDIENTS

4 Jerusalem artichokes

1 bunch fresh cilantro, about 1 cup

4 large radishes, tailed and trimmed

3 medium carrots, trimmed

Yields: 1 cup

Per 1 cup serving • Calories: 303 • Fat: 0.5g • Protein: 8g • Sodium: 159mg • Sugar: 38g • Carbohydrates: 71g

1. Process the Jerusalem artichokes, one at a time, through your electronic juicer according to the manufacturer's directions.

2. Roll the cilantro into a ball to compress and add.

3. Add the radishes and carrots.

4. Mix the juice thoroughly to combine and serve over ice as desired.

Cilantrophobia

Cilantro is the fresh leaves of the coriander plant. Sometimes known as Chinese parsley, its strong aroma and unusual flavor tends to polarize opinion on its use as a seasoning. Food scientists believe that whether you like it or hate it may have something to do with genetics. Famous chef Julia Child was once quoted as saying she would just pick it out and throw it on the floor!

AVOCADO SMOOTHIE

Avocados don't juice well, but can be blended with fresh-pressed juice for an elegant smoothie. In hospitals, avocados are often blended with infant formula or breast milk and fed to premature infants with immature digestive systems to help build them up.

INGREDIENTS

2 leaves kale or Swiss chard, chopped

½ cup mango chunks

¼ avocado

½ cup coconut water

½ cup ice

Yields: 1½ cups

Per 1 cup serving • Calories: 281 • Fat: 5.3g • Protein: 2.5g • Sodium: 35mg • Sugar: 11g • Carbohydrates: 18g

1. Process the kale or Swiss chard and the mango chunks through an electronic juicer according to the manufacturer's directions.

2. Transfer the mixture to a blender and add the avocado, coconut water, and ice.

3. Blend until smooth.

The Awesome Avocado

Avocados contain more than 20 nutrients, are rich in vitamin K and monosaturated fats, and are thought to assist in reducing high blood pressure and bad cholesterol.

THE FRENCH CONNECTION

Fresh haricots vert, or green beans, are juiced and flavored with fresh tarragon in this elegant concoction.

INGREDIENTS

½ pound haricots vert

1 large cucumber

¼ cup fresh tarragon

3 scallions, trimmed

Yields: 1 cup

Per 1 cup serving • Calories: 91 • Fat: 0.7g • Protein: 5g • Sodium: 20mg • Sugar: 10g • Carbohydrates: 20g

1. Process the beans through an electronic juicer according to the manufacturer's directions.

2. Add the cucumber, followed by the tarragon and the scallions.

3. Whisk or shake the juice to combine the ingredients and serve over ice.

Bring on the Beans!

In addition to the protein that green beans provide, the antioxidant capacity of green beans has been shown to be greater than similar foods in the pea and bean families, for example, snow peas or winged beans.

GOLDEN GLOW

Yellow tomatoes, yellow summer squash, and yellow wax beans combine for a beautiful color and a mild, pleasing flavor.

INGREDIENTS

4 yellow pear tomatoes

1 yellow summer squash

1 cup fresh yellow wax beans

Yields: 1 cup

Per 1 cup serving • Calories: 232 • Fat: 1g •
Protein: 14g • Sodium: 59mg • Sugar: 8.5g •
Carbohydrates: 44g

1. Process the tomatoes through an electronic juicer according to the manufacturer's directions.

2. Add the squash, followed by the beans.

3. Stir the juice to combine the ingredients and serve alone or over ice.

Let the Sunshine In

Yellow fruits and vegetables are teeming with carotenoids and bioflavonoids, which are a class of plant pigments that function as antioxidants. Sunny-colored foods also have an abundance of vitamin C. These nutrients will help your heart, vision, digestion, and immune systems. Other benefits of naturally yellow foods include maintenance of healthy skin, wound healing, and stronger bones and teeth.

BEAN SPROUT BLISS

Simplicity itself, this light and lovely combination has powerful nutritional benefits.

INGREDIENTS

1 cup bean sprouts

2 stalks celery, with leaves

1 medium cucumber

Yields: 1 cup

Per 1 cup serving • Calories: 111 • Fat: 1.3g
• Protein: 10g • Sodium: 81mg • Sugar: 6.5g
• Carbohydrates: 20g

1. Process the bean sprouts and celery through an electronic juicer according to the manufacturer's directions.

2. Add the cucumber.

3. Mix the juice to combine the ingredients and serve over ice.

Why Sprouts Are So Healthy

As a seed sprouts, it activates many different metabolic systems. It converts some of its sugar content into vitamin C, to act as an anti-oxidant above the soil. It also begins to synthesize a variety of new enzymes, many of them necessary to handle oxygen metabolism.

BEET BLISS

Adding onion and garlic to this root veggie combo results in great flavor and extra nutrients, too!

INGREDIENTS

2 large carrots, trimmed

1 medium beet, trimmed and tailed

½ cup watercress

¼ cup red onion, peeled and chopped

1 clove garlic, peeled

Yields: 1 cup

Per 1 cup serving • Calories: 116 • Fat: 0.5g
• Protein: 3.6g • Sodium: 172mg • Sugar:
14g • Carbohydrates: 26g

1. Process the carrots, beet, and watercress through an electronic juicer according to the manufacturer's directions.

2. Add the onion and the garlic. Whisk or shake the juice to combine the ingredients and serve over ice.

For the Love of Garlic

Sautéed, fresh, or roasted, garlic is an excellent source of minerals, vitamins, and enzymes essential to good health. The bulbs are one of the richest sources of potassium, iron, calcium, magnesium, manganese, zinc, and selenium.

BERRY BEET SPECIAL

Substitute milk or yogurt for the water in this recipe for a smoothie variation.

INGREDIENTS

1 cup blueberries

½ cup strawberries

½ medium beet

1 large leaf rainbow chard

½ cup spring water

Yields: 1 cup

Per 1 cup serving • Calories: 131 • Fat: 0.8g • Protein: 2.8g • Sodium: 110mg • Sugar: 21g • Carbohydrates: 32g

1. Process the berries through an electronic juicer according to the manufacturer's directions.

2. Add the beet and the chard.

3. Whisk the juice together with the water to blend and enjoy!

THE BEET MASTER

Author Tom Robbins once described the beet as "the world's most serious vegetable." When it comes to all-around good health, increased energy, and healing powers, he might well have been right! Beet juice cleanses the liver and kidneys, helps lower blood pressure, and also helps to replenish the body's red blood cells.

INGREDIENTS

2 medium beets

2 apples, cored

1 medium orange, peeled

2 stalks celery, with leaves

Yields: 1 cup

Per 1 cup serving • Calories: 283 • Fat: 1g • Protein: 5g • Sodium: 191mg • Sugar: 54g • Carbohydrates: 70g

1. Scrub and trim the beets. Cut into chunks.

2. Process beet chunks through the feed tube of an electronic juicer according to the manufacturer's directions.

3. Cut the apples into chunks and add to the juicer, along with the orange and the celery.

4. Mix the juice thoroughly and serve over ice.

Sweeten It Up!

For best juicing results, use sugar beets, a hybrid beet that is sweeter than other varieties. Even at their best, however, beets can have an earthy flavor, and so are best combined with apples or carrots for a tastier juice.

BLUES BUSTER

Fasting can bring on some mood swings, so if you feel your good humor slipping away, try this.

INGREDIENTS

1 cup broccoli florets

½ cup spinach leaves

4 leaves Swiss chard

½ red bell pepper, seeded

Yields: 1 cup

Per 1 cup serving • Calories: 89 • Fat: 1g • Protein: 7g • Sodium: 339mg • Sugar: 6g • Carbohydrates: 17g

1. Process the broccoli through an electronic juicer according to the manufacturer's directions.

2. Add the spinach, followed by the chard.

3. Add the bell pepper.

4. Mix the juice thoroughly to combine the ingredients and serve alone or over ice.

SUPER SPROUT

Sprouts are milder in flavor, so if you don't like radishes, you can use radish sprouts instead, as sprouts don't significantly change the flavor of any of your juices. Further, most sprouts contain much higher concentrations of micronutrients than the mature vegetable and are an easy way to pack your juice with an extra healthy punch.

INGREDIENTS

½ cup broccoli sprouts

½ cup bean sprouts

½ cup alfalfa sprouts

3 medium carrots, trimmed

1 medium apple, cored

1 medium orange, peeled

Yields: 1 cup

Per 1 cup serving • Calories: 211 • Fat: 1.5g • Protein: 8.2g • Sodium: 170mg • Sugar: 27g • Carbohydrates: 48g

1. Process the sprouts through the feed tube of an electronic juicer according to the manufacturer's directions.

2. Add the carrots, one at a time, maintaining speed.

3. Cut the apple into chunks and add.

4. Add the orange segments.

5. Mix the juice thoroughly before serving.

CABBAGE AND CARROT COMBO

You may also substitute red cabbage in this recipe, but be aware that while red cabbage is slightly higher in nutrients than the white or green varieties, it does have a stronger flavor.

INGREDIENTS

8 ounces white or green cabbage, chopped

3 large carrots, trimmed

Yields: 1 cup

Per 1 cup serving • Calories: 144 • Fat: 0.7g • Protein: 4.8g • Sodium: 189mg • Sugar: 17g • Carbohydrates: 33g

1. Process the cabbage and carrots through an electronic juicer according to the manufacturer's directions.

2. Whisk or shake the juice to combine the ingredients and serve over ice.

Read the Directions . . .

Cabbage, because of its high fiber content, can be challenging to some juicers, so be sure to check the manufacturer's guidelines.

CABBAGE KALE CLEANSE

Not just for cleansing, cabbage has beneficial effects for hair, skin, and nails, too!

INGREDIENTS

1 cup broccoli florets

1 small head red cabbage

3 large leaves kale or Swiss chard

Yields: 1½ cups

Per 1 cup serving • Calories: 135 • Fat: 0.8g • Protein: 7g • Sodium: 166mg • Sugar: 15g • Carbohydrates: 31g

1. Process the broccoli through an electronic juicer according to the manufacturer's directions.

2. Cut the cabbage into chunks and add to the juicer.

3. Add the kale or chard.

4. Mix the juice thoroughly and serve alone or over ice.

Swiss Chard

There are several varieties of chard available, and while they don't carry all of the nutritional benefits of kale, many juicers prefer chard to kale because it has a milder flavor.

CARROT CLEANSE

When it comes to cleansing and detoxifying, you can't go wrong with carrots. They are especially beneficial for colon health, and are a rich source of vitamin A, which is essential to the health of all the mucous membranes of the body. The addition of lemon to this recipe adds vitamin C and balances the carrots with a brighter note of flavor.

INGREDIENTS

½ pound carrots, trimmed

1 large apple, cored

1 lemon, peeled and seeded

Yields: 1 cup

Per 1 cup serving • Calories: 212 • Fat: 1g • Protein: 3.5g • Sodium: 155mg • Sugar: 33g • Carbohydrates: 54g

1. Process the carrots, one at a time, through your electronic juicer according to the manufacturer's directions.

2. Cut the apple into chunks and add.

3. Add the lemon.

4. Whisk the juice to combine and enjoy immediately.

Toxic Toppers

Unlike other root veggies such as beets and turnips, never use carrot greens in your juice. They are not only bitter, they contain elements that can be toxic.

CARROT MANGO CUP

This is a great combination of flavors that is both tasty and filling.

INGREDIENTS

3 large carrots, trimmed

1 mango, peeled and seeded

Yields: 1 cup

Per 1 cup serving • Calories: 223 • Fat: 1g • Protein: 3g • Sodium: 153mg • Sugar: 40g • Carbohydrates: 55g

1. Process the carrots and mango through an electronic juicer according to the manufacturer's directions.

2. Serve the juice alone or over ice.

FAST FEAST

Substitute mustard greens for the turnip greens in this recipe for a peppery flavor.

INGREDIENTS

6 medium carrots, trimmed

1 cup turnip greens

1 red bell pepper, seeded

½ cup kale

Yields: 2 cups

Per 1 cup serving • Calories: 140 • Fat: 0.4g • Protein: 4.6g • Sodium: 141mg • Sugar: 18g • Carbohydrates: 31g

1. Process the carrots through an electronic juicer according to the manufacturer's directions.

2. Add the turnip greens, followed by the pepper.

3. Add the kale.

4. Stir or shake the juice to combine the ingredients and enjoy!

Storing Juice

If you make more juice than you can drink at once, use a vacuum seal device and store the juice in the refrigerator. Most juices will retain their nutrients for at least twenty-four hours when sealed and refrigerated, the exception being the more volatile, citrus- based juices, which should be consumed as soon as possible.

THE IRON MAIDEN

This juice is named the Iron Maiden because of its rich supply of the mineral.

INGREDIENTS

4 carrots, trimmed

½ cup chopped spinach

4 romaine lettuce leaves

½ turnip, including greens

¼ cup chopped fresh parsley

Yields: 2 cups

Per 1 cup serving • Calories: 88 • Fat: 0.3g • Protein: 3.3g • Sodium: 105mg • Sugar: 11.3g • Carbohydrates: 20g

1. Process the carrots through an electronic juicer according to the manufacturer's directions.

2. Add the spinach, followed by the romaine.

3. Add the turnip and greens, followed by the parsley.

4. Whisk or shake the juice to combine the ingredients and serve over ice.

SUNSET SUPPER

This juice has great color and a fantastic flavor perfect for any time of the day! For easier juicing, cut the greens from the beets and add them separately.

INGREDIENTS

5 carrots, trimmed

2 cucumbers

2 medium sugar beets, complete with greens

Yields: 1½ cups

Per 1 cup serving • Calories: 227 • Fat: 0.6g • Protein: 8g • Sodium: 255mg • Sugar: 31g • Carbohydrates: 52g

1. Process the carrots through an electronic juicer according to the manufacturer's directions.

2. Add the cucumbers, one at a time.

3. Add the beets, followed by the greens.

4. Mix the juice to combine the ingredients and serve over ice.

CELERY ASPARAGUS TONIC

Two superfoods combine in one great juice that tastes like springtime!

INGREDIENTS

5 stalks celery, with leaves

10 to 12 asparagus stalks, woody ends removed

¼ cup mint leaves

Yields: 1½ cups

Per 1 cup serving • Calories: 66 • Fat: 0.6g • Protein: 4.8g • Sodium: 178mg • Sugar: 5.7g • Carbohydrates: 12.6g

1. Process the celery through an electronic juicer according to the manufacturer's directions

2. Add the asparagus, followed by the mint.

3. Mix the juice to combine the ingredients and serve alone or over ice.

SUPER CAROTENE COMBO

Carotene is especially helpful for the eyes, but also helps the liver. In addition to providing a great energy boost, it's also believed to be helpful in preventing the onset of Type 2 diabetes.

INGREDIENTS

3 medium carrots, trimmed

½ large cantaloupe, peeled and seeded

1 medium sweet potato, peeled and cut into chunks

1 tablespoon fresh mint leaves

Yields: 1½ cups

Per 1 cup serving • Calories: 250 • Fat: 0.5g • Protein: 5.7g • Sodium: 155mg • Sugar: 35g • Carbohydrates: 60g

1. Process the carrots through an electronic juicer according to the manufacturer's directions.

2. Cut the cantaloupe into chunks and add.

3. Add the sweet potato.

4. Roll the mint leaves into a ball to compress and add to the juicer.

5. Whisk the juice together and serve over ice, if desired.

Mint and Melon

The classic combination of flavors is the perfect summertime refreshment. Not only do fresh mint leaves add wonderful flavor, they add chlorophyll and a touch of green goodness to this bright orange juice. Garnish with additional mint leaves for extra eye appeal.

CELERY CHERVIL COCKTAIL

Mild-mannered celery gets a whole new character with the addition of fresh chervil.

INGREDIENTS

6 stalks celery, with leaves

½ cup fresh chervil

Yields: 1½ cups

Per 1 cup serving • Calories: 48 • Fat: 0.6g • Protein: 2.4g • Sodium: 216mg • Sugar: 4.2g • Carbohydrates: 9g

1. Process the celery though an electronic juicer according to the manufacturer's directions.

2. Add the chervil.

3. Serve the juice alone or over ice.

Chervil

Related to and with many of the same nutritional properties as parsley, chervil has a faint flavor of licorice.

GINGER CELERY COOLER

Distinctly Asian flavor makes this perfect for a summer snack! Add a dash of soy sauce for added zip.

INGREDIENTS

3 stalks celery, with leaves

1 small clove of fresh garlic, peeled

1" ginger, peeled

1 cucumber

2 scallions, trimmed

Yields: 1 cup

Per 1 cup serving • Calories: 94 • Fat: 1g • Protein: 3.7g • Sodium: 107mg • Sugar: 8g • Carbohydrates: 20g

1. Process the celery through an electronic juicer according to the manufacturer's directions.

2. Add the garlic and the ginger, followed by the cucumber and the scallions.

3. Mix the juice to combine the ingredients and serve.

POWERHOUSE

This juice provides powerful nutrition in a glass.

INGREDIENTS

4 celery stalks, with leaves

1 bunch parsley

2 cups spinach

⅓ medium cucumber

2 carrots, trimmed

1 beet, trimmed and tailed

2 leaves Swiss chard

Yields: 1½ cups

Per 1 cup serving • Calories: 126 • Fat: 0.8g • Protein: 5.8g • Sodium: 302mg • Sugar: 15g • Carbohydrates: 27g

1. Process the celery and parsley through an electronic juicer according to the manufacturer's directions.

2. Add the spinach, followed by the cucumber and the carrots.

3. Add the beet and the Swiss chard.

4. Mix the juice thoroughly to combine the ingredients and serve alone or over ice.

Give It a Squeeze

Some people find the flavor of greens-based juices less than appetizing, but adding a healthy squeeze of lemon juice or a dash of hot sauce can do a lot to perk up the flavor and tickle your taste buds.

CAULIFLOWER COMBO

Another feast for your fast, this is the juicing equivalent of a big chef's salad!

INGREDIENTS

1 cup cauliflower florets

1 cup red cabbage

1 sweet orange pepper, seeded

4–5 scallions

½ head romaine lettuce

1 cup cherry tomatoes

Yields: 2 cups

Per 1 cup serving • Calories: 139 • Fat: 1.5g • Protein: 7.8g • Sodium: 705mg • Sugar: 9.9g • Carbohydrates: 30g

1. Process the cauliflower through an electronic juicer according to the manufacturer's directions.

2. Add the cabbage, followed by the pepper and the scallions.

3. Add the romaine and the tomatoes.

4. Whisk or shake the juice thoroughly to combine the ingredients and serve alone or over ice.

Cauliflower Caution

Like other members of the cruciferous family, excessive consumption of cauliflower may cause swelling of the thyroid gland and thyroid hormone deficiency. This is due to the presence of certain plant compounds known as goitrogens. So if you have a history of thyroid dysfunction, limit your cruciferous intake.

CAULI-CARROT COMBO

This combination of vegetable juices is a tasty choice for diabetics who steer clear of sugary juices.

INGREDIENTS

1 cup cauliflower florets

3 carrots, trimmed

1 celery stalk, with leaves

Yields: 1½ cups

Per 1 cup serving • Calories: 95 • Fat: 0.2g • Protein: 3.7g • Sodium: 135mg • Sugar: 11g • Carbohydrates: 21g

1. Process the cauliflower and carrots through your juicer according to the manufacturer's directions.

2. Add the celery.

3. Serve the juice alone or over ice.

CHAYOTE JUICE

There are myriad claims among chayote fans about its fantastic abilities to lower blood pressure and regulate blood sugar levels in those who suffer from diabetes.

INGREDIENTS

1 medium chayote squash, peeled and pitted

1 cucumber

1 carrot, trimmed

Yields: 1½ cups

Per 1 cup serving • Calories: 79 • Fat: 0.4g • Protein: 3g • Sodium: 33mg • Sugar: 9g • Carbohydrates: 19g

1. Process the chayote through an electronic juicer according to the manufacturer's directions.

2. Add the cucumber, followed by the carrot.

3. Mix the juice to combine the ingredients, and serve over ice.

Chayote Squash

Chayote squash belongs to the summer squash family and is considered, along with corn and beans, by indigenous peoples of Mexico and the Southwest to be one of the "three sisters," the staples of their diet for centuries.

COLLARD CLASSIC

Red pepper and tomato provide a nice flavor balance for the greens in this recipe.

INGREDIENTS

1 kale leaf

1 collard leaf

1 celery stalk, with leaves

1 carrot, trimmed

½ red pepper, seeded

1 large tomato

½ cup arugula

¼ cup parsley

Yields: 1½ cups

Per 1 cup serving • Calories: 75 • Fat: 0.6g • Protein: 3.3g • Sodium: 85mg • Sugar: 9g • Carbohydrates: 16g

1. Process the kale and collard leaves through an electronic juicer according to the manufacturer's directions.

2. Add the celery, followed by the carrot and the red pepper.

3. Add the tomato, the arugula, and the parsley.

4. Mix the juice to combine the ingredients and serve over ice.

Collard Greens

A staple of traditional Southern cooking, collards are rich in nutrition. They contain protein, thiamine, niacin, and potassium, as well as vitamin A, vitamin C, vitamin E, vitamin K, riboflavin, vitamin B_6, folate, calcium, and manganese. It doesn't get much healthier than that!

CUCUMBER PEAR PLUS!

The plus in this recipe comes from sugar snap peas, a rich source of folates. Snap peas have 150 percent more vitamin C than regular garden peas and also contain phytosterols, which help lower cholesterol.

INGREDIENTS

3 medium pears, cored

1 medium cucumber, peeled

2 cups spinach

6 leaves kale

½ leaf Swiss chard

½ lemon, peeled

1 cup sugar snap peas

Yields: 1½ cups

Per 1 cup serving • Calories: 282 • Fat: 3g • Protein: 8g • Sodium: 75mg • Sugar: 38g • Carbohydrates: 65g

1. Process the pears through an electronic juicer according to the manufacturer's directions.

2. Add the cucumber, followed by the spinach.

3. Roll the kale and chard leaves together to compress and add to the juicer.

4. Add the lemon and the snap peas.

5. Whisk the juice to combine the ingredients and serve immediately.

Snap!

Sugar snap peas also are a good source of riboflavin, vitamin B_6, pantothenic acid, magnesium, phosphorus, and potassium, in addition to fiber, vitamin A, vitamin K, thiamine, iron, and manganese.

CUCUMBER PEPPER POTION

Sweet bell peppers are an excellent source of vitamins A and C. Choose cucumbers with firm skin and no shriveling or soft spots.

INGREDIENTS

1 cucumber, peeled

1 celery stalk, with leaves

½ green bell pepper, seeded

Yields: 1 cup

Per 1 cup serving • Calories: 63 • Fat: 0.5g • Protein: 2.7g • Sodium: 39mg • Sugar: 7g • Carbohydrates: 15g

1. Process the cucumber through an electronic juicer according to the manufacturer's directions.

2. Add the celery, followed by the bell pepper.

3. Stir the juice to combine the ingredients and serve over ice.

Cucumbers

Cucumbers are available year round. Store them unwashed in your refrigerator for up to ten days. Wash them just before using. Leftover cucumbers can be refrigerated again; just tightly wrap them in plastic and they will keep for up to five days.

CUCUMBER HONEYDEW PUNCH

Seedless green grapes are best in this recipe because their more delicate flavor doesn't overwhelm the other ingredients.

INGREDIENTS

½ cucumber

¼ small honeydew melon

1 cup seedless green grapes

2 kiwis, peeled

¾ cup of spinach

Sprig of mint

1 lemon, peeled

Yields: 2 cups

Per 1 cup serving • Calories: 163 • Fat: 0.8g • Protein: 3g • Sodium: 43mg • Sugar: 30g • Carbohydrates: 42g

1. Process the cucumber and melon through an electronic juicer according to the manufacturer's directions.

2. Add the grapes and the kiwis.

3. Add the spinach and the mint, followed by the lemon.

4. Mix the juice thoroughly to combine ingredients and serve immediately.

Grapes and Phytochemicals

All grapes are high in phytochemicals, plant-derived compounds that are not classified as vitamins or minerals but remain active in the body working to help prevent strokes, cancer, and diabetes.

DILLED CUCUMBER COCKTAIL

Try this juice for a gorgeous mane and a magnificent manicure. It tastes great, too.

INGREDIENTS

1 large cucumber

5 to 6 stalks asparagus

½ bunch fresh dill

Yields: 1 cup

Per 1 cup serving • Calories: 30 • Fat: 0.2g • Protein: 2.4g • Sodium: 6mg • Sugar: 3g • Carbohydrates: 6.5g

1. Process the cucumber through an electronic juicer according to the manufacturer's directions.

2. Add the asparagus, followed by the dill.

3. Whisk the juice to combine the ingredients and serve over ice.

Delicious Dill

Not just for pickles, dill is related to the cilantro family and contains many essential volatile oils such as d-carvone, dillapiol, DHC, eugenol, limonene, terpinene, and myristicin.

LIQUID PICKLE

Cucumbers are almost all water, yet hold a wealth of restorative powers. This recipe is wonderful for a hot summer's day, because this dill-flavored juice contains none of the salt of regular pickles.

INGREDIENTS

2 medium cucumbers

½ cup fresh dill

4 scallions, trimmed

½ cup chopped Swiss chard

Yields: 1½ cups

Per 1 cup serving • Calories: 77 • Fat: 0.6g • Protein: 3.7g • Sodium: 42mg • Sugar: 8g • Carbohydrates: 18g

1. Process the cucumbers through an electronic juicer according to the manufacturer's directions.

2. Add the dill, followed by the scallions and the Swiss chard.

3. Whisk or shake the juice to combine the ingredients and serve over ice.

Cucumber Benefits

Cucumber has high alkaline levels, and helps to regulate the body's blood pH to neutralize acidity. It also helps with overall hydration and regulates blood pressure. The hard skin of the cucumber is rich in fiber and a range of minerals that include magnesium, molybdenum, silica, and potassium.

SPICY CUCUMBER

Cucumbers are rich in chlorophyll and silica. They are a natural diuretic and benefit the digestion.

INGREDIENTS

1 cucumber

1 garlic clove, peeled

2 green onions, trimmed

½ jalapeño pepper

2 small key limes or Mexican limes

Yields: 1 cup

Per 1 cup serving • Calories: 98 • Fat: 1g • Protein: 3.5g • Sodium: 12mg • Sugar: 9g • Carbohydrates: 27g

1. Process the ingredients in any order through an electronic juicer according to the manufacturer's directions.

2. Stir to mix the juice and serve over ice.

TROPICAL CUCUMBER

This drink provides skin benefits. Cucumber contains silica, a trace mineral that helps provide strength to the connective tissues of the skin. Cucumbers help with swelling of the eyes and water retention. They are high in vitamins A and C and folate.

INGREDIENTS

1 cup pineapple, peeled, cored, and cut into chunks

1 mango, pitted

1 cucumber, peeled

½ lemon, rind intact

Yields: 2 cups

Per 1 cup serving • Calories: 158 • Fat: 0.9g • Protein: 2.6g • Sodium: 5mg • Sugar: 32g • Carbohydrates: 40g

1. Process the pineapple through your electronic juicer according to the manufacturer's directions.

2. Add the mango, followed by the cucumber.

3. Cut lemon into thin slices and add it last.

4. Stir the juice well before serving.

VITAMIN MIXER

Alfalfa sprouts are low in calories but high in protein, with a fabulous mix of vitamins to boot.

INGREDIENTS

1 lemon, peeled

2 cups alfalfa sprouts

1" ginger, peeled

2 carrots, trimmed

3 cucumbers

½ cup parsley

Yields: 1½ cups

Per 1 cup serving • Calories: 167 • Fat: 1.3g
• Protein: 8g • Sodium: 80mg • Sugar: 18g
• Carbohydrates: 39g

1. Process the lemon through an electronic juicer according to the manufacturer's directions.

2. Add the sprouts, followed by the ginger and the carrots.

3. Add the cucumbers one at a time, followed by the parsley.

4. Mix the juice thoroughly to combine the ingredients and serve alone or over ice.

DANDELION DANDY

Got dandelions? Juice them! Dandelion greens rank in the top four green vegetables in overall nutritional value. If you prefer, you can substitute a tomato for the lemon.

INGREDIENTS

1 pound carrots, trimmed

1 lemon, peeled

¾ cup dandelion greens, chopped

Yields: 2 cups

Per 1 cup serving • Calories: 119 • Fat: 0.2g
• Protein: 3.8g • Sodium: 132mg • Sugar:
15g • Carbohydrates: 28g

1. Process the carrots, lemon, and dandelion greens through an electronic juicer according to the manufacturer's directions.

2. Whisk or shake the juice to combine the ingredients and serve over ice.

Dandelions

Dandelions are also nature's richest green vegetable source of beta-carotene, from which vitamin A is created, as well as being particularly rich in fiber, potassium, iron, calcium, magnesium, phosphorus, and the B vitamins, thiamine, and riboflavin, and a good source of protein.

DANDELION DELIGHT

So called "wild" foods such as dandelions and the nettle greens included in this recipe are not just inexpensive to the point of being free, depending on where you live, but can serve as a reminder of just how bountiful Nature is.

INGREDIENTS

1 cup chopped dandelion greens

1 cup chopped nettle greens

1 cucumber

Yields: 2 cups

Per 1 cup serving • Calories: 53 • Fat: 0.4g
• Protein: 3g • Sodium: 26mg • Sugar: 3g •
Carbohydrates: 11g

1. Wash the greens thoroughly before chopping. Process the greens through an electronic juicer according to the manufacturer's directions.

2. Add the cucumber.

3. Whisk the juice thoroughly to combine the ingredients and serve over ice.

How to Pick Nettle Greens

If nettles aren't available at your local farmers' market, choose young plants and take only the top 4 or 5 inches from each plant. Wear gloves and long pants to avoid getting "stung." As for nutrition? A lot like spinach, but better. High in iron, calcium, vitamin C, and a slew of other nutrients, nettles have been used fresh and dried for nutritional and medical uses over the years.

ANOTHER GREEN MACHINE

This savory green juice is also great with a dash of lemon juice or hot sauce.

INGREDIENTS

½ cup romaine lettuce, chopped

½ cup green beans

¾ cup Brussels sprouts

½ cup chopped Jerusalem artichokes

2 large carrots, trimmed

Yields: 1½ cups

Per 1 cup serving • Calories: 108 • Fat: 0.5g • Protein: 4.2g • Sodium: 82mg • Sugar: 12g • Carbohydrates: 25g

1. Process the romaine and green beans through an electronic juicer according to the manufacturer's directions.

2. Add the Brussels sprouts and Jerusalem artichokes, followed by the carrots.

3. Whisk or shake the juice to combine the ingredients and serve over ice.

Jerusalem Artichokes

Jerusalem artichokes are actually the tubers of a tall flowering plant. They have a taste and texture much like that of water chestnuts.

EASY GREENS

Romaine lettuce is great for juicing because it tends to be more substantial than some other lettuces and therefore yields more juice! If greens are just not your thing, this one's great because it has a light easy flavor with no cabbage-y tasting undertone.

INGREDIENTS

2 hearts of romaine lettuce

1 bunch arugula, about 1 cup

½ cup spinach

1 bunch parsley

3 stalks celery, with leaves

½ lemon, peeled

Yields: 1½ cups

Per 1 cup serving • Calories: 69 • Fat: 0.2g • Protein: 3.7g • Sodium: 157mg • Sugar: 8g • Carbohydrates: 15g

1. Process the romaine hearts through an electronic juicer according to the manufacturer's directions.

2. Add the arugula, followed by the spinach and the parsley.

3. Add the celery and the lemon.

4. Mix the juice thoroughly and enjoy over ice, if desired.

GREEN JUICE

This flavorful juice is good for reducing cravings for sour foods, which can be caused by a lack of acetic acid. Green vegetables are high in chlorophyll and help with these types of cravings.

INGREDIENTS

3 celery stalks, leaves intact

½ cucumber

1 red apple, cored

1 cup spinach leaves

1 cup beet greens

Yields: 1½ cups

Per 1 cup serving • Calories: 90 • Fat: 0.5g • Protein: 2.6g • Sodium: 140mg • Sugar: 13.5g • Carbohydrates: 21g

1. Process the celery and cucumber through an electronic juicer according to the manufacturer's directions.

2. Add the apple.

3. Add the spinach and beet greens.

4. Whisk the juice to combine the ingredients, and serve alone or over ice.

GREEN GODDESS

If the flavor of this kale-based juice seems too intense, add distilled water, or half a container of Greek yogurt.

INGREDIENTS

2 medium apples, cored

2 medium carrots, trimmed

2 medium pears, cored

½ cucumber

6 to 8 leaves fresh kale

Yields: 1 cup

Per 1 cup serving • Calories: 474 • Fat: 3g • Protein: 12.5g • Sodium: 190mg • Sugar: 58g • Carbohydrates: 115g

1. Process the apples and carrots through an electronic juicer according to the manufacturer's directions.

2. Add the pears, followed by the cucumber.

3. Roll the kale leaves together to compress and add to the juicer.

4. Stir or shake the mixture to combine ingredients.

LETTUCE PLAY

Some say lettuce has a sedative effect, so this makes a good nightcap.

INGREDIENTS

½ head romaine lettuce

½ head red leaf lettuce

2 stalks celery, with leaves

Yields: 1½ cups

Per 1 cup serving • Calories: 60 • Fat: 1g • Protein: 4.3g • Sodium: 85mg • Sugar: 4g • Carbohydrates: 11g

1. Process the lettuces and celery through an electronic juicer according to the manufacturer's directions.

2. Serve the juice alone or over ice.

LUSCIOUS LIQUID LUNCH

Gorgeous color and lively flavor! If cilantro is not to your liking, substitute fresh parsley, or a combination of parsley and mint.

INGREDIENTS

2 kale leaves

½ cup spinach

½ cup cilantro

2 apples, cored

1 pear, cored

½ lemon, peeled

1" ginger, peeled

Yields: 1½ cups

Per 1 cup serving • Calories: 212 • Fat: 0.9g • Protein: 2.7g • Sodium: 23mg • Sugar: 36g • Carbohydrates: 55g

1. Process the kale, spinach, and cilantro through an electronic juicer according to the manufacturer's directions.

2. Add the apples, followed by the pear.

3. Add the lemon and the ginger.

4. Stir or shake the juice to combine the ingredients and enjoy!

MEAN GREEN MACHINE

Got a full day ahead? This one will make sure you get through it with energy to spare.

INGREDIENTS

1 cup fresh pineapple, peeled and chopped

1 medium Granny Smith apple, cored

2 cups baby spinach leaves

¼ cup parsley

2 tablespoons mint leaves

½ pink grapefruit, peeled and seeded

1 cup coconut water

Yields: 2½ cups

Per 1 cup serving • Calories: 118 • Fat: 0.3g • Protein: 1.8g • Sodium: 54mg • Sugar: 18g • Carbohydrates: 30g

1. Process the pineapple chunks in an electronic juicer according to the manufacturer's directions.

2. Slice the apple and add pieces to the juicer, maintaining the juicer speed.

3. Wash the spinach, parsley, and mint. Add to the juicer.

4. Add the grapefruit segments.

5. Whisk the juice together with the coconut water until well blended. Chill or serve immediately over ice.

Coconut Water

Inside the humble coconut is a tropical elixir that's packed with a unique compound of simple sugars, vitamins, minerals, electrolytes, enzymes, amino acids, and more. The benefits associated with coconut water are believed to be good for the heart, anti-aging, and anti-carcinogenic. Use fresh or canned coconut water in your juice recipes depending on availability.

POPEYE'S SECRET BLEND

This juice is high in magnesium, which is a natural muscle relaxant. Spinach is very rich in iron and a great source of vitamins A and C. The leaves tend to be gritty, so rinse them thoroughly.

INGREDIENTS

1 cup spinach leaves

1 cucumber, peeled

2 carrots, trimmed and peeled

Yields: 1 cup

Per 1 cup serving • Calories: 111 • Fat: 0.7g
• Protein: 4g • Sodium: 129mg • Sugar: 12g
• Carbohydrates: 25g

1. Process the spinach through an electronic juicer according to the manufacturer's directions.

2. Add the cucumber, followed by the carrots.

3. Mix or shake the juice to combine the ingredients and serve alone, or over ice.

SPINACH CANTALOUPE COCKTAIL

In a recent study, spinach showed evidence of significant protection against the occurrence of aggressive prostate cancer—more reason to eat this beneficial green.

INGREDIENTS

1 cup spinach

2 medium carrots, trimmed

1 cup cantaloupe chunks

Yields: 1 cup

Per 1 cup serving • Calories: 109 • Fat: 0.7g
• Protein: 3.3g • Sodium: 132mg • Sugar: 18g • Carbohydrates: 25g

1. Process the spinach through an electronic juicer according to the manufacturer's directions.

2. Add the carrots, followed by the cantaloupe.

3. Stir or shake the juice to combine the ingredients and serve.

WATERCRESS COCKTAIL

Watercress adds a peppery punch to the taste of this juice along with some powerful nutrients.

INGREDIENTS

4 ounces watercress

3 large carrots, trimmed

2 stalks of celery, with leaves

Yields: 1 cup

Per 1 cup serving • Calories: 113 • Fat: 0.8g
• Protein: 5g • Sodium: 258mg • Sugar: 12g
• Carbohydrates: 24g

1. Process the watercress and carrots through an electronic juicer according to the manufacturer's directions.

2. Add the celery.

3. Whisk or shake the juice to combine the ingredients and serve over ice.

KOHLRABI CURE-ALL

Kohlrabi is a root vegetable that tastes like a cross between turnips, radishes, and cabbage. For that reason, it's best to combine it with milder veggies or water to dilute the strong flavor a bit.

INGREDIENTS

1 small kohlrabi, cut into quarters, with greens

1 medium cucumber

1 medium zucchini

1 clove garlic, peeled

Yields: 1 cup

Per 1 cup serving • Calories: 117 • Fat: 1g •
Protein: 5.6g • Sodium: 103mg • Sugar: 14g
• Carbohydrates: 25g

1. Process the kohlrabi and its greens through an electronic juicer according to the manufacturer's directions.

2. Add the cucumber, followed by the zucchini and the garlic.

3. Shake the juice to combine the ingredients, dilute with water to taste, or serve over ice.

Kohlrabi Facts

Cultivated since Roman times, kohlrabi can be found in a purple globe variety or a lighter apple green. Kohlrabi leaves or tops, like the bulbs, are very nutritious, abundant in carotenes, vitamin A, vitamin K, minerals, and B-complex vitamins.

THE RADICAL RADISH

Radishes are rich in folate, vitamin C, and anthocyanins. These nutrients make it a very effective cancer-fighting food. It is said that radish is effective in fighting oral cancer, colon cancer, and intestinal cancer as well as kidney and stomach cancers.

INGREDIENTS

1 cup radishes, trimmed and tailed

½ cup parsley

1 medium zucchini

Yields: 1 cup

Per 1 cup serving • Calories: 62 • Fat: 1g • Protein: 4g • Sodium: 77mg • Sugar: 7g • Carbohydrates: 12g

1. Process the radishes through an electronic juicer according to the manufacturer's directions.

2. Add the parsley, followed by the zucchini.

3. Mix or shake the juice to combine the ingredients and serve alone, or over ice.

ROOT VEGETABLE CLEANSE

Root vegetables are a staple for any juice fast because of their soluble fiber.

INGREDIENTS

½ medium beet, tailed and trimmed

3 medium carrots, trimmed

2 apples, cored

1 medium sweet potato, cut into chunks

¼ sweet Spanish or Vidalia onion, peeled

Yields: 1½ cups

Per 1 cup serving • Calories: 304 • Fat: 0.6g • Protein: 5g • Sodium: 153mg • Sugar: 43g • Carbohydrates: 75g

1. Process the beet and carrots through an electronic juicer according to the manufacturer's directions.

2. Add the apples and sweet potato, followed by the onion.

3. Mix the juice thoroughly to combine ingredients and serve immediately.

LIQUID CRUCIFEROUS

Simply adding cruciferous veggies like broccoli, cauliflower, cabbage, and kale can give your weight loss juice recipes real fat-fighting clout.

INGREDIENTS

2 small zucchini

¼ red cabbage

2 red apples, cored

4 kale leaves

½ cup cauliflower florets

1 cup blueberries

1 orange, peeled

½ medium cucumber

½ cup coconut water

Yields: 2 cups (2 servings)

Per 1 cup serving • Calories: 254 • Fat: 1.6g • Protein: 6.6g • Sodium: 71mg • Sugar: 42g • Carbohydrates: 62g

1. Process the zucchini through an electronic juicer according to the manufacturer's directions.

2. Add the cabbage, followed by the apples and kale.

3. Add cauliflower, followed by the blueberries and the orange.

4. Add the cucumber and the coconut water.

5. Whisk the juice to combine and enjoy!

Weight and Hormones

Hormone disruptors called xenoestrogens mimic the effect of natural estrogen, which affects fat storage in the body. Apart from adding to cancer risks, xenoestrogens are known to cause our bodies to store more fat than usual, while at the same time making it very difficult to lose extra weight. The phytochemicals contained in cruciferous veggies help metabolize and eliminate xenoestrogens, putting the body back in hormonal balance.

SUMMER SQUASH SPECIAL

All the summer squashes—zucchini, yellow squash, Mexican gray squash, and patty pan squash—are excellent sources of protein, which is important to keep up during any weight loss program. Juicing is also a good way to use larger squashes because they contain much more liquid.

INGREDIENTS

1 cup spinach

1 zucchini or other summer squash

1 cucumber

2 carrots, trimmed

½ apple, cored

Yields: 1 cup

Per 1 cup serving • Calories: 139 • Fat: 1g • Protein: 5g • Sodium: 108mg • Sugar: 18g • Carbohydrates: 32g

1. Process the spinach through an electronic juicer according to the manufacturer's directions.

2. Add the squash, followed by the cucumber.

3. Add the carrots and the apple.

4. Whisk the juice thoroughly to combine ingredients and enjoy!

Other Squash Varieties

You can also choose crookneck, straightneck, scallop squash, yellow squash, or any of the round zucchini hybrids for this recipe.

GOOD OLD GAZPACHO JUICE

Here is the pure juice form of the traditional cold soup.

INGREDIENTS

2 large tomatoes

½ green pepper, seeded

½ red pepper, seeded

1 fresh jalapeño pepper, seeded

4 scallions, trimmed

1 clove garlic, peeled

Yields: 2 cups

Per 1 cup serving • Calories: 62 • Fat: 0.6g • Protein: 3 g • Sodium: 16mg • Sugar: 8g • Carbohydrates: 13g

1. Process the tomatoes through an electronic juicer according to the manufacturer's directions.

2. Add the peppers, followed by the scallions and the garlic.

3. Whisk or shake the juice to combine the ingredients and serve over ice.

Heat in Jalapeños

Most of the fiery heat of fresh jalapeños is avoided if you carefully remove the seeds and ribs of the pepper before juicing.

HEIRLOOM TOMATO JUICE

Tomatoes are indeed a fruit and are available in many low-acid heirloom varieties. Combine them with other fruit treasures for a great-tasting juice!

INGREDIENTS

3 heirloom tomatoes, such as Yellow Pear
or Cherokee Purple

2 sweet heirloom apples, such as Lady
Sweet or Gala, cored

Yields: 2 cups

Per 1 cup serving • Calories: 129 • Fat: 0.6g
• Protein: 2.4g • Sodium: 14mg • Sugar: 23g
• Carbohydrates: 33g

1. Process the tomatoes through an electronic juicer according to the manufacturer's directions.

2. Add the apples.

3. Whisk or shake the juice to combine the ingredients and serve alone or over ice.

Heirlooms

The resurgence of interest in heirloom varieties of fruits and vegetables has largely come about with the interest in locally grown foods. Commercial farming tends to erode varietals because of its emphasis on consistency. But heirloom varietals are essential, because they frequently have distinct regional characteristics in their ability to withstand climate conditions, pests, and diseases specific to different areas.

HOT TOMATO

The pungent addition of horseradish to this recipe doesn't just add flavor; horseradish is anti-inflammatory and antioxidant, and has been found to have soothing effects on the nerves.

INGREDIENTS

1 cup red or yellow cherry tomatoes

1 large carrot, trimmed

1 stalk celery, with leaves

1" ginger, peeled

1" piece horseradish root

¼ lemon, peeled

3 to 4 sprigs fresh cilantro

1 radish

1 garlic clove, peeled

Yields: 1½ cups

Per 1 cup serving • Calories: 71 • Fat: 0.7g • Protein: 2.8g • Sodium: 79mg • Sugar: 7g • Carbohydrates: 16g

1. Process the tomatoes through an electronic juicer according to the manufacturer's directions.

2. Add the carrot, followed by the celery.

3. Add the ginger, horseradish, and lemon.

4. Add the cilantro, the radish, and the garlic.

5. Mix the juice thoroughly to combine ingredients and serve over ice.

Yellow Tomatoes

The only significant nutritional difference between red tomatoes and yellow is that the yellow varieties tend to be somewhat lower in acids. So if you have a sensitive stomach, they're a good choice.

TERRIFIC TURNIP JUICE

Like many root vegetables, turnips can be a bit earthy tasting, but inclusion of the fennel bulb in this concoction imparts a wonderful flavor!

INGREDIENTS

½ turnip, peeled

3 carrots, trimmed

1 apple, cored

¼ fennel bulb

Yields: 1 cup

Per 1 cup serving • Calories: 165 • Fat: 0.7g • Protein: 2.8g • Sodium: 154mg • Sugar: 24g • Carbohydrates: 41g

1. Process the turnip and carrots through an electronic juicer according to the manufacturer's directions.

2. Add the apple and the fennel bulb.

3. Mix the juice thoroughly to blend and serve over ice.

Fabulous Fennel

In addition to wonderful flavor, fennel is a good source of niacin, calcium, iron, magnesium, phosphorus, and copper, and also contains vitamin C, folate, potassium, and manganese.

VEGETABLE SUPER JUICE

Add a generous dash of hot sauce to this juice for extra zip! It's great on the rocks for a fast summer lunch.

INGREDIENTS

1 whole cucumber

6 leaves romaine lettuce

4 stalks of celery, including leaves

2 cups fresh spinach

½ cup alfalfa sprouts

½ cup fresh parsley

Yields: 1½ cups

Per 1 cup serving • Calories: 95 • Fat: 1.3g • Protein: 6g • Sodium: 146mg • Sugar: 7g • Carbohydrates: 19g

1. Cut the cucumber into pieces and process through your juicer according to the manufacturer's directions.

2. Wrap the romaine leaves around the celery stalks and add to the feeding tube.

3. Add the spinach, sprouts, and parsley in any order you desire.

4. Mix the juice thoroughly before serving.

Sandy Spinach?

Spinach grows best in sandy soils, but can be tough to really rinse well. Rather than rinsing spinach through a colander, place it in a deep bowl or kettle and cover it with water. Gently toss to allow any sand or grit to fall to the bottom and lift the greens out.

YAMTASTIC

If juice fasting leaves you a bit low on get-up-and-go, use this juice for an energy boost!

INGREDIENTS

3 oranges, peeled

2 Anjou pears, cored

1 large yam, peeled

Yields: 1½ cups

Per 1 cup serving • Calories: 345 • Fat: 0.5g • Protein: 5g • Sodium: 50mg • Sugar: 49g • Carbohydrates: 87g

1. Process the orange segments through an electronic juicer according to the manufacturer's directions.

2. Add the pears.

3. Cut the yam into pieces and add to the juicer. Serve over ice.

Not the Same

Although similar in taste, yams and sweet potatoes don't belong to the same botanical family. Yams are closely related to the lily, while sweet potatoes belong to the morning glory family.

GADZOOKS

As this recipe proves, sometimes the simplest combinations provide maximum benefits.

INGREDIENTS

3–4 medium zucchini

2 stalks celery, with leaves

Yields: 1 cup

Per 1 cup serving • Calories: 112 • Fat: 2g • Protein: 7.6g • Sodium: 111mg • Sugar: 16g • Carbohydrates: 20g

1. Process the squash and the celery through an electronic juicer according to the manufacturer's directions.

2. Mix or shake the juice to combine the ingredients and serve alone or over ice.

Zucchini Benefits

If you grow a garden, juicing is a wonderful way to rid yourself of too many zucchini. Very low in calories, zucchini is rich in vitamin A and potassium, a heart-friendly electrolyte that helps reduce blood pressure and heart rates by countering the effects of sodium.

CHAPTER 12

KID-FRIENDLY JUICES

APPLE FANTASTIC

For kids' juice, milder apples like Delicious or Baldwin will do just fine.

INGREDIENTS

4 Delicious or Golden Delicious apples, cored

½ cup filtered water

Yields: 1½ cups (3 servings)

Per ½ cup serving • Calories: 164 • Fat: 0.5g • Protein: 0.8g • Sodium: 3.3mg • Sugar: 34g • Carbohydrates: 46g

1. Process the apples through an electronic juicer according to the manufacturer's directions.

2. Dilute with water and mix.

Variation

If your kids flatly refuse anything but their favorite apple juice, try adding just a few grapes or a bit of melon, a little at a time until they get accustomed to the variation in flavor.

APPLE GRAPE MAGIC

Perennial favorites in kidland, this combination is a guaranteed winner with the younger set.

INGREDIENTS

1 cup Concord grapes

2 apples, cored

½ cup water

Yields: 1 cup (2 servings)

Per ½ cup serving • Calories: 209 • Fat: 0.5g • Protein: 1.6g • Sodium: 3mg • Sugar: 45g • Carbohydrates: 55g

1. Process the grapes through an electronic juicer according to the manufacturer's directions.

2. Add the apples.

3. Dilute with water to taste.

APPLE PIE

Juice for dessert? Why not? A great way to introduce kids to juicing is by substituting juice for dessert after meals.

INGREDIENTS

2 apples, cored

8 stalks celery, with leaves

Dash of cinnamon

Yields: 1½ cups (3 servings)

Per ½ cup serving • Calories: 52 • Fat: 0.2g • Protein: 0.9g • Sodium: 85mg • Sugar: 9g • Carbohydrates: 12g

1. Process the apples and celery through an electronic juicer according to the manufacturer's directions.

2. Add the cinnamon.

3. Mix the juice to combine the ingredients and serve.

APPLE WATERMELON SHAKE

Kids who play hard need hydration, especially in the summer, and this one's a great choice.

INGREDIENTS

2 apples, cored

3 cups watermelon chunks

Yields: 1½ cups (3 servings)

Per ½ cup serving • Calories: 80 • Fat: 0.3g • Protein: 1g • Sodium: 1.5mg • Sugar: 16g • Carbohydrates: 20g

1. Process fruit through an electronic juicer according to the manufacturer's directions.

2. Shake the juice together with ice and serve.

BEDTIME SNACK

If your child is hyper at bedtime, try this lettuce-based juice for a calming effect.

INGREDIENTS

1 cup chopped romaine or iceberg lettuce

1 apple, cored

Yields: 1 cup (2 servings)

Per ½ cup serving • Calories: 30 • Fat: 0.1g • Protein: 0.4g • Sodium: 1.8mg • Sugar: 5.8g • Carbohydrates: 7.7g

Process the lettuce and apple through your juicer according to the manufacturer's directions and serve.

BUNNY JUICE

Everyone knows that bunnies love carrots, right? This one will teach your little one to love them, too.

INGREDIENTS

3 carrots, trimmed

1 Gala apple, cored

Yields: 1 cup (2 servings)

Per ½ cup serving • Calories: 70 • Fat: 0.3g • Protein: 1g • Sodium: 74mg • Sugar: 10g • Carbohydrates: 17g

Process the carrots and apples through an electronic juicer according to the manufacturer's directions and serve.

GREEN GOBLIN JUICE

Pronounced grape flavor and great green color—they'll never suspect there's spinach in there!

INGREDIENTS

2 cups white or green seedless grapes

½ cup fresh spinach

1 cup filtered water

Yields: 2 cups (4 servings)

Per ½ cup serving • Calories: 211 • Fat: 0.5g
• Protein: 2.6g • Sodium: 17mg • Sugar: 46g
• Carbohydrates: 55g

1. Process the grapes through an electronic juicer according to the manufacturer's directions.

2. Add the spinach.

3. Dilute with water and mix.

GREEN SLIME SUPER JUICE

There are times when a little reverse psychology works wonders when it comes to getting kids to try new things. Call it slime and dare them to try it—they'll like it!

INGREDIENTS

1½ cups collard greens

1 lemon, peeled

2 tablespoons agave nectar

Yields: 1½ cups (3 servings)

Per ½ cup serving • Calories: 53 • Fat: 0.1g •
Protein: 0.6g • Sodium: 4.5mg • Sugar: 12g •
Carbohydrates: 14g

1. Process the collard greens through an electronic juicer according to the manufacturer's directions.

2. Add the lemon.

3. Stir the juice to combine the ingredients and sweeten with the agave nectar.

Agave Nectar

Agave nectar has become a popular alternative to artificial sweeteners, because it has little impact on blood sugar.

HONEY MELON JUICE

This delicious juice is high in vitamins C and B$_2$, which strengthen immunity—plus kids love it!

INGREDIENTS

½ honeydew melon, peeled and seeded

1 cup black grapes

½ medium seedless watermelon, cut into chunks

1 cup low-fat milk

Yields: 3 cups (6 servings)

Per ½ cup serving • Calories: 177 • Fat: 1g • Protein: 4g • Sodium: 37mg • Sugar: 36g • Carbohydrates: 42g

1. Process the honeydew through an electronic juicer according to the manufacturer's directions.

2. Add the grapes, followed by the watermelon.

3. Combine the juice with the milk and serve.

JOY JUICE

A winning combo that tastes like fruit, but sneaks in a cucumber for good measure.

INGREDIENTS

1 small seedless watermelon, peeled and cubed

1 medium cucumber

1 large lime, or medium lemon, peeled

Yields: 3 cups (6 servings)

Per ½ cup serving • Calories: 236 • Fat: 1.2g • Protein: 4.9g • Sodium: 9mg • Sugar: 47g • Carbohydrates: 59g

1. Process the watermelon and cucumber through an electronic juicer according to the manufacturer's directions.

2. Add the lime.

3. Stir the juice to combine the ingredients and serve.

JUNGLE JUICE

When busy kids don't have time to eat, this juice will keep them going.

INGREDIENTS

¼ cup fresh mint

1 pineapple, peeled and cut into chunks

1 papaya, peeled and seeded

1 small mango, peeled and seeded

Yields: 3 cups (6 servings)

Per ½ cup serving • Calories: 119 • Fat: 0.3g
• Protein: 1.4g • Sodium: 4.8mg • Sugar: 22g
• Carbohydrates: 30g

1. Process the mint and fruits in any order through an electronic juicer according to the manufacturer's directions.

2. Mix the juice to combine the ingredients and serve.

KID'S CHOICE

Mild melon, juicy cherries, and grapes make for great taste and a really appealing color in this combination.

INGREDIENTS

1 cup cantaloupe chunks

½ cup sweet cherries, pitted

1 cup white or green seedless grapes

Yields: 1½ cups (3 servings)

Per ½ cup serving • Calories: 68 • Fat: 0.2g
• Protein: 1g • Sodium: 9mg • Sugar: 15g •
Carbohydrates: 17g

1. Process the fruits in any order through an electronic juicer according to the manufacturer's directions.

2. Mix the juice to combine the ingredients and serve.

KIWI PEAR POTION

This juice is especially great in cold and flu season to arm your little ones with extra vitamin C.

INGREDIENTS

2 kiwis

2 pears, cored

½ cup water or skim milk

Yields: 1 cup (2 servings)

Per ½ cup serving • Calories: 264 • Fat: 1g • Protein: 2.6g • Sodium: 10mg • Sugar: 29g • Carbohydrates: 68g

1. Process the kiwis through an electronic juicer according to the manufacturer's directions.

2. Add the pears.

3. Dilute with water or skim milk and mix.

MANGO PEAR PUNCH

Yummy! The pears nicely offset the sharper notes of mango here in a way that's sure to please the less than sophisticated kiddie palate.

INGREDIENTS

2 small mangos, seeded

2 medium pears, cored

2 medium carrots, trimmed

2 medium apples, cored

Yields: 1½ cups (3 servings)

Per ½ cup serving • Calories: 226 • Fat: 0.7g • Protein: 1.8g • Sodium: 32mg • Sugar: 44g • Carbohydrates: 59g

1. Process the mangos through an electronic juicer according to the manufacturer's directions.

2. Add the pears, followed by the carrots.

3. Add the apples.

4. Mix the juice to combine the ingredients and serve.

Kid-Sized Portions

While older kids can handle a full serving of undiluted fresh juice, reduce portion size for young ones, limiting servings to ½ to ¾ cup. Too much more than that can lead to stomach or gastrointestinal upset.

MIGHTY GRAPE

An old standby with a new twist—mellow honeydew melon.

INGREDIENTS

1 cup Concord grapes

1 cup honeydew melon

½ cup water

Yields: 1 cup (2 servings)

Per ½ cup serving • Calories: 165 • Fat: 0.5g
• Protein: 2g • Sodium: 33mg • Sugar: 37g •
Carbohydrates: 42g

1. Process the grapes through an electronic juicer according to the manufacturer's directions.

2. Add the melon.

3. Dilute with water to taste and serve.

MINT SHAKE

Most kids love the sweet and minty flavor, and will never suspect the chlorophyll and phytonutrients this juice contains.

INGREDIENTS

2 cups pineapple chunks

½ cup fresh mint

½ cup filtered water or skim milk

Yields: 1 cup (2 servings)

Per ½ cup serving • Calories: 95 • Fat: 0.3g •
Protein: 1.6g • Sodium: 8mg • Sugar: 16g •
Carbohydrates: 23g

1. Process the pineapple through an electronic juicer according to the manufacturer's directions.

2. Roll the mint into a ball and add to the juicer.

3. Dilute the juice with water or milk, and shake until foamy.

Pineapple Sensitivity

Very young kids can have sensitivity to fresh pineapple, but you can use canned, packed in its own juice.

OJ FOOLER

Imagine their faces when you ask them to taste, and then tell them there aren't any oranges in this one!

INGREDIENTS

3–4 tangerines or clementines, peeled

½ cup water

Yields: 1 cup (2 servings)

Per ½ cup serving • Calories: 139 • Fat: 0.8g • Protein: 2g • Sodium: 5mg • Sugar: 27g • Carbohydrates: 35g

1. Process the fruit through an electronic juicer according to the manufacturer's directions.

2. Dilute with water to taste.

Easy on the Tummy

Tangerines or clementines have just as much nutrition and vitamin C as oranges, but are friendlier for younger kids, who may be sensitive to orange's higher acid content.

ORANGEBERRY JUICE

This juice contains an array of nutrients to give kids energy, making it an excellent breakfast juice.

INGREDIENTS

1 cup fresh raspberries

2 oranges, peeled

2 nectarines, pitted

Yields: 1½ cups (3 servings)

Per ½ cup serving • Calories: 89 • Fat: 0.6g • Protein: 2g • Sodium: 0.41mg • Sugar: 14g • Carbohydrates: 21g

1. Process the raspberries and oranges through an electronic juicer according to the manufacturer's directions.

2. Add the nectarines.

3. Whisk or shake the juice and serve alone or diluted with ½ cup skim milk.

Oranges and Calcium

Just one of the reasons orange-based juices are important for kids is that the calcium they contain helps build strong bones. A medium-sized orange has 52mg of calcium.

PEPPERMINT JUICE

In addition to great flavor, peppermint is a great natural cure for upset tummies.

INGREDIENTS

½ cup fresh peppermint leaves

½ cucumber

½ cup bean sprouts

2 leaves romaine lettuce

1 teaspoon raw honey (optional—do not give honey to children under 1 year of age)

Yields: 1½ cups (3 servings)

Per ½ cup serving • Calories: 26 • Fat: 0.3g • Protein: 2.3g • Sodium: 8.8mg • Sugar: 1g • Carbohydrates: 5g

1. Process the peppermint and cucumber through an electronic juicer according to the manufacturer's directions.

2. Add the sprouts and the romaine.

3. Sweeten the juice with honey as desired.

PLAIN PEAR

An excellent choice for toddlers, this one is just right for a sippy cup.

INGREDIENTS

2 pears, cored

½ cup filtered water

Yields: 1 cup (2 servings)

Per ½ cup serving • Calories: 85 • Fat: 0.1g • Protein: 0.5g • Sodium: 1.4mg • Sugar: 14g • Carbohydrates: 22g

1. Process the pears through an electronic juicer according to the manufacturer's directions.

2. Dilute with water and serve.

Make Your Own

Kids are likely to enjoy their juice more when you let them pick their own combinations. Simply put an array of prepared fruits and veggies out on the table and let them make their choices.

PUMPKIN JUICE

Though generally thought of as a fruit, pumpkin is actually a squash, belonging to the same family as other summer squashes. Use a heavier duty juicer for this one, especially if you're tackling a bigger pumpkin!

INGREDIENTS

2 cups chopped pumpkin

½ cup water

1" ginger, peeled

3 tablespoons raw honey

Yields: 1 cup

Per 1 cup serving • Calories: 272 • Fat: 0.5g • Protein: 3g • Sodium: 10mg • Sugar: 55g • Carbohydrates: 71g

1. Process the pumpkin through an electronic juicer according to the manufacturer's directions.

2. Add the water, ginger, and honey.

3. Mix or shake the juice to combine the ingredients and serve alone or over ice.

Don't Toss That Pumpkin!

Once your pumpkin has done its Halloween duty, slice it into segments and freeze. The squash can be repurposed for all kinds of uses. When juicing pumpkin, reserve the pulp and freeze to use in pies, baking, or other recipes. Just be sure to use or freeze your pumpkin within 24 hours.

PURPLE MOO JUICE

If your child is allergic to dairy, use soy or rice milk instead.

INGREDIENTS

1 cup blueberries

½ cup blackberries

1 cup skim milk or soymilk

Yields: 1½ cups (3 servings)

Per ½ cup serving • Calories: 72 • Fat: 1g • Protein: 3.4g • Sodium: 36mg • Sugar: 10g • Carbohydrates: 13g

1. Process the berries through an electronic juicer according to the manufacturer's directions.

2. Mix the juice with the milk to combine and serve.

Soymilk

As an alternative to dairy, soymilk is also a good source of copper, vitamin D, riboflavin, vitamin B_{12}, and calcium.

SPAPPLE JUICE

Just call it that; they'll never suspect the spinach.

INGREDIENTS

1 cup spinach

2 Gala or Pink Lady apples, cored

1 lemon, peeled

3–4 drops stevia (optional)

Yields: 1 cup (2 servings)

Per ½ cup serving • Calories: 64 • Fat: 0.2g • Protein: 1g • Sodium: 12mg • Sugar: 11g • Carbohydrates: 17g

1. Process the spinach through an electronic juicer according to the manufacturer's directions.

2. Add the apples and the lemon.

3. Sweeten the juice with stevia as desired.

Stevia

Stevia is a popular sweetener used in place of sugar or artificial sweeteners. It's available as an extract or in powdered form. It comes from an herb in the sunflower family.

WATERMELON MIX

Kids love watermelon, and the addition of a few cherries only makes it better!

INGREDIENTS

2 cups watermelon chunks

½ cup sweet cherries, pitted

1 cup filtered water

Yields: 2 cups (4 servings)

Per ½ cup serving • Calories: 139 • Fat: 0.6g • Protein: 2.6g • Sodium: 3mg • Sugar: 28g • Carbohydrates: 35g

1. Process the watermelon through an electronic juicer according to the manufacturer's directions.

2. Add the cherries.

3. Dilute with water and mix.

WHITE GRAPE WONDER

This juice provides wonderful nutrition and doesn't stain kids' clothes like some other grape juices can.

INGREDIENTS

2 cups white or green seedless grapes

½ cup filtered water

Yields: 1½ cups (3 servings)

Per ½ cup serving • Calories: 208 • Fat: 0.4g • Protein: 2g • Sodium: 6mg • Sugar: 46g • Carbohydrates: 54g

1. Process the grapes through an electronic juicer according to the manufacturer's directions.

2. Dilute with water and mix.

CHAPTER 13

JUICES FOR HEALTHY LIVING

7-UP

These seven ingredients combine in a powerful vegetable juice for cancer prevention, because of their ability to fight free radicals and inflammation.

INGREDIENTS

3 tomatoes

2 medium carrots, trimmed

1 celery stalk, leaves intact

½ cup parsley

2 green onions

1 cup cauliflower florets

2 garlic cloves, peeled

Yields: 1½ cups

Per 1 cup serving • Calories: 135 • Fat: 1g • Protein: 6.4g • Sodium: 136mg • Sugar: 16g • Carbohydrates: 29g

1. Process the tomatoes through an electronic juicer according to the manufacturer's directions.

2. Add the carrots, celery, and parsley.

3. Next add the onions, the cauliflower, and the garlic.

4. Mix the juice to combine the ingredients. Serve alone or over ice.

ACNE BLASTER

Whether you're troubled by long-term acne problems or annoying little monthly breakouts, this one will help clear your skin fast!

INGREDIENTS

2 medium carrots, trimmed

1 medium cucumber

1 cup spinach

Yields: 1 cup

Per 1 cup serving • Calories: 102 • Fat: 0.7g • Protein: 4g • Sodium: 113mg • Sugar: 10g • Carbohydrates: 23g

1. Process the carrots through your electronic juicer according to the manufacturer's directions.

2. Add the cucumber, followed by the spinach.

3. Stir or shake the juice thoroughly to combine and serve alone or over ice.

Spinach and Memory

A recent study showed that when elderly people ate spinach, it prevented memory loss and even reversed it. So don't forget to eat your spinach!

ALL CLEAR

If your sensitive skin is prone to upsets such as rashes or reactions to cosmetics, try this sweet and refreshing juice.

INGREDIENTS

1½ cups pineapple chunks

1 large cucumber

1 apple, cored

Yields: 1½ cups

Per 1 cup serving • Calories: 176 • Fat: 0.6g
• Protein: 2.5g • Sodium: 7mg • Sugar: 32g
• Carbohydrates: 46g

1. Process the pineapple through an electronic juicer according to the manufacturer's directions.

2. Add the cucumber, followed by the apple.

3. Stir or shake the juice to combine the ingredients and enjoy!

THE ANTI-AGING BODY BOOSTER

Cherries contain lutein. Lutein plus vitamins A and C up collagen production, which results in stronger bones and younger-looking skin.

INGREDIENTS

1 medium apple, cored

2 medium pears, cored

½ cup Bing or Queen Anne cherries, pitted

Yield: 1½ cups

Per 1 cup serving • Calories: 226 • Fat: 1.9g
• Protein: 2g • Sodium: 1.2mg • Sugar: 41g
• Carbohydrates: 58g

1. Process the apple through an electronic juicer according to the manufacturer's directions.

2. Add the pears, followed by the cherries.

3. Whisk the juice to combine ingredients and enjoy!

Antioxidants, Anyone?

Cherries are extraordinarily high in the nutrients necessary to help the body destroy free radicals. Data from the USDA's 2007 Oxygen Radical Absorbance Capacity table gives sweet cherries a total ORAC score of 3,365 per 3.5 ounces.

ASPARAGUS ZUCCHINI MEDLEY

There's nothing better than asparagus for regulating blood sugar levels.

INGREDIENTS

8 stalks asparagus, trimmed

2 medium zucchini, trimmed

Yields: 1½ cups

Per 1 cup serving • Calories: 94 • Fat: 1.5g •
Protein: 7.5g • Sodium: 37mg • Sugar: 12g •
Carbohydrates: 17g

1. Process the vegetables through your juicer according to the manufacturer's directions.

2. Mix the juice to combine the ingredients and serve over ice.

BANANA GRAPEFRUIT REFRESHER

The potassium found in bananas is very heart healthy. Make this one in a blender for best results.

INGREDIENTS

1 large pink grapefruit, peeled

1 banana, peeled

½ cup skim milk or coconut water

Yields: 1 cup

Per 1 cup serving • Calories: 223 • Fat: 1.7g
• Protein: 6.8g • Sodium: 54mg • Sugar: 36g
• Carbohydrates: 49g

1. Place the grapefruit sections, the banana, and the milk or coconut water in a blender and purée until smooth.

2. Serve the smoothie immediately.

BASIL BLAST

Better than a trip to the Mediterranean! Well, maybe not quite . . .

INGREDIENTS

1 cup fresh basil leaves

4 Roma tomatoes

1 garlic clove, peeled

½ medium cucumber

Yields: 1½ cups

Per 1 cup serving • Calories: 54 • Fat: 0.6g
• Protein: 3g • Sodium: 12mg • Sugar: 6g •
Carbohydrates: 11g

1. Process the basil and tomatoes through an electronic juicer according to the manufacturer's directions.

2. Add the garlic and cucumber.

3. Serve the juice alone or over ice.

BEAN MACHINE

Any variety of green beans will do for this recipe, but the flat, Roma variety does yield more juice.

INGREDIENTS

2 cups fresh green beans

5 large leaves romaine lettuce

1 cucumber

1 lemon cut into quarters, peeled

Yields: 1 cup

Per 1 cup serving • Calories: 137 • Fat: 1g •
Protein: 8g • Sodium: 30mg • Sugar: 13g •
Carbohydrates: 30g

1. Process the beans through your electronic juicer according to the manufacturer's directions.

2. Add the romaine, followed by the cucumber and the lemon.

3. Mix the juice thoroughly to combine the ingredients and serve alone or over ice.

Green Bean Facts

Green beans provide a good source of protein, thiamine, riboflavin, niacin, vitamin B_6, calcium, iron, magnesium, phosphorus, potassium, and copper.

BEET HIGH BLOOD PRESSURE

High blood pressure happens when the flow of blood puts too much pressure on your arteries. Fresh fruits and vegetables have a wonderful effect on lowering blood pressure, and beets are especially effective.

INGREDIENTS

1 medium beet, tailed and trimmed

1 medium carrot, trimmed

3 stalks celery, with leaves

Yields: 1 cup

Per 1 cup serving • Calories: 74 • Fat: 0.4g • Protein: 2.6g • Sodium: 194mg • Sugar: 10g • Carbohydrates: 16g

1. Process the beet through an electronic juicer according to the manufacturer's directions.

2. Add the carrot and the celery.

3. Stir the juice to combine the ingredients. Serve alone or over ice.

Celery and Blood Pressure

The phthalides in celery have been shown to lower blood pressure. Celery is also a great source of potassium, calcium, and magnesium, each of which help to control hypertension, according to the Linus Pauling Institute.

BEST OF BOTH WORLDS

Some of the best fruits are combined with the best veggies in a winning combination for maximum benefit.

INGREDIENTS

4–6 medium carrots, trimmed

1 medium sweet potato, peeled

1 red bell pepper, seeded

2 kiwis

1" ginger, peeled

½ lemon, peeled

2 stalks celery, with leaves

Yields: 1½ cups

Per 1 cup serving • Calories: 310 • Fat: 0.9g • Protein: 7.8g • Sodium: 257mg • Sugar: 36g • Carbohydrates: 71g

1. Process the carrots through an electronic juicer according to the manufacturer's directions.

2. Add the sweet potato, followed by the pepper.

3. Add the kiwis and the ginger.

4. Add the lemon and the celery.

5. Whisk or shake the juice thoroughly to combine and serve alone or over ice.

BLOOD PRESSURE BUSTER

Science Daily reports that researchers from the London School of Medicine discovered that beet juice can lower blood pressure within an hour of drinking it and keep blood pressure down for up to twenty-four hours.

INGREDIENTS

1 medium beet, tailed and trimmed

1 medium orange, peeled

1 medium apple, cored

Yields: 1 cup

Per 1 cup serving • Calories: 133 • Fat: 0.4g • Protein: 2.5g • Sodium: 63mg • Sugar: 25g • Carbohydrates: 33g

1. Process the beet through an electronic juicer according to the manufacturer's directions.

2. Add the orange and the apple.

3. Stir the juice to combine the ingredients. Serve alone or over ice.

BLUE HAWAII

Try this in your fight against Father Time. The super combination of blueberries and pineapple will make you feel like a kid again!

INGREDIENTS

¼ pineapple, peeled

1 cup blueberries

½" ginger, peeled

Yields: 1 cup

Per 1 cup serving • Calories: 216 • Fat: 1g • Protein: 3g • Sodium: 5mg • Sugar: 37g • Carbohydrates: 54g

1. Process the pineapple and blueberries through an electronic juicer according to the manufacturer's directions.

2. Add the ginger.

3. Whisk the juice to combine the ingredients and serve over ice.

BOK CHOY BLEND

For those who can't abide cabbage, the milder-flavored bok choy is a great substitute. Reducing blood pressure is just one of the many health benefits it has to offer, as it also includes antioxidants and vitamin C, and is a rich source of potassium.

INGREDIENTS

2 large leaves bok choy

2 stalks celery, with leaves

1 cup spinach

3 leaves romaine lettuce

Yields: 1½ cups

Per 1 cup serving • Calories: 30 • Fat: 0.5g • Protein: 2.2g • Sodium: 77mg • Sugar: 2g • Carbohydrates: 5.5g

1. Process the bok choy through your juicer according to the manufacturer's directions.

2. Add the celery, followed by the spinach and the romaine.

3. Serve the juice alone or over ice.

BOOST JUICE

It's too bad that so many people are relying on so-called energy drinks when the juice alternative is so much healthier! Try this the next time you need a boost.

INGREDIENTS

1 small sweet potato, peeled

1 large carrot, trimmed

2 ripe pears, cored

3 medium oranges, peeled

Yields: 1½ cups

Per 1 cup serving • Calories: 351 • Fat: 1.8g • Protein: 5.6g • Sodium: 81mg • Sugar: 53g • Carbohydrates: 86g

1. Wash fruits and vegetables thoroughly. Cut the sweet potato into pieces.

2. Process the carrot and sweet potato through your juicer according to manufacturer's directions.

3. Add the pears and orange segments and process.

4. Mix the juice thoroughly before serving.

Pears for Good Health

A great flavor complement and sweetener for many juices, pears are also rich in vitamins B_1 and B_2 and are considered by food experts to be hypoallergenic. When juicing pears, choose harder varieties, such as Bosc or Anjou. Softer pears yield less juice and more pulp to your mixture.

BOOSTING BODY CLEANSE

One of the first places the need for detox shows up is in the complexion. This one is especially recommended for calming down skin flare-ups and restoring a healthy glow.

INGREDIENTS

1 cup broccoli florets

3 medium carrots, trimmed

1 medium apple, such as Granny Smith, cored

1 celery stalk, including leaves

½ cup spinach leaves

Yields: 1 cup

Per 1 cup serving • Calories: 206 • Fat: 1g • Protein: 5g • Sodium: 222mg • Sugar: 28g • Carbohydrates: 49g

1. Process the broccoli, carrots, and apple through an electronic juicer according to the manufacturer's directions.

2. Add the celery stalk and spinach leaves.

3. Mix the juice thoroughly and drink as soon as possible after preparation for maximum effect.

Cheers to Broccoli!

Less than 50 calories' worth of broccoli contains more than 150 percent of our daily requirements of vitamin C, 60 percent of vitamin A, 5 percent of iron, and 5 percent of calcium. It's also rich in sulforaphane, an enzyme that is essential in removing potentially harmful carcinogens from the body. Finally, other phytonutrients help protect and balance estrogen cells, which some scientists believe are particularly susceptible to cancer-causing agents.

BORSCHT IN A GLASS

Add plain yogurt to this recipe for a more authentic borscht experience!

INGREDIENTS

2 small sugar beets, including greens

1 medium apple, cored

1 medium orange, peeled

3 green onions, including tops

1 large cucumber

2 tablespoons fresh mint leaves

Yields: 1 cup

Per 1 cup serving • Calories: 220 • Fat: 1g • Protein: 5g • Sodium: 138mg • Sugar: 39g • Carbohydrates: 53g

1. Process the beets and greens through your electronic juicer according to the manufacturer's directions.

2. Add the apple, followed by the orange segments.

3. Add the onions and cucumber.

4. Add the mint leaves.

5. Mix the juice thoroughly to combine and serve over ice.

More on Beet Greens

Like beets themselves, beet greens are a powerful cleanser of the liver, blood, and kidneys. Beet juice and juice made with beet greens should always be taken in moderation and always combined with other ingredients to avoid the ill effects sometimes associated with a high oxalic acid content.

BREATHE EASY

This recipe is especially good for older adults afflicted with COPD, allergies, or asthma. It also has the added benefit of aiding eyesight.

INGREDIENTS

2 cups broccoli florets

1 large cucumber

1 medium zucchini

10 stalks asparagus, trimmed

Yields: 1 cup

Per 1 cup serving • Calories: 118 • Fat: 1.2g • Protein: 9.7g • Sodium: 73mg • Sugar: 9.7g • Carbohydrates: 23g

1. Process the broccoli through an electronic juicer according to the manufacturer's directions.

2. Add the cucumber.

3. Add the zucchini, followed by the asparagus.

4. Mix the juice thoroughly to combine ingredients and drink immediately.

BRUSSELS BEAN JUICE

Brussels sprouts and beans are both good sources of natural insulin, and so are considered beneficial for people with diabetes and pre-diabetes.

INGREDIENTS

1 cup green beans

6 Brussels sprouts

1 lemon, peeled

Yields: 1 cup

Per 1 cup serving • Calories: 99 • Fat: 0.7g • Protein: 6.5g • Sodium: 36mg • Sugar: 7.5g • Carbohydrates: 23g

1. Process the beans through an electronic juicer according to the manufacturer's directions.

2. Add the Brussels sprouts, followed by the lemon.

3. Mix the juice to combine the ingredients. Serve alone or over ice.

Turning Up Your Nose?

The stronger flavors of cabbages and Brussels sprouts are greatly mitigated by the lemon juice.

CABBAGE PATCH COMBO

The great thing about cabbage, aside from its health benefits, is that it's inexpensive year-round.

INGREDIENTS

¼ head red cabbage

1 cup green cabbage

2 large apples, cored

Yields: 1½ cups

Per 1 cup serving • Calories: 209 • Fat: 0.8g
• Protein: 3.3g • Sodium: 49mg • Sugar: 36g
• Carbohydrates: 54g

1. Process the cabbages through your juicer according to the manufacturer's directions.

2. Add the apples.

3. Stir the juice to combine the ingredients. Serve alone or over ice.

CELLULITE BUSTER

Any juice with high diuretic properties is going to help eliminate cellulite by reducing the water content of fat cells, thereby lessening those dreaded "dimples."

INGREDIENTS

1 apple, cored

1 grapefruit, peeled

2 stalks celery, with leaves

½ cucumber

2 tablespoons fresh mint leaves

Yields: 1 cup

Per 1 cup serving • Calories: 161 • Fat: 0.8g
• Protein: 3.7g • Sodium: 78mg • Sugar: 29g
• Carbohydrates: 39g

1. Process the apple through an electronic juicer according to the manufacturer's directions.

2. Add the grapefruit sections, followed by the celery.

3. Add the cucumber and mint leaves.

4. Whisk or shake the juice to blend and enjoy!

Weight Loss and Calcium

Many studies have proven there's a direct relationship between calcium intake and the ability to lose weight easily. So when juicing for weight loss, look for fruits and veggies with a high calcium content including spinach, broccoli, bok choy, oranges, and grapefruit.

CITRUS BLEND

The fruits in the citrus family can work wonders at reducing high blood pressure.

INGREDIENTS

1 medium orange, peeled

2 limes, peeled

1 lemon, peeled

1 tablespoon raw honey

Yields: 1 cup

Per 1 cup serving • Calories: 166 • Fat: 0.5g • Protein: 2.5g • Sodium: 4.6mg • Sugar: 30g • Carbohydrates: 48g

1. Process the fruits in any order through an electronic juicer according to the manufacturer's directions.

2. Add the honey to the resulting juice.

3. Stir the juice to combine the ingredients. Serve alone or over ice.

Citrus and Blood Pressure

Studies suggest that vitamin C reduces systolic blood pressure. A glass of orange juice at every meal can significantly lower your blood pressure. Any citrus fruit will do, but if you are also taking cholesterol medication, check with your doctor before drinking grapefruit juice.

COLLARDS AGAINST CANCER

When it comes to fighting or preventing cancer remember the four c's—collards, cabbage, carrots, and cauliflower.

INGREDIENTS

1 cup chopped collard greens

1 cup chopped cabbage

1 cup cauliflower florets

2 carrots, trimmed

Yields: 1½ cups

Per 1 cup serving • Calories: 83 • Fat: 0.4g • Protein: 4g • Sodium: 87mg • Sugar: 8g • Carbohydrates: 18g

1. Process the greens through an electronic juicer according to the manufacturer's directions.

2. Add the cabbage and cauliflower, followed by the carrots.

3. Mix the juice to combine the ingredients. Serve alone or over ice.

The Right Stuff

Cabbage and cauliflower contain several chemical compounds that research indicates provide protection against cancer. One of these, indole-3-carbinol, may deactivate estrogen and reduce the risk of breast cancer, while the compound sulforaphane helps degrade free radicals and some carcinogenic substances.

COMBAT DEPRESSION

For some, seasonal depression can be a problem, for others it can result from external stressors. In any event, when juiced, these foods can provide a healthy lift when you're battling the blues.

INGREDIENTS

4 broccoli spears

½ cup spinach leaves

3 Swiss chard leaves

1 red bell pepper, seeded

Yields: 1 cup

Per 1 cup serving • Calories: 109 • Fat: 1g • Protein: 7.6g • Sodium: 364mg • Sugar: 8g • Carbohydrates: 21g

1. Process the broccoli, spinach, and chard through an electronic juicer according to the manufacturer's directions.

2. Add the bell pepper.

3. Stir the juice to combine the ingredients. Serve alone or over ice.

Look to the B Group for Treating Mood

Folate, as well as increasing and maintaining levels of B vitamins in the blood, has been shown to improve mood and energy levels. All green leafy vegetables such as spinach and chard are excellent sources of B complex, while broccoli and peppers are rich in folate.

COMMON COLD ADE

Vitamin C helps to alleviate cold symptoms.

INGREDIENTS

2 oranges, peeled

3 leaves rainbow chard

½ lemon, peeled

Yields: 1½ cups

Per 1 cup serving • Calories: 115 • Fat: 0.5g • Protein: 3.6g • Sodium: 206mg • Sugar: 17g • Carbohydrates: 29g

1. Process the oranges and the chard through an electronic juicer according to the manufacturer's directions.

2. Add the lemon.

3. Mix the juice to combine the ingredients. Serve alone or over ice.

ANTI-CANCER CRUCIFERS

All these cruciferous vegetables, members of the cabbage family, are rich in the vitamins, mineral, and fiber believed essential to preventing and fighting cancer.

INGREDIENTS

1 stalk of broccoli

¼ head of cabbage

¼ head of cauliflower

2 kale leaves

½ lemon

2 apples, cored

Yields: 1½ cups

Per 1 cup serving • Calories: 227 • Fat: 1.7g • Protein: 8.6g • Sodium: 125mg • Sugar: 25g • Carbohydrates: 54g

1. Process the broccoli segments through an electronic juicer according to the manufacturer's directions.

2. Add the cabbage, followed by the cauliflower.

3. Add the kale, followed by the lemon and the apples.

4. Whisk the juice together to combine and serve over ice.

Broccoli Caution

If you're a Type 2 diabetic, consult with your doctor about juicing. Broccoli juice has been seen to interfere with some diabetic medications.

CUCUMBER COMPLEXION TONIC

Cucumbers are known to help the skin from becoming overly dry. Cucumbers contain silica, which helps improve the complexion.

INGREDIENTS

½ large cucumber, peeled

1 celery stalk, leaves intact

2 sprigs fresh baby dill, for garnish

Yields: 1¼ cups

Per 1¼ cup serving • Calories: 18 • Fat: 0.2g • Protein: 0.9g • Sodium: 34mg • Sugar: 2g • Carbohydrates: 3.4g

1. Process the cucumber through your electronic juicer according to the manufacturer's directions.

2. Add the celery.

3. Mix the juice thoroughly to combine and add fresh sprigs of dill to the top of the drink for garnish.

C-WATER DETOX

Don't forget that good old aqua pura *is one of the best and most efficient ways to detox and cleanse your body. The recipe uses kiwi and grapefruit for a nice vitamin C blast as well.*

INGREDIENTS

3 kiwis

2 pink grapefruits, peeled and seeded

4 ounces water

Yields: 1½ cups

Per 1 cup serving • Calories: 205 • Fat: 1g • Protein: 3.2g • Sodium: 10mg • Sugar: 12g • Carbohydrates: 52g

1. Process the kiwis and the grapefruit through your electronic juicer according to the manufacturer's directions.

2. Add the water and mix thoroughly.

3. Drink as soon as possible after preparation, as fresh vitamin C deteriorates quickly.

Peel It?

Despite the kiwi's fuzzy exterior, it really isn't necessary to peel them before processing. If you find the fuzz too off putting, scrub the fruit lightly with a brush to remove it before juicing.

THE DETOX SPECIAL

Any worthwhile detox regimen will pay special attention to fruits and veggies that benefit the liver. Not only is it the largest organ in the body, it's one of the most important for its abilities to eliminate toxins, filter the blood, metabolize nutrients, and perform hundreds of other functions.

INGREDIENTS

3 medium sugar beets, including greens, trimmed

1 medium carrot, trimmed

½ pound black seedless grapes

Yields: 1 cup

Per 1 cup serving • Calories: 289 • Fat: 1g • Protein: 6g • Sodium: 246mg • Sugar: 54g • Carbohydrates: 70g

1. Cut the beets and greens into pieces.

2. Process the beets, greens, and carrots through your electronic juicer according to the manufacturer's directions.

3. Add the grapes.

4. Whisk the juice to combine the ingredients completely. Drink immediately.

EDEN ELIXIR

Some say Eve ate an apple, others say a pomegranate. Either way, this will put you in paradise.

INGREDIENTS

6 carrots, trimmed

2 kale leaves

4 Brussels sprouts

1 apple or ¼ cup pomegranate pips

Yields: 1½ cups

Per 1 cup serving • Calories: 219 • Fat: 0.4g • Protein: 6.5g • Sodium: 178mg • Sugar: 31g • Carbohydrates: 51g

1. Process the carrots through an electronic juicer according to the manufacturer's directions.

2. Add the kale, followed by the Brussels sprouts and the apple or pomegranate.

3. Whisk the juice to combine the ingredients and serve alone or over ice.

Brussels Sprouts and Cancer Prevention

Three major systems in the body that figure into cancer risk are the body's detox system, its antioxidant system, and its anti-inflammatory system. Chronic imbalances in any of these three systems can increase risk of cancer, and when imbalances in all three systems occur simultaneously, the risk of cancer increases. The good news is that Brussels sprouts have been seen to have a significant impact on the health of each of these systems without the negative impact on the thyroid sometimes associated with the cruciferous group.

THE ENERGIZER

Need a jolt? This concoction will perk you up and keep you on your toes.

INGREDIENTS

2 apples, cored

½ cucumber

¼ bulb fennel

3 stalks celery, including leaves

½ lemon, peeled

¼" ginger

½ cup of kale

½ cup of spinach

6 leaves romaine lettuce

Yields: 2 cups

Per 1 cup serving • Calories: 142 • Fat: 0.8g • Protein: 3g • Sodium: 81mg • Sugar: 22g • Carbohydrates: 36g

1. Slice the apples and process through the feed tube of an electronic juicer according to the manufacturer's directions.

2. Follow with pieces of cucumber and fennel.

3. Add the celery, followed by the lemon and the ginger.

4. Lightly tear the remaining greens into pieces and process.

5. Mix the juice thoroughly before serving. Serve over ice if desired.

Balance the Flavor

Adding citrus, apples, and ginger to predominantly green juices brightens the flavor to offset the sometimes bitter taste of greens such as kale.

THE EYES HAVE IT

When carrots are eaten raw, you only absorb 1 percent of the carrot's available beta-carotene. When you juice your carrots, that amount is increased by almost a hundredfold. Plus, the sweet potato included in this recipe is rich in vitamin B$_6$, which has been shown to be essential in the maintenance of healthy blood vessels.

INGREDIENTS

4 medium carrots, trimmed

1 sweet potato, peeled

1 cup pineapple chunks

2 medium oranges, peeled

Yields: 1½ cups

Per 1 cup serving • Calories: 314 • Fat: 0.5g • Protein: 6.3g • Sodium: 157mg • Sugar: 44g • Carbohydrates: 779g

1. Process the carrots, one at a time, through an electronic juicer according to the manufacturer's directions.

2. Cut the sweet potato into chunks and add to the juicer.

3. Add the pineapple chunks, followed by the orange segments.

4. Whisk the juice together to combine and serve immediately.

Feeling Ravaged by Time?

The nutrients in fresh fruit and vegetable juice are also responsible for reducing or eliminating high cholesterol, carpal tunnel, constipation, gallstones, glaucoma, hypertension, indigestion, insomnia, kidney stones, macular degeneration, menopause, osteoporosis, prostate enlargement, psoriasis, and varicose veins.

FEEL THE BURN FAT BURNER

This hot and spicy concoction will perk up your taste buds and your metabolism. Hot peppers help to speed up metabolic systems and increase circulation.

INGREDIENTS

2 large tomatoes, quartered

2 stalks celery

3–4 radishes, tailed and trimmed

1 sweet red bell pepper, seeded

1 yellow banana pepper, or 1 fresh jalapeño pepper, seeded

3 green onions

½ teaspoon cayenne pepper

Generous dash of Tabasco sauce, or to taste

Yields: 2½ cups (2 servings)

Per 1¼ cup serving • Calories: 129 • Fat: 1.7g • Protein: 5.5g • Sodium: 460mg • Sugar: 17g • Carbohydrates: 26g

1. Process the tomatoes and the celery through an electronic juicer according to the manufacturer's directions.

2. Add the radishes and peppers.

3. Add the green onions.

4. Add the cayenne and hot sauce.

5. Whisk the juice to combine and enjoy!

Spice It Up!

Capsaicin is a chemical found in jalapeño, cayenne, and other varieties of hot peppers. It's thought to aid weight loss because eating or juicing the peppers temporarily stimulates your body to release more stress hormones, which speeds up the metabolism in response.

FOUNTAIN OF YOUTH COCKTAIL

This refreshing anti-aging juice is packed with vitamins and antioxidants. Start your morning with all the nutritious benefits this juice has to offer.

INGREDIENTS

1 pint blackberries

1 pint raspberries

½ lemon, peeled

¼" ginger

Yields: ¾ cup

Per ¾ cup serving • Calories: 261 • Fat: 3g • Protein: 7g • Sodium: 6mg • Sugar: 25g • Carbohydrates: 60g

1. Process the berries through an electronic juicer according to the manufacturer's directions.

2. Add the lemon and ginger.

3. Mix the juice thoroughly and enjoy over ice if desired.

What Are Antioxidants?

Antioxidants are nutrients that can prevent or slow oxidative damage to your body. When your body's cells use oxygen, they naturally produce free radicals that can cause damage. Antioxidants work as scavengers, gobbling up the free radicals and preventing and repairing the damage they cause.

GINGER ZINGER

Another great choice for your morning wakeup call.

INGREDIENTS

3 medium Granny Smith apples, cored

½ medium cucumber

1" ginger, peeled

Yields: 1 cup

Per 1 cup serving • Calories: 312 • Fat: 1g • Protein: 2.5g • Sodium: 9mg • Sugar: 59g • Carbohydrates: 82g

1. Process the apple through your electronic juicer according to the manufacturer's directions.

2. Add the cucumber and ginger.

3. Mix the juice thoroughly and enjoy!

GLAMOROUS GREENS

Watercress and arugula both help activate enzymes in the liver, while acting as a natural diuretic. Plus, they contribute a lively, peppery flavor that makes this one taste like it's fresh from the spa!

INGREDIENTS

½ bunch spinach, about 2 cups

1 cup watercress

1 cup arugula

1 medium apple, cored

½ lemon, peeled

2 stalks celery, with leaves

½" slice ginger

Yields: 1½ cups

Per 1 cup serving • Calories: 92 • Fat: 0.6g • Protein: 2.9g • Sodium: 89mg • Sugar: 14g • Carbohydrates: 22g

1. Rinse the spinach, watercress, and arugula well to ensure greens are free of grit.

2. Process the apple through an electronic juicer according to the manufacturer's directions.

3. Add the lemon and celery stalks.

4. Add the greens and ginger in any order.

5. Whisk the juice to combine and serve well-chilled or over ice.

Juicing Greens

To make juicing green leafy vegetables like lettuce and spinach easier, roll the greens into balls before adding to the juicer.

GREEN GLOW

No, it won't make you glow green, but it will give your skin and hair a marvelously healthy new look.

INGREDIENTS

1 head romaine lettuce

5 leaves of kale

2 pears, cored

1 lemon peeled, cut into quarters

Yields: 1½ cups

Per 1 cup serving • Calories: 226 • Fat: 2.9g
• Protein: 7.9g • Sodium: 43mg • Sugar: 29g
• Carbohydrates: 53g

1. Process the romaine through your electronic juicer according to the manufacturer's directions.

2. Add the kale, followed by the pears and lemon.

3. Stir or shake the juice thoroughly to combine ingredients and serve.

More about Kale

Kale is very rich in vitamin A, which not only fights cancer but also is required for maintaining healthy mucous membranes and skin.

GREEN POWER

These dark leafy greens are rich in carotenoids, a specific group of antioxidants.

INGREDIENTS

1 cup spinach

½ cup kale

3 large leaves romaine lettuce

1 cup mustard greens

Yields: 1 cup

Per 1 cup serving • Calories: 52 • Fat: 0.7g •
Protein: 4.5g • Sodium: 58mg • Sugar: 2g •
Carbohydrates: 10g

1. Process the greens through an electronic juicer according to the manufacturer's directions.

2. Stir the juice to combine the ingredients and serve over ice.

Antioxidants and Free Radicals

Free radicals are elements thought to damage cells, which in turn can lead to the onset of cancerous growths. Antioxidants fight free radicals and reduce the risk of cellular damage.

HAPPINESS IN A GLASS

Pineapple contains manganese and thiamine, which when metabolized translate to increased energy and higher spirits.

INGREDIENTS

1 cup pineapple chunks

2 cups grapes

Yields: 1½ cups

Per 1 cup serving • Calories: 135 • Fat: 1g • Protein: 1.5g • Sodium: 1mg • Sugar: 31g • Carbohydrates: 36g

1. Process the fruits through an electronic juicer according to the manufacturer's directions.

2. Stir the juice to combine the ingredients. Serve alone or over ice.

All about Iron

Iron is such an important mineral because it transports life-sustaining nutrients throughout the body. It also increases oxygen in the blood while removing carbon dioxide. Iron ensures a healthy immune system and creates energy. Iron deficiency can cause a variety of health problems, including fatigue, irritability, and headaches.

HEADACHE CURE

Try this juice the next time you feel a headache coming on.

INGREDIENTS

¾ cup cantaloupe, cut into chunks

½" ginger, peeled

2 small key or Mexican limes

Yields: 1 cup

Per 1 cup serving • Calories: 41 • Fat: 0.2g • Protein: 1g • Sodium: 3mg • Sugar: 2g • Carbohydrates: 14g

1. Process the cantaloupe, ginger, and limes through an electronic juicer according to the manufacturer's directions.

2. Stir the juice to combine the ingredients. Serve alone or over ice.

HEALTH HARVEST SPECIAL

In late summer and early autumn, it's hard to come home from the farmers' market without feeling that you've just bought more than you could ever eat! Juicing is a great way to manage Nature's bounty and take advantage of all the goodness the season provides!

INGREDIENTS

1 small sugar beet, greens optional

6 carrots, trimmed

2 stalks celery, with leaves

1 cucumber

1 grapefruit, peeled

1 kiwi

1 red or black plum, pitted

2 Bosc or Anjou pears, cored

2 apples, cored

Yields: 2½ cups

Per 1 cup serving • Calories: 568 • Fat: 1.3g • Protein: 11g • Sodium: 253mg • Sugar: 93g • Carbohydrates: 140g

1. Process the beet and carrots through an electronic juicer according to the manufacturer's directions.

2. Add the celery and cucumber.

3. Add the grapefruit sections, followed by the kiwi.

4. Add the plum, and the pears, followed by the apple.

5. Whisk or shake the juice to combine and serve over ice, if desired.

A HIDDEN CLOVE

The sweetness of the carrots will offset the strong taste of garlic, and the dill adds a touch of green. This juice is great for reducing water retention.

INGREDIENTS

4 carrots, peeled

2 garlic cloves, peeled

1 sprig baby dill

Yields: 1 cup

Per 1 cup serving • Calories: 91 • Fat: 0.5g • Protein: 2g • Sodium: 139mg • Sugar: 9g • Carbohydrates: 21g

1. Process carrots and garlic through an electronic juicer according to the manufacturer's directions.

2. Garnish juice with baby dill.

HIGH CALCIUM COCKTAIL

For those at risk of osteoporosis, extra calcium never hurts.

INGREDIENTS

1 large orange, peeled

1 tangerine, peeled

2 kiwis

Yields: 1 cup

Per 1 cup serving • Calories: 219 • Fat: 1g • Protein: 3.8g • Sodium: 9mg • Sugar: 25g • Carbohydrates: 54g

1. Process the fruits in any order through an electronic juicer according to the manufacturer's directions.

2. Stir the juice to combine the ingredients. Serve immediately.

Extra Calcium Needn't Come from Milk

If you're in search of ways to add extra calcium to your diet, consider dried fruits such as apricots, dates, and prunes.

INSOMNIA CURE

Going through a rough time? Carrots, zucchini, cabbage, and ginger all contain nutrients that help to alleviate anxiety, a major cause of troubled sleep.

INGREDIENTS

3 carrots, trimmed

1 apple, cored

1 whole head romaine lettuce

1 cup broccoli florets

1 zucchini

½ head green cabbage

1" ginger, peeled

Yields: 2 cups (2 servings)

Per 1 cup serving • Calories: 402 • Fat: 3.6g • Protein: 19g • Sodium: 275mg • Sugar: 46g • Carbohydrates: 89g

1. Process the carrots and the apple through an electronic juicer according to the manufacturer's directions.

2. Add the romaine a few leaves at a time, followed by broccoli.

3. Add the zucchini, followed by the cabbage and the ginger.

4. Mix the juice thoroughly to combine ingredients and drink immediately before bedtime.

Catching Your ZZZZZs

As they age, most people will be inclined to fall asleep earlier and wake up earlier. However, most cases of insomnia are caused by underlying treatable causes. Stress, anxiety, and depression can cause insomnia, but the most common causes in seniors are a poor sleep environment or poor daytime habits.

IRON MAN (OR WOMAN)

Truth is, many more women tend to suffer from low iron and anemia than men do. Symptoms of a low red blood cell count can include fatigue, decreased energy, and dizziness. One of the principal causes of low iron is poor nutrition, so be sure to include this iron booster in your body's good housekeeping plan.

INGREDIENTS

4 large oranges, peeled

4 medium lemons, peeled

¼ cup raw honey, or to taste

4 cups red, black, or green seedless grapes

Yields: 3 cups (2 servings)

Per 1½ cup serving • Calories: 922 • Fat: 2g • Protein: 10g • Sodium: 20mg • Sugar: 204g • Carbohydrates: 245g

1. Process the oranges and lemons in an electronic juicer according to the manufacturer's directions.

2. Add the honey, followed by the grapes.

3. Whisk the juice to combine completely and enjoy! If you prefer, add cold water to thin the juice slightly and lessen the intensity of the flavor.

Oranges for Juicing?

Some oranges are bred for ease of eating, like the easy-peeling navel. But other oranges yield more juice. Valencia is a great choice, with Hamlins and blood oranges also favored to yield more juice per fruit.

JUICE FOR SUPPER COCKTAIL

When juicing for weight loss, sweeter juices in the evening help fight fatigue and keep up energy levels until bedtime rolls around.

INGREDIENTS

1 medium apple, cored

¼ honeydew melon, peeled and seeded

½ cup raspberries

1 medium pear, cored

Yields: 1½ cups

Per 1 cup serving • Calories: 211 • Fat: 1.4g • Protein: 2.3g • Sodium: 32mg • Sugar: 39g • Carbohydrates: 53g

1. Process the apple through an electronic juicer according to the manufacturer's directions.

2. Add the melon, cut into chunks, followed by the raspberries.

3. Add the pear.

4. Whisk the juice to combine ingredients; serve in a chilled glass or over ice.

Great Flavor Combos

The predominant notes of pear and raspberry in the recipe complement each other perfectly and are nicely rounded out by the apple and melon. For a special treat, serve in an elegantly iced martini or margarita glass that's been pre-chilled in the freezer.

LIBIDO LIFTER

Great for getting back some of the old spark, this juice is best prepared in a blender or bullet-type juicer.

INGREDIENTS

2 stalks celery, with leaves

½ banana, frozen, peeled

½" ginger

½ avocado, peeled and pitted

½ cup basil leaves

3 fresh figs

2 cups coconut water

Yields: 2½ cups (2 servings)

Per 1¼ cup serving • Calories: 160 • Fat: 7.8g
• Protein: 2.5g • Sodium: 37mg • Fiber: 6.7
• Sugar: 13g • Carbohydrates: 23g

Place all ingredients in the work bowl of a blender or bullet-type juicer and purée until smooth.

Getting Fresh

When fresh figs aren't available, reconstitute dried figs in plain water or coconut water until soft.

MAGIC MEDICINE

Winnie the Pooh knew what's what. The raw honey used in this recipe has antibacterial qualities, and can contain antimicrobial properties. It's been found useful for digestion, bronchitis, and increased energy and longevity. If you think of your body as an engine, raw unrefined honey qualifies as one of the superfuels.

INGREDIENTS

1 mango, peeled and cored

½ cup peaches

½ cup pineapple chunks

2 tablespoons raw honey

1 teaspoon fresh grated ginger

1 cup blueberries

Yields: 1 cup

Per 1 cup serving • Calories: 425 • Fat: 1.5g • Protein: 3.5g • Sodium: 9mg • Sugar: 94g • Carbohydrates: 110g

1. Process the mango through your electronic juicer according to the manufacturer's directions.

2. Add the peaches and pineapple chunks, a few at a time.

3. Mix the honey with the ginger and blueberries and add to the juicer.

4. Mix the juice thoroughly before serving.

Mango Mania?

Everything about the mango has medicinal properties. The roots and bark are anti-inflammatory. The leaves have astringent and styptic properties. The flowers help to increase red blood cells. The fruits help with digestion and help to reduce gas. The seed kernel is effective against parasites and is thought to act as a tonic on the female organs.

MAGIC PARSLEY POTION

Magic? Well almost. Parsley is so rich in chlorophyll and phytonutrients, one juice aficionado claims it's a true natural high, because it imparts such a boost of energy.

INGREDIENTS

1 bunch flat leaf Italian parsley

2 carrots, trimmed

1 apple, cored

2 stalks celery, with leaves

Yields: 1 cup

Per 1 cup serving • Calories: 138 • Fat: 1g • Protein: 3.6g • Sodium: 166mg • Sugar: 20g • Carbohydrates: 32g

1. Compress the parsley by rolling it into a ball. Process through an electronic juicer according to the manufacturer's directions.

2. Add the carrots and the apple, followed by the celery.

3. Mix the juice thoroughly to blend and serve over ice.

MEMORY ENHANCER

Zinc has been shown by numerous studies to improve memory. The cauliflower in this juice provides zinc, and the vitamin E found in the tomatoes protects your cell membranes.

INGREDIENTS

1 tomato

3 red lettuce leaves

½ cup cauliflower

Yields: 1 cup

Per 1 cup serving • Calories: 56 • Fat: 0.6g • Protein: 3.5g • Sodium: 44mg • Sugar: 6g • Carbohydrates: 11.5g

1. Process the tomato through an electronic juicer according to the manufacturer's directions.

2. Add the lettuce and cauliflower.

3. Mix the juice thoroughly and enjoy over ice if desired.

How to Wash Lettuce

Wash and drain lettuce very well. You should blot the lettuce with a towel to ensure that you have removed all of the excess moisture. Do not soak lettuce. This will make the leaves soft. Even if you buy organic lettuce, it is important to rinse it before eating it.

MINTY REFRESHER

Fresh mint is not just good for your breath, it's great for your digestion.

INGREDIENTS

4 stalks celery, with leaves

1 apple, cored

5 sprigs of mint

1 lime, peeled

Yields: 1 cup

Per 1 cup serving • Calories: 135 • Fat: 0.8g • Protein: 3g • Sodium: 137mg • Sugar: 20g • Carbohydrates: 34g

1. Process the celery through an electronic juicer according to the manufacturer's directions.

2. Add the apple, followed by the mint and lime.

3. Serve alone or over ice.

Luscious Limes

Between 1795 and 1815, some 1.6 million gallons of lime juice drastically reduced the mortality rate of seamen from scurvy. That's why British seamen became known as "limeys."

NUTRITION STAR

The starfruit, also known as carambola, is cultivated throughout the tropics. It provides vitamins C and A, as well as iron and dietary fiber.

INGREDIENTS

3 starfruit

1 slice honeydew melon

Yields: 1 cup

Per 1 cup serving • Calories: 145 • Fat: 1g • Protein: 3.5g • Sodium: 36mg • Sugar: 24g • Carbohydrates: 33g

1. Process the starfruit and melon through an electronic juicer according to the manufacturer's directions.

2. Mix or shake the juice to combine the ingredients and serve alone or over ice.

NIGHT ON THE TOWN TONIC

Whether it's a holiday special, a family celebration, or an all-nighter with friends, even the best of us overindulge on occasion. So if you spent the night partying and woke up with the world's worst hangover, this is one to restore your good humor and digestive health.

INGREDIENTS

1 small beet

6 medium carrots, trimmed

1 green pepper, seeded

1 red bell pepper, seeded

½ cup kale

2 cups baby spinach leaves

3 large tomatoes

¼ head fresh cabbage

3 stalks celery

4 green onions, trimmed

1 small garlic clove, peeled

1 teaspoon salt

Hot pepper sauce, to taste

Yields: 2½ cups (2 servings)

Per 1¼ cup serving • Calories: 468 • Fat: 3.8g • Protein: 18g • Sodium: 2357mg • Sugar: 57g • Carbohydrates: 103g

1. Process the beet and the carrots through your electronic juicer according to the manufacturer's directions.

2. Add the peppers, followed by the kale and spinach.

3. Add the tomatoes, cabbage, and celery

4. Last, add the onions and garlic and salt.

5. Whisk the juice thoroughly to combine, season to taste with hot sauce and serve over ice to increase hydration.

Don't Procrastinate!

Always remember that the nutrients in fresh juice are fragile. Every minute the juice stands, you lose enzymes and other micronutrients. Retain the full benefits of your freshly made juice by drinking your power cocktails as soon as possible after you make them.

OSTEO JUICE

Osteoporosis is a medical condition that results in the weakening of bones. It primarily affects females, although some males may also experience osteoporosis. Over half of all American women have some degree of this condition.

INGREDIENTS

1 cup broccoli florets

1 turnip, including greens

2 green onions

1 cup spinach

Yields: 1 cup

Per 1 cup serving • Calories: 61 • Fat: 0.6g • Protein: 4.2g • Sodium: 98mg • Sugar: 5g • Carbohydrates: 12g

1. Process the broccoli through an electronic juicer according to the manufacturer's directions.

2. Add the turnip and its greens, followed by the onions and the spinach.

3. Stir the juice to combine the ingredients. Serve alone or over ice.

Bone Builders

While juicing is not a substitute for medical treatment of osteoporosis, some fruits and veggies are high in both sulfur and magnesium, both of which prevent loss of calcium from the body. They are broccoli, kale, spinach, onions, and turnips; and fruits high in magnesium, such as bananas, cantaloupe, and avocados.

PEPPER UP!

Bell peppers come in an array of colors: red, green, yellow, orange, and even purple. Each contains different levels of the pepper's basic nutrients, so mix it up and enjoy!

INGREDIENTS

½ red bell pepper, cored and seeded

½ green bell pepper, cored and seeded

½ yellow bell pepper, cored and seeded

3 tomatoes

2 stalks celery, with leaves

½ cup parsley

½ lemon, peeled

Yields: 1 cup

Per 1 cup serving • Calories: 140 • Fat: 1.5g • Protein: 6.6g • Sodium: 105mg • Sugar: 17g • Carbohydrates: 30g

1. Process the pepper sections through an electronic juicer according to the manufacturer's directions.

2. Add the tomatoes, followed by the celery.

3. Roll the parsley into a ball to compress and add to the juicer, followed by the lemon.

4. Whisk the juice to combine and serve in a chilled glass or over ice.

Ring the Bell

Bell peppers are packed with vitamin C and contain other nutrients that have been shown to be essential in preventing heart attacks and stroke.

POWER PAC

Proanthocyanidins (or PACs) are powerful cancer fighters and are found in beets, blueberries, and grapes as well as some other foods.

INGREDIENTS

1 cup blueberries

1 cup grapes

2 plums, pitted

Yields: 1 cup

Per 1 cup serving • Calories: 52 • Fat: 0.7g • Protein: 4.5g • Sodium: 58mg • Sugar: 2g • Carbohydrates: 10g

1. Process the fruits in any order through an electronic juicer according to the manufacturer's directions.

2. Serve immediately.

POWER PUNCH

Punch up your energy levels with this sharp and citrusy potion.

INGREDIENTS

1 medium yam, peeled

4 medium oranges, peeled

2 medium carrots, trimmed

½ fresh pineapple, peeled and cut into chunks

Yields: 1½ cups

Per 1 cup serving • Calories: 455 • Fat: 1g • Protein: 7.7g • Sodium: 107mg • Sugar: 72g • Carbohydrates: 115g

1. Cut the yam into pieces as required. Process through your electronic juicer according to the manufacturer's directions.

2. Add the orange segments, a few at a time.

3. Add the carrots and pineapple chunks.

4. Mix resulting juice thoroughly before serving.

PURPLE PERFECTION

Healthy berries help make your complexion merry and bright!

INGREDIENTS

1 cup Queen Anne or other sweet cherries, pitted

2 cups blueberries

Yields: 1½ cups

Per 1 cup serving • Calories: 177 • Fat: 0.9g
• Protein: 2.6g • Sodium: 2mg • Sugar: 33g
• Carbohydrates: 45g

1. Process the cherries through an electronic juicer according to the manufacturer's directions.

2. Add the blueberries.

3. Mix the juice to combine the ingredients and serve alone or over ice.

RED, WHITE, AND BLACK

Commercial cultivation of black currants was once banned by many states in the United States because the bushes can carry a fungus that is lethal for many pine trees. But in 2001, those bans began to be lifted, bringing these highly nutritious berries back on the market.

INGREDIENTS

1 cup red grapes

1 cup white grapes

½ cup black currants

Yields: 1½ cups

Per 1 cup serving • Calories: 162 • Fat: 0.5g
• Protein: 2g • Sodium: 5mg • Sugar: 31g •
Carbohydrates: 42g

1. Process the grapes through an electronic juicer according to the manufacturer's directions.

2. Add the currants.

3. Serve the juice alone or over ice.

Black Currants

Studies have shown that black currants have potential benefits against cancer, aging, inflammation, and neurological diseases.

RED, WHITE, AND BLUE

Great for looking gorgeous in short order! Red and blue berries combined with white-fleshed apple make a great-tasting combination for looking good.

INGREDIENTS

2 cups strawberries

2 cups blueberries

1½ cups raspberries

1 apple, cored

Yields: 1½ cups

Per 1 cup serving • Calories: 293 • Fat: 2.2g
• Protein: 4.6g • Sodium: 6mg • Sugar: 45g
• Carbohydrates: 73g

1. Process the berries through an electronic juicer according to the manufacturer's directions.

2. Add the apple.

3. Stir or shake the juice to combine ingredients and enjoy!

RELAXING COOLER

Some phytonutrients in fruits and vegetables actually help muscles and blood vessels relax. This is a great one to try at the end of a hectic day or a long workout.

INGREDIENTS

4 apples, cored

2 cups sweet cherries, pitted

1 cup blueberries

½ lemon, peeled

Yields: 2½ cups (2 servings)

Per 1¼ cup serving • Calories: 488 • Fat: 1.5g
• Protein: 5.8g • Sodium: 2mg • Sugar: 99g
• Carbohydrates: 129g

1. Process the apples through an electronic juicer according to manufacturer's directions.

2. Add the cherries, followed by the blueberries and the lemon.

3. Whisk the juice to blend, and serve alone or over ice.

Lemon Zest

Lemon juice really helps perk up the flavor of sweet juices like this. By adding a note of tartness, the sweetness is enhanced.

SALTY DOG

Cucumbers are considered especially beneficial for those with type 2 diabetes. Beta cells within the pancreas produce insulin, and cucumbers help to increase the hormone required by the beta cells in insulin production.

INGREDIENTS

2 cucumbers

1 lemon, peeled

¼"ginger, peeled

Pinch of kosher or sea salt

Yields: 1 cup

Per 1 cup serving • Calories: 125 • Fat: 1g • Protein: 5g • Sodium: 309mg • Sugar: 11g • Carbohydrates: 31g

1. Process the cucumbers and lemon through your juicer according to the manufacturer's directions.

2. Add the ginger.

3. Add salt to the juice according to your taste.

4. Serve alone or over ice.

Grains of Salt

It's always a good idea to substitute kosher or sea salt in your recipes. Neither contain additives, and they have lower sodium overall than commercial table salt.

SASSY SNACK

Celery is a great diuretic, spinach is full of iron, and the sweet potato in this recipe is sure to fill you up when your stomach is telling you it's time to eat!

INGREDIENTS

1 sweet potato, peeled

4 stalks celery, with leaves

½ cup of spinach

1 zucchini

1 cucumber

Yields: 1½ cups

Per 1 cup serving • Calories: 146 • Fat: 0.9g • Protein: 5g • Sodium: 155mg • Sugar: 12g • Carbohydrates: 32g

1. Cut the sweet potato into chunks and process through an electronic juicer according to the manufacturer's directions.

2. Add the celery and spinach.

3. Cut the zucchini into chunks and add it to the juicer, followed by the cucumber.

4. Whisk the juice thoroughly to combine and serve over ice as desired.

SILKY SKIN

Pineapple has long been known for its benefits to the skin. Add the silica-rich cucumber, and you've got an unbeatable combination.

INGREDIENTS

1 cup pineapple chunks, peeled

1 mango, pitted

1 cucumber

½ lemon, rind intact, thinly sliced

Yields: 1 cup

Per 1 cup serving • Calories: 270 • Fat: 1g • Protein: 4g • Sodium: 12mg • Sugar: 52g • Carbohydrates: 70g

1. Process the pineapple through an electronic juicer according to the manufacturer's directions.

2. Add the mango and the cucumber.

3. Add the lemon.

4. Stir or shake the juice well to combine ingredients and enjoy!

Pineapple Benefits for Skin

Pineapple contains enzymes that improve skin's elasticity. It also improves skin hydration, and speeds up the process that removes damaged and dead cells. In addition, the enzymes in pineapples fight free-radical damage and can reduce age spots and fine lines.

SIMPLE PLEASURE

If you had to pick one juice to incorporate regularly into your diet for its all-around health benefits, this one should be it. Simple and delicious.

INGREDIENTS

4 large carrots, trimmed

1 orange, peeled

Yields: 1 cup

Per 1 cup serving • Calories: 179 • Fat: 1g • Protein: 4g • Sodium: 198mg • Sugar: 25g • Carbohydrates: 42g

1. Process the carrots through an electronic juicer according to the manufacturer's directions.

2. Add the orange segments.

3. Whisk or shake the juice to combine, and serve.

SLIM FEST

This one has so many of the right ingredients for losing weight, you are all but guaranteed results!

INGREDIENTS

1 small to medium beet, trimmed and tailed

1 medium tomato

4 medium carrots, trimmed

4 Brussels sprouts

½ cup cauliflower florets

¾ cup broccoli florets

2 pears, cored

2 apples, cored

½ cup pineapple chunks

Yields: 2½ cups (2 servings)

Per 1¼ cup serving • Calories: 665 • Fat: 2.5g • Protein: 13g • Sodium: 329mg • Sugar: 99g • Carbohydrates: 157g

1. Process the first three ingredients through an electronic juicer according to the manufacturer's directions.

2. Add the Brussels sprouts, cauliflower, and broccoli.

3. Add the pears, followed by the apples and pineapple.

4. Whisk the juice to combine ingredients and serve alone or over ice!

STRAWBERRY PAPAYA JUICE

Thought to be beneficial in reducing the risk of colon cancer, the soluble fiber in papaya is able to bind itself with cancer-causing toxins in the colon and aids in their elimination.

INGREDIENTS

1 cup strawberries

1 papaya, seeded

1 cup cantaloupe chunks

Yields: 1 cup

Per 1 cup serving • Calories: 153 • Fat: 1g • Protein: 3g • Sodium: 27mg • Fiber: 7g • Sugar: 27g • Carbohydrates: 37g

1. Process the berries and the papaya through an electronic juicer according to the manufacturer's directions.

2. Add the cantaloupe.

3. Stir the juice, and enjoy alone or over ice.

STRESS BUSTER

If good health is the goal, stress is its enemy. This one helps to offset the effects of stress.

INGREDIENTS

½ honeydew melon, peeled

1 cup watermelon chunks

1 orange, peeled

Yields: 1½ cups

Per 1 cup serving • Calories: 191 • Fat: 0.7g • Protein: 3.2g • Sodium: 61mg • Sugar: 42g • Carbohydrates: 28g

1. Process the fruits in any order through an electronic juicing machine according to the manufacturer's directions.

2. Whisk the juice to combine ingredients and enjoy!

How to Pick a Melon

You've probably heard about melon thumping as a measure of ripeness, but there are others, too. One of the best for cantaloupe and honeydew melons is simply to smell them. If they don't smell like melon, they're not ripe. The same holds true of peaches and nectarines.

SUPER IMMUNITY BOOSTER

When cold and flu season comes around, this citrus powerhouse is better than a flu shot!

INGREDIENTS

2 medium grapefruits, peeled

2 Valencia oranges, peeled

2 Mineola tangelos, peeled

1 small lime, quartered

Pips of 2 pomegranates, white pith removed

Yields: 2 cups

Per 1 cup serving • Calories: 463 • Fat: 4.2g • Protein: 8.7g • Sodium: 13mg • Sugar: 62g • Carbohydrates: 112g

1. Process the grapefruit and oranges through an electronic juicer according to the manufacturer's directions.

2. Add the tangelos and the lime.

3. Add the pomegranate pips.

4. Stir the juice to combine the ingredients and serve immediately.

SWEET SHAKE

All the flavor of a fattening dessert, with none of the consequences!

INGREDIENTS

1 banana, frozen or fresh, peeled

1 apple, cored

½ cup coconut milk

¼ teaspoon nutmeg

1 teaspoon pumpkin pie spice

Yields: 1 cup

Per 1 cup serving • Calories: 373 • Fat: 24g • Protein: 3.8g • Sodium: 16mg • Sugar: 23g • Carbohydrates: 42g

1. Combine all the ingredients in a blender and purée until smooth.

2. Serve immediately.

Bananas in the Blender

Use a bullet-type juicer or blender to combine pulpy fruits such as bananas and avocados.

SUPER WEIGHT LOSS COCKTAIL

Vary the greens in this recipe according to your tastes and the season. It's guaranteed to fill you up, without filling you out!

INGREDIENTS

2 stalks celery, including leaves

½ cucumber

¼ head green cabbage

2 stalks bok choy

½ medium apple, cored

½ lemon, peeled

½" ginger, peeled

½ cup parsley

5 kale or collard leaves

1 cup spinach

Yields: 2 cups (2 servings)

Per 1 cup serving • Calories: 214 • Fat: 2g • Protein: 11g • Sodium: 188mg • Sugar: 17g • Carbohydrates: 47g

1. Process the celery and cucumber through an electronic juicer according to the manufacturer's directions.

2. Cut the cabbage into chunks and add to the juicer, followed by the bok choy, apple, and lemon.

3. Add the ginger and parsley.

4. Add the kale or collards, and the spinach.

5. Serve alone or over ice.

SWEET TART

Pears provide a nice balance to the tart grapefruit in this juice.

INGREDIENTS

1 large pink grapefruit, peeled

2 Anjou pears, cored

Yields: 1 cup

Per 1 cup serving • Calories: 235 • Fat: 0.5g
• Protein: 2.3g • Sodium: 3mg • Sugar: 42g
• Carbohydrates: 61g

1. Process the grapefruit and pears through an electronic juicer according to the manufacturer's directions.

2. Whisk the juice to combine the ingredients and serve over ice.

Pear ABCs

When it comes to picking perfect pears, remember that they ripen off the tree, so if you don't plan to use them right away, there's no harm in buying them rock hard. The best pears for juicing are simple as ABC: Anjou, Bartlett, and Comice.

THREE, TWO, ONE!

Count down your cleanse with this easy recipe. The high fiber content of this combo will help readjust your digestion to solid foods as you're coming off a fast.

INGREDIENTS

3 apples, cored

2 carrots, trimmed

1 yam, peeled

Yields: 1½ cups

Per 1 cup serving • Calories: 310 • Fat: 0.7g
• Protein: 3.6g • Sodium: 105mg • Sugar:
48g • Carbohydrates: 78g

1. Process the apples through an electronic juicer according to the manufacturer's directions.

2. Add the carrots, followed by the yam.

3. Whisk the juice to combine the ingredients and serve alone or over ice.

Yams, a Rich Source of Vitamin K

Most people are aware that vitamin K is essential to proper blood clotting, but you may not know that it also contributes to heart and bone health.

TOTAL BODY DETOX

Veggies such as asparagus and celery are natural diuretics that are especially beneficial to the kidneys, another of the body's most important organs. This one is especially useful for those suffering side effects from certain medications.

INGREDIENTS

1 large tomato

2 stalks asparagus

1 medium cucumber

½ lemon, peeled

Yields: 1 cup

Per 1 cup serving • Calories: 91 • Fat: 1g • Protein: 4.5g • Sodium: 16mg • Sugar: 10g • Carbohydrates: 21g

1. Process the tomato and asparagus through your electronic juicer according to the manufacturer's directions.

2. Add the cucumber and lemon.

3. Mix the juice to combine and served chilled or over ice.

Asparagus: A Super Food

Thought to be one of the superfoods, asparagus will not, as some sources insist, cure cancer. But it is extremely rich in folate, vitamins A and E, and iron.

TROPIC WEIGHT LOSS ADE

Mango is highly rated as a weight loss aid, partially due to its high concentration of soluble fiber.

INGREDIENTS

2 mangos, seeded

1 apple, cored

1 grapefruit, peeled

1 (½") piece of ginger

Yields: 1½ cups

Per 1 cup serving • Calories: 381 • Fat: 2g • Protein: 4.7g • Sodium: 7mg • Sugar: 70g • Carbohydrates: 97g

1. Process the mangos through an electronic juicer according to the manufacturer's directions.

2. Add the apple, followed by the grapefruit segments and the ginger.

3. Whisk or shake the juice to combine ingredients and serve.

Ginger Tips

Store ginger in your vegetable bin in the fridge to prolong freshness. It's also extremely useful in preventing the nausea associated with morning sickness during pregnancy.

TROPICAL TREAT

It's said that Christopher Columbus called papayas "the fruit of the angels."

INGREDIENTS

1 small papaya, seeded

2 small key limes or Mexican limes

1 cup unsweetened coconut milk

Yields: 2 cups

Per 1 cup serving • Calories: 281 • Fat: 18g • Protein: 3g • Sodium: 41mg • Sugar: 12g • Carbohydrates: 28g

1. Process the papaya and limes through an electronic juicer according to the manufacturer's directions.

2. Stir in the coconut milk and serve alone or over ice.

Papaya Facts

Papaya is an excellent source of vitamin A and vitamin C. It is a very good source of folate and potassium. In addition, it is a good source of dietary fiber, vitamin E, and vitamin K.

UP AND AT 'EM

Just not a morning person? If you're the type who has to drink a pot of coffee before you can make a pot of coffee, this uncomplicated juice is easy to make and will get you going faster than you ever thought possible!

INGREDIENTS

3 carrots, trimmed

1 apple, cored

2 medium oranges, peeled

1 (1") piece fresh ginger

Yields: 1½ cups

Per 1 cup serving • Calories: 214 • Fat: 0.5g • Protein: 4g • Sodium: 83mg • Sugar: 36g • Carbohydrates: 53g

1. Process the carrots and the apple through your electronic juicer according to the manufacturer's directions.

2. Add the oranges, a few sections at a time.

3. Add the ginger.

4. Mix the juice thoroughly and enjoy!

All about Ginger

Fresh ginger is great for the digestion, but did you also know it's great for circulation and improves blood flow to the brain? A piece held under the tongue is also helpful in curing motion sickness, and the nausea that can accompany rough airline flights or boat trips.

WEIGHT GOAL SHAKE

Definitely a substitute for lunch or dinner, 2 or 3 glasses of this per week and you'll reach your weight goal in no time! Two servings make this ideal for sharing with a weight loss juice buddy, too!

INGREDIENTS

1 medium sugar beet, tops optional

5 carrots, trimmed

2 stalks celery, including leaves

1 cucumber, cut into chunks

1 grapefruit, peeled

1 kiwi

1 plum, pitted

2 pears, cored

2 apples, cored

Yields: 2½ cups (2 servings)

Per 1¼ cup serving • Calories: 606 • Fat: 2.4g • Protein: 10g • Sodium: 276mg • Sugar: 94g • Carbohydrates: 152g

1. Process the beet and carrots through an electronic juicer according to the manufacturer's directions.

2. Add the celery and cucumber.

3. Add the grapefruit and kiwi, followed by the plum.

4. Add the pears and apples.

5. Whisk or shake the juice to combine the ingredients. Serve straight up or over ice.

Alternating Ingredients

When using a recipe like this one, which includes quite a few ingredients, always alternate harder fruits and veggies with softer ones to avoid overworking your juicer.

VAMPIRE CHASER

Not only does garlic chase away vampires and werewolves, it's wonderful for your health. No worries though—the parsley will counteract any bad breath.

INGREDIENTS

1 large cucumber

2 garlic cloves, peeled

½ cup parsley

Yields: 1½ cups

Per 1 cup serving • Calories: 43 • Fat: 0.4g • Protein: 2.2g • Sodium: 16mg • Sugar: 3.6g • Carbohydrates: 10g

1. Process the cucumber, garlic, and parsley through an electronic juicer according to the manufacturer's directions.

2. Serve the juice alone or over ice.

WHEATGRASS BLEND

Wheatgrass juice contains thirteen vitamins. The chlorophyll and beta-carotene in wheatgrass juice is beneficial in fighting and preventing cancer.

INGREDIENTS

1 beet, greens included

1 cup cauliflower florets

1 carrot, trimmed

½ cup wheatgrass

Yields: 1½ cups

Per 1½ cup serving • Calories: 125 • Fat: 0.5g • Protein: 5g • Sodium: 143g • Sugar: 10g • Carbohydrates: 19g

1. Process the beet and its greens through an electronic juicer according to the manufacturer's directions.

2. Add the cauliflower, followed by the carrot and the wheatgrass.

3. Mix the juice to combine the ingredients. Serve alone or over ice.

Wheatgrass Tip

To derive maximum juice and benefit from wheatgrass, use a masticating juicer.

YOUTH JUICE

This one helps restore energy and packs a real nutritional punch. The parsley not only adds necessary chlorophyll, but great flavor for those who may not take to the taste of cauliflower.

INGREDIENTS

4 medium carrots, trimmed

1 cup cauliflower florets

½ cup parsley

Yields: 1 cup

Per 1 cup serving • Calories: 117 • Fat: 1g • Protein: 4.5g • Sodium: 184mg • Sugar: 11g • Carbohydrates: 26g

1. Process the carrots through an electronic juicer according to the manufacturer's directions.

2. Add the cauliflower florets.

3. Roll the parsley leaves into a ball to compact them, and process.

4. Whisk the ingredients thoroughly to combine and enjoy!

Cauliflower Power

Cauliflower is packed with boron, which contributes to proper brain function, helps lower cholesterol levels in the blood, helps prevent arthritis, and protects against fungal infections.

STANDARD U.S./METRIC MEASUREMENT CONVERSIONS

VOLUME CONVERSIONS

U.S. Volume Measure	Metric Equivalent
⅛ teaspoon	0.5 milliliter
¼ teaspoon	1 milliliter
½ teaspoon	2 milliliters
1 teaspoon	5 milliliters
½ tablespoon	7 milliliters
1 tablespoon (3 teaspoons)	15 milliliters
2 tablespoons (1 fluid ounce)	30 milliliters
¼ cup (4 tablespoons)	60 milliliters
⅓ cup	90 milliliters
½ cup (4 fluid ounces)	125 milliliters
⅔ cup	160 milliliters
¾ cup (6 fluid ounces)	180 milliliters
1 cup (16 tablespoons)	250 milliliters
1 pint (2 cups)	500 milliliters
1 quart (4 cups)	1 liter (about)

WEIGHT CONVERSIONS

U.S. Weight Measure	Metric Equivalent
½ ounce	15 grams
1 ounce	30 grams
2 ounces	60 grams
3 ounces	85 grams
¼ pound (4 ounces)	115 grams
½ pound (8 ounces)	225 grams
¾ pound (12 ounces)	340 grams
1 pound (16 ounces)	454 grams

OVEN TEMPERATURE CONVERSIONS

Degrees Fahrenheit	Degrees Celsius
200 degrees F	95 degrees C
250 degrees F	120 degrees C
275 degrees F	135 degrees C
300 degrees F	150 degrees C
325 degrees F	160 degrees C
350 degrees F	180 degrees C
375 degrees F	190 degrees C
400 degrees F	205 degrees C
425 degrees F	220 degrees C
450 degrees F	230 degrees C

BAKING PAN SIZES

U.S.	Metric
8 × 1½ inch round baking pan	20 × 4 cm cake tin
9 × 1½ inch round baking pan	23 × 3.5 cm cake tin
11 × 7 × 1½ inch baking pan	28 × 18 × 4 cm baking tin
13 × 9 × 2 inch baking pan	30 × 20 × 5 cm baking tin
2 quart rectangular baking dish	30 × 20 × 3 cm baking tin
15 × 10 × 2 inch baking pan	30 × 25 × 2 cm baking tin (Swiss roll tin)
9 inch pie plate	22 × 4 or 23 × 4 cm pie plate
7 or 8 inch springform pan	18 or 20 cm springform or loose bottom cake tin
9 × 5 × 3 inch loaf pan	23 × 13 × 7 cm or 2 lb narrow loaf or pâté tin
1½ quart casserole	1.5 liter casserole
2 quart casserole	2 liter casserole

INDEX

Note: Recipe titles followed by 🅟 indicate Pregnant-Friendly recipes. Recipe titles followed by 🅥 indicate Vegan recipes.